The Child and the Machine

The Child and the Machine

Why Computers May Put Our Children's Education at Risk

Alison Armstrong and Charles Casement

KEY PORTER BOOKS

Canadian Cataloguing in Publication Data

Armstrong, Alison, 1955-
   The child and the machine: why computers may put our children's education at risk

Includes index.
ISBN 1-55263-004-8

1. Education-Data processing. I. Casement, Charles. II. Title.

LB1028.43.A75 1998   371.33'4   C98-931419-7

THE CANADA COUNCIL | LE CONSEIL DES ARTS
FOR THE ARTS | DU CANADA
SINCE 1957 | DEPUIS 1957

The publisher gratefully acknowledges the support of the Canada Council for the Arts and the Ontario Arts Council for its publishing program.

Key Porter Books Limited
70 The Esplanade
Toronto, Ontario
Canada M5E 1R2

www.keyporter.com

Electronic formatting: Kyle Gell Art & Design

Printed and bound in Canada

98 99 00 01 6 5 4 3 2 1

Excerpts from Theodore Roszak, *The Cult of Information: A Neo-Luddite Treatise on High Tech, Artificial Intelligence, and the True Art of Thinking* (University of California Press, 1994). Copyright © Theodore Roszak, 1986, 1994. Reprinted with permission; excerpts from Douglas Sloan (Ed.), *The Computer in Education: A Critical Perspective* (New York: Teachers College Press © 1985 by Teachers College, Columbia University. All rights reserved.), pp. 3, 7-8, 58. Reprinted by permission of the publisher; excerpts from Jane M. Healy, *Endangered Minds: Why Our Children Don't Think* (Simon & Schuster, 1990). Copyright © Jane M. Healy, 1990; excerpts from Seymour Papert, *Mindstorms: Children, Computers, and Powerful Ideas* (Basic Books, 1980). Copyright © Seymour Papert, 1980; and from Seymour Papert, *The Children's Machine: Rethinking School in the Age of the Computer* (Basic Books, 1993). Copyright © Seymour Papert, 1993; excerpt from David A. Dockterman, "Interactive Learning: It's Pushing the *Right* Buttons," *Educational Leadership*, October 1995. Copyright © David A. Dockterman. Reprinted with permission; excerpt from Daniel Goleman, *Emotional Intelligence* (Bantam Books, 1995). Copyright © Daniel Goleman, 1995. Reprinted by permission of Bantam Books, a division of Bantam Doubleday Dell Publishing Group, Inc.

This is for Alex, Anthony and Deirdre.
A.A.

To the children of the Parent-Child Mother Goose Program.
C.C.

Contents

Acknowledgments

Many people helped us in a variety of ways in the course of our research and writing. We would first like to thank Douglas F. Noble, whose writing on the subject of computers in education was a formative influence, for giving us access to his work in press. Stephen Fast read the first draft and guided us through the history of computer languages. Don Rutledge, Corinne Manley, Ron Stringer and Brenda Linn Stringer read the chapters on reading and writing and made valuable comments. Dr. Mark Gilbert of the Repetitive Strain Injury Clinic in Toronto read the chapter on the physical effects of computer use. Teachers Sandra Campbell, Steve Hanson, and Roma Lupenec were available for discussions. Richard Sugarman at the Hospital for Sick Children, Toronto, provided us with many valuable insights into the nature of child development. Beaty Popescu, at Memorial University, Cornerbrook, Newfoundland, and Martin von Mirbach were available for discussions on art, technology, and the environment and sent us useful studies. Maria Miller and Louis Slesin drew our attention to many studies on electromagnetic fields. Christopher Schmitt passed along many useful articles.

We would like especially to thank Ursula Franklin, Distinguished Professor Emeritus at the University of Toronto, David Livingstone of the Ontario Institute for Studies in Education, and Karl Pribram of the Brain Research Center, Radford University, Virginia, for giving their valuable time to review the manuscript. Judah Schwartz of Harvard University and the Massachusetts Institute of Technology gave generously of his time for interviews and discussion about the nature of education and technology, and also read the draft manuscript and suggested many valuable changes.

We also thank Patrick Crean who had faith in this book from the beginning, Jennifer Glossop for her judicious editing, and our agent Jennifer Barclay for her support. Barbara Berson saw the project through to completion, and Catherine Marjoribanks was both prompt and meticulous in her attention to detail.

The authors would like to acknowledge the assistance of The Canada Council for the Arts, The Ontario Arts Council, and the Toronto Arts Council.

David Noble and Mary Ann O'Connor encouraged this project from the beginning. Carole Corbeil and Susan Rogers wrote letters of support to the Canada Council. Marilyn Dickson was generous in her assistance, especially in California. Teresa Eckart and Robin Lee were most welcoming in San Francisco. Thanks to Christine Smith for her hospitality in Denver and Andrea Armstrong for help in Boston. Suzanne Sherkin assisted with research and also put me up in Vancouver. Thanks also to Margot Armstrong, Jeff Krymalowski, Joan Sweeney Marsh, Nona Lupenec, Sarah Scott and Dinah Power. I am especially grateful to my family for putting up with me and this project for the past five years; to Anthony for helping me to navigate the Internet and to Alex and Deirdre on whose behalf this book was undertaken. And most of all to Sean for his unstinting support.
A. A.

I would like to thank my wife, Olive, for her unwavering patience and support during the four years I worked on this book.
C. C.

Preface

L ike many schools across Canada and the United States, the public elementary school my children attend has been preoccupied with the issue of technological change. In the past five years, our home and school association has spent tens of thousands of dollars—money often matched by provincial government grants—on computer technology. At a typical home and school meeting, a parent or teacher will ask for funds to purchase a new computer, printer, or software package that someone has seen advertised in a magazine or heard about through a colleague or friend. Almost every time, parents vote, usually unanimously, to spend the money.

Parents routinely say things like: "We have to prepare our children for the future and computers are part of that future. They have to learn sometime—they may as well start sooner rather than later." Or: "Computers help kids to learn the basics. We don't want them to be left behind." Or: "Computers are fun. Kids just love them."

At another Toronto school, parents voted to spend thousands to buy networked computers for the primary classes. When a parent attempted to start a debate about the objectives behind this decision, he was told by another parent, "I'm a judge, and all the judges have computers."

Underlying such discussions is the tacit assumption that computer technology is the biggest shot in the arm that education could get. Parents are genuinely motivated by a belief that their children will receive a better education if they have access to computers. Missing from these discussions are questions about the quality or suitability of this technology or concern about how it might affect the students, physically, socially, or intellectually.

Scenes like this have no doubt been reenacted all across North America and in many countries around the world in what appears to be a headlong rush to computerize classrooms so as to equip our children for survival in the future we are creating for them. But are computers really so essential to children's education?

As a journalist who had written about education issues and as a parent who had served on a school's executive committee, I felt a responsibility to find out just what we were buying. I examined some of the software to which our increasingly scarce education dollars were being devoted and discovered that much of it was little more than electronic games dressed up to look like math or language instruction. How, I asked myself, could we be voting so much money to buy this material and yet take so little time to evaluate it? While we were spending a bundle on computers, our library was in need of new books, and many students received little or no art instruction.

Parents, I noticed, were often much more enthusiastic about bringing computer technology into the classroom than the teachers. Often there were grumblings about the failure to teach "computer literacy" in teachers' colleges and about the necessity of holding special workshops for teachers to bring them up to speed. At one school in Montreal, parents were so keen to have their children use computers that they went out and bought a lot of pricey equipment which then sat unused because no one knew how to install it.

The media have, until very recently, also been caught up in the enthusiasm for high-tech education, to the extent that it was often difficult to determine where reporting ended and advertising began. Critical coverage was in fact so hard to find (beyond the pages of specialist journals) that when I wrote an article for *The Toronto Star* questioning the benefits of computer use with young children, a number of readers responded with outrage. Several readers suggested that the problem lay not with the technology but with the teachers. If we turn our backs on computer technology, the argument goes, our children will suffer: they will miss out on wonderful learning opportunities that are out of reach of conventional classrooms, and because of these lost opportunities they will fall behind in the competitive global struggle, the outcome of which will determine the course of their future lives. It is heady stuff.

As I began my research, I discovered that what had been effectively excluded from the debate was the evidence of scientific research, which supposedly bolstered the argument for computer-based education but which, in reality, struck a far more cautious, if not critical, note. I wrote several more articles, and in the spring of 1994 I asked Charles Casement, a writer specializing in education, with a strong background in children's and family literacy, if he wanted to collaborate on a book. (The volume of research in this field is extensive, and I realized it would take both of us to wade through it.)

As we dug deeper into the history of computer-based education and researched various aspects of computer use in elementary schools, it became increasingly clear that there were important questions that were not being asked, let alone answered. I set out to visit as many schools as possible in Canada and the United States in order to get a feel for what is actually going on, always selecting schools that are recognized as exemplary in their use of computer technology. I focused on elementary schools, because we believe that it is young children who will be most affected by the current obsession with computers as a medium for learning. Meanwhile, Charles concentrated on the published research in North American, European, and international journals. (We both have anecdotes to tell and, so as not to interrupt the narrative flow, we have used the first person singular, without distinguishing which one of us is doing the telling.)

One question was uppermost in our minds while working on this book: Do computers improve the quality of instruction in schools?

This question was no doubt far from the minds of those parents who so forcefully argued for the purchase of computers for our local elementary school. It also seemed to be far from the minds of the educational administrators and decision-makers who have taken the need to computerize so much to heart. Yet this question is the one in need of an answer. Public education should be accountable to the citizens who pay for it. People are entitled to know whether their money is being well spent. So far, the best that can be said about computer-based instruction is that vast sums have been lavished on a technology whose educational potential has not yet been proven. As for the long-term effects of computer use on young children's development, we can only guess what these might be.

We hope that this book will provide the framework for a necessary debate about the role of computer technology in schools.

1

Educational Technology and Illusions of "Progress"

A prudent society controls its own infatuation with "progress" when planning for its young.

Jane Healy[1]

In April 1997, Canadian Prime Minister Jean Chrétien paid an official visit to President Bill Clinton in Washington. While their husbands held talks, Aline Chrétien and Hillary Rodham Clinton went to an elementary school in a poor neighborhood where, as *The Globe and Mail* reported, "through the wonders of technology, they watched the students of twinned schools in Washington and Ottawa share their hopes on a live, audio-visual Internet hook-up."[2] It was the kind of photo opportunity politicians love to stage these days: virtually every public figure, in North America at least, wants to be associated with the latest developments in information technology. In this instance, however, the scene created was a sham. The equipment had been installed for the First Ladies' visit and would be removed immediately after their departure. Before the day was over, as *The Globe and Mail*'s article sadly concluded, the students would be back to taking turns on the school's single aging computer with an Internet connection.

We mention this story not to underline the thoroughgoing cynicism of political posturing, but to draw attention to the way in which computer technology seems to have taken over the public's perception of what education is all about. It's almost as if nothing worthwhile goes on in schools unless computers are involved. Yet some of the most elementary questions about the educational use of computers remain unanswered. Why should children be exposed to computer technology from an early age? Are computers and computer software so essential to children's education? What can we expect them to gain? What do they stand to lose? Not only are these issues unresolved, for the most part the questions themselves have never been asked.

Schools throughout the developed world are currently undergoing the most dramatic change to occur in education since the introduction of compulsory schooling. A host of new and emerging computer technologies, which drive industry and commerce and have radically altered the workplace, are now establishing themselves in our homes and schools, transforming the education of the young in unimagined and, as yet, unimaginable ways. A generation of children have become the unwitting participants in what can only be described as a huge social experiment. This experiment calls for a radical restructuring of the educational system and with it a fundamental change in the way children learn about and experience the world.

The impetus for this reform stems largely from two beliefs. The first is that computer technology can make education more productive, more relevant, and more interesting for students of all ages. Students will learn more, and more quickly, the argument goes, because they will be more motivated to learn. They will be more motivated because they like working with computers and because their intellectual horizons will no longer be limited to the resources of their school and local community or by the knowledge of their teachers.

The second belief is that computers should be a part of education because they are very much a part of life. According to this belief, since computers play an ever larger role in our lives, students must understand and be able to take advantage of the potential of the technology if they are to participate fully in society. In particular, a familiarity with computer technology is seen as a prerequisite for a successful career.

Arising from both these beliefs is the conviction that an essential part of our children's schooling is the acquisition of computer literacy, and that to be computer literate children must have access to computers in the school. But the airy optimism and sense of certainty with which computers have been acquired for educational use are not matched by what has been happening in schools. Computer use in the classroom, in fact, has been largely a matter of trying to keep up with the pace of technological change, with educational goals running a poor second. The greater the capabilities of the technology, the more eagerly it has been embraced. Yet its use has seldom been targeted at specific problems in the classroom that have been identified in advance. The main thing has been to get the machines installed; the benefits would emerge later. It is, as Joseph Weizenbaum, one of the most influential researchers in artificial intelligence, has pointed out, a case of "a solution in search of problems."[3]

When computers were first introduced into classrooms in the late 1970s and early 1980s, the computer language BASIC (Beginners' All-purpose Symbolic Instruction Code) was in widespread use. Unlike earlier programming languages, which, because of their perceived complexity, were taught only at universities, BASIC was simple enough to allow beginners to program a computer. Teachers from kindergarten through high school were encouraged to master BASIC in order to pass along the necessary technical skills to their students, the rationale being that it was "the language that comes with your computer."[4] Parents were warned that children must learn to program in BASIC in order to become competent computer operators when they graduate to their computerized workplaces, or else risk a life of under- or unemployment.

But BASIC did not remain "the language that comes with your computer" for long. With the development of operating systems such as MS-DOS and the graphic user interface of the Macintosh, computer operators could do all sorts of things without knowing how to program at all. Consequently, the advantages of learning to program in BASIC or mastering other languages like Fortran, Pascal, Cobol, or PL-1 became minimal. (In fact, this kind of technical knowledge is now required for less than one-quarter of all occupations within the high-tech field.) Far from being skilled technicians, many computer operators today are little more than typists, since the software packages they use require them to perform repetitive, machine-like tasks. Advances in software have thus resulted in a deskilling of jobs, the reverse of what had been anticipated.

This was not the end of teaching programming in schools, however. By 1984, educational reformers had become swept up in a new notion of what to do with computers. Instead of merely programming a computer for the sake of acquiring technical expertise, children would use computers to teach them how to think. It was reasoned that the step-by-step sequential thinking involved in programming would make the computer the perfect tutor for this type of learning.

The idea of using a computer to teach children to think originated with Seymour Papert and was put forward in his book *Mindstorms: Children, Computers and Powerful Ideas.* Back in the 1960s, Papert, who along with Marvin Minsky co-founded artificial intelligence studies at the Massachusetts Institute of Technology, developed a new programming language called Logo. Dismayed by the boring, repetitive nature of much computer-based instruction, which at the time consisted mostly of drill-and-practice lessons, Papert believed that this new programming language could revolutionize the way children learn. Through the process of programming, they would come to see computers "as instruments to work with and to think with, as the means to carry out projects, the source of concepts to think new ideas," which was precisely the way Papert saw them himself.[5]

At its simplest, programming with Logo involves formulating a set of instructions that cause a "turtle" to move about on the screen, for example, to create a square. By observing the movement of the turtle, children can see whether executing their program has had the desired effect. If it hasn't, they must go back and debug the program—in other words, they must find out where their thinking has gone wrong in order to correct the program. This is a very basic example—Logo can be used to explore much more sophisticated concepts—but it illustrates the principle that made Logo such an attractive learning tool:

children become aware of how they think in solving particular types of problems.

Along with its spinoff, Turtle Graphics, Logo has played a key role in the widespread adoption of computer programming in elementary schools throughout North America, and to a lesser extent in Europe and Africa. Recent years have seen the development of the Logo Writer program and Lego/Logo, which combines Logo programming with Lego building materials and allows children to manipulate their constructions electronically.

Claims made for the educational value of Logo have been instrumental in persuading thousands of educators to see computers as a tool for enhancing cognitive development in young children. Whether the use of Logo has actually had this effect is, however, greatly in doubt. Much depends on the way it is used, and while Logo was conceived of as a creative tool, it is often used as just another medium for drill and practice, an application that must horrify Papert himself. (Logo is discussed in more detail in chapter 3.)

The introduction of Logo, then, did not mean the end of drill and practice. In fact, quite the opposite. Concern about declining levels of academic performance, which sparked a call for a return to "the basics," gave rise to renewed interest in drill-and-practice programs as a means of improving test scores. Computers were seen as an ideal medium for drill and practice because they allowed for individualized instruction, provided immediate feedback to students, and never became impatient with even the most reluctant learner. Software packages such as *Math Blaster* and *Reader Rabbit*, which promised to improve math and language skills respectively, became big sellers.

Initially, students used drill-and-practice programs as a supplementary activity. But as schools began to network their computers, they turned to Integrated Learning Systems (ILSs), which, as their name implies, provide computer-based lessons that are meant to be an integral part of the curriculum. Rather than having students spend short periods of time in the computer lab, with an ILS they spend hours a day at their own computers in the classroom, each student going through the lessons at his or her own pace. Because everything is recorded on the computer and tests are already laid out, teachers need not mark papers or tally up a report card, and the system's sophisticated management capabilities make it easy for them to keep track of each student's progress and thus provide individual assistance where needed. Although ILSs offer other forms of computer use, such as word processing and simulations, their emphasis is on drill-and-practice and tutorial programs in reading, writing, and math, and their success has been measured largely by their effect on standardized test scores.

According to *Teachers and Technology*, a report published by the U.S. Office of Technology Assessment in April 1995, basic skills practice remains one of the most common uses of computers in the elementary and middle school years.[6] Yet it appears that computer-based drill-and-practice programs are seldom properly integrated into the existing curriculum.

By the late 1980s, the concept of the computer as a drill-and-practice machine was being challenged by another view. In its new incarnation, the computer was seen as a tool for getting things done, its most widespread use being associated with word processing. Keyboarding has become the focus of much school computer use, even though many primary school children do not possess sufficient eye-hand coordination for the task until they are eight or nine years of age.

The educational scope of "the computer-as-useful-tool" was given a dramatic boost by the development of CD-ROM technology, which greatly expanded the amount of information that could be delivered in a small package. Since CD-ROMs offered content in a wide range of subject areas, schools were encouraged to integrate their use throughout the curriculum, which meant having computers in every classroom instead of keeping them in the lab or the library. Progressive teachers and school boards dropped the "drill and kill" software packages in favor of simulation programs and historical and scientific data bases. The market for educational CD-ROMs grew, and schools purchased them in large quantities.

As the software became more sophisticated, acquiring hypertext and multimedia capabilities, interest began to focus on the "products" that students could create with computer technology, such as hyper-text documents, which allow users to branch from one related topic to another by clicking on key words, and multimedia presentations, combining text, graphics, and sound. It was thought that the creation of such products, besides demonstrating students' technical expertise, would encourage learning because it enabled students to communicate with audiences beyond the classroom. It is now quite common for students to use hypertext and multimedia to create electronic portfolios of their work, and schools that have invested heavily in computers often encourage their students to create CD-ROM material that can be used throughout a school board or sold in order to raise funds for high-tech equipment.

Since the mid-1990s, another development has been poised to revolutionize our classrooms all over again. This is the rise of the Internet as a universal communications and research tool which, it is claimed, will bring students' learning into the real world of global telecommunications. It can also expose students to less-desirable aspects of the real world, such as pornography, pedophilia, and hate literature, which up to now have been screened from educational materials. Internet use thus confronts educators with a dilemma: on one hand, the promise of greater freedom; on the other, a greater need for control.

With multimedia presentations and Internet access, we have come a long way from the educational software of the early 1980s, and there is no sign that the pace of change is slowing down. Each time a new technological development takes place, schools will be pushed into teaching their students the associated skills. Our love affair with a rapidly changing technology has left teachers and parents breathless in their attempts to revise the school curriculum in order to keep up to date, and the end of the race is nowhere in sight.

The fact that there are so many uses for computers in schools is a tribute to the machine's power and versatility, but it also points to a major drawback to an over-reliance on such technology. The capabilities of computer hardware and software change constantly. Machines that were once state-of-the-art become obsolete within a year or so of being installed and are unable to run the latest programs or applications.

Many schools have been left far behind and have to make do with old machines of limited usefulness.

Along with changes in the way computers are used, there has been a continual shift in the meaning educators attach to "computer literacy." At each stage of technological innovation, the term has been associated with a particular kind of computer use. In the early days it often referred simply to the ability to turn on the machine, load a disk, and get a program up and running. Proficiency in applications such as word processing and electronic spreadsheets became another common definition. In high schools especially, computer literacy was equated with knowledge about how computers actually worked. Now it is most likely to be associated with e-mail use and surfing the Internet. One thing, however, is clear: there is no consensus as to what computer literacy entails.

This much has been admitted by Andrew Molnar, the person who first thought up the term in 1972. At the time, Molnar was director of the Office of Computing Activities at the National Science Foundation, which was then engaged in spending what would amount to $500 million to promote the use of technology in education. In a 1991 interview, by then painfully aware that computers had failed to have much positive effect on education, Molnar explained: "We started computer literacy in '72. We coined that phrase. It's sort of ironic. Nobody knows what computer literacy is. Nobody could define it, and nobody knew what it was."[7]

Despite the lack of definition, computer literacy became an umbrella term for more concepts than even Molnar and his colleagues could have imagined. It has provided the theme for many prestigious conferences and academic journals, and it is often invoked by politicians concerned that their schools are not performing up to standard. In 1983, California began a national trend in the United States when it required all of its high school students to take computer literacy courses before they could graduate. Many states soon followed California's lead, although none was successful in defining what computer literacy meant. In Canada, New Brunswick requires all its high school students to be computer literate, whatever that may mean, before graduating.

The arguments for computer literacy focus mainly on the wonders of the technology itself, and the need for students to get their hands on it, rather than on what educational purpose it might actually serve. Cleborne Maddux of the University of Nevada, Reno, who has written extensively on the educational use of computer technology, has noted about the current Internet craze that *"far too many educators seem concerned only with making the Internet accessible to students, and far too few seem concerned with making sure that teachers and students can and will use it in educationally appropriate ways."*[8]

Related to the emphasis on access is a trend that Maddux calls the "Everest Syndrome." This is the belief that computers should be used in schools "simply *because they are there.*"[9] Underlying this belief is a perception in the public mind that computer use is equated with high intelligence, leading-edge technology, and future success. As a result, computers tend to have what has been referred to as a "halo effect," whereby any activity or enterprise in which computers are involved acquires an intellectual luster and significance it would not otherwise have. It is as if "computerizing" an activity automatically improves it.

Interestingly, although Papert remains perhaps the greatest advocate for the use of computers by children, his definition of computer literacy reflects a need for balance. In Papert's view, "true computer literacy is not just knowing how to make use of computers and computational ideas. It is knowing when it is appropriate to do so."[10] By placing computers so much at the center of children's lives, and encouraging a kind of techno–tunnel vision, we may well be undermining our children's ability to make such a judgment.

Electronic media, as Harold Innis, political economist and author of *The Bias of Communications*, was first to realize, have had a profound impact on our perceptions of the world and our place in it. When communications theorist Marshall McLuhan proclaimed that "the medium is the message," he was telling us that television wasn't just a new source of information, it changed the nature of the information we received and thus shaped our responses to it. Indeed, it would create types of information that had not previously been considered. In a very real sense, nothing would ever be quite the same again.

A lesson to be drawn from the writings of Innis and McLuhan is that electronic technology can affect us in ways that at first are not always obvious to us. In the early days of television, no one expected that the average North American would spend four to six hours watching it every day. Indeed, there was some doubt as to whether there would even be that much daily programming. Certainly, no one foresaw that television would become an essential forum for election campaigns, or that it would bring live coverage of warfare directly into people's living rooms. But it did, and both developments have had a profound effect on politics, especially in the United States.

Television has now been around long enough for us to be aware of its influence. Love it or hate it, and there are good reasons to do both, we have learned to live with it. It is in fact hard to think of life without it. Now the same thing is happening with personal computers and the new forms of communications and entertainment they make possible. Computer use, in fact, is beginning to rival television as a way of spending leisure time.

A significant number of households in Canada, the United States, and Britain now have personal computers. By the end of 1995, the proportion of American homes with a computer was almost 35 percent (and about 50 percent for families with an income of more than $50,000); in Britain the figure was 26 percent.[11] In 1996, one in four Canadian families owned a home computer. Recently acquired home computers tend to have multimedia capabilities that lure viewers away from their television sets. Many parents have noticed that their children prefer to spend time at the computer rather than watch TV, and often they regard this as a good thing.

Public opinion about television is generally much less favorable than it is about computers. This may simply be because television has been around longer. But in the public perception there are essential differences between television and computers. Television is *watched*; it evokes a passive response. Computers are *used*; they require active involvement. Television is synonymous with mindless relaxation; it produces couch potatoes. Computers are associated with skills needed for a successful career; they help to develop tomorrow's leading-edge computer scientists. There is widespread concern about how much time children spend in front of the television, but the time children are prepared to spend on computer games is seen as proof that their attention spans have not declined.

Yet in one important way computers and television are far more similar than is often acknowledged: they both involve people sitting more or less motionless in front of a screen which feeds them with a rapid succession of images that make up what one commentator has called a "surrogate reality."[12]

Back in 1978, Jerry Mander, author of *Four Arguments for the Elimination of Television*, argued that watching television constituted "the replacement of experience." People thought they were experiencing real life, whereas in fact they were "sitting in a darkened room, staring at a flickering light, ingesting images which had been edited, cut, rearranged, sped up, slowed down, and confined in hundreds of ways."[13] The technical capabilities that lie behind the screen have advanced considerably since then, yet the images conveyed are even more artfully contrived than ever. However absorbing they may be, both computers and television present us with an artificial world that undermines our ability to experience the real one. We should bear this in mind when contemplating the possible effects of computer use on young children.

Children, as is now recognized, can be especially vulnerable to the effects of television because they have not built up enough experience of real life against which they can judge what they see on the screen. Moreover, once these effects have taken hold, they tend to exert a permanent influence. In Bill McKibben's evocative phrase, anyone who grew up with television has been "flavored for life."[14]

It seems, in fact, that we have learned little, if anything, from our experience with television. Its pervasive influence could not have been foreseen when it was introduced; now we know better. In integrating computers into our classrooms we should, therefore, proceed with caution. This is especially important in the case of young children in elementary schools, who are most susceptible to the influences of electronic media.

Caution, however, has been in short supply. Governments, encouraged by the prospect of corporate partnerships, have climbed eagerly aboard the bandwagon. Between 1989 and 1992, U.S. schools acquired 1.1 million computers, increasing the number in use by nearly 50 percent, from 2.4 million to 3.5 million; by 1995, the total was expected to reach 5.8 million, about one computer for every nine students,[15] and there is no sign that the pace of computerization is abating. The Clinton administration is firmly behind the move to computerize classrooms and has pledged to connect every school in the nation to the information highway. When President Clinton, Vice-President Al Gore, and a host of volunteers strung electrical wire through California classrooms on what was billed as the first "NetDay,"[16] in March 1996, they were signalling the Clinton administration's commitment to make Internet access a priority. If Al Gore has his way, every school, library, and hospital in the United States will be online by the year 2000.

The situation is much the same in Canada, where provincial ministries of education have laid out ambitious school technology plans. In British Columbia, for example, the aim is that all teachers and students "will acquire computer literacy" and that there will be "one computer for every three students in secondary schools, and one computer for every six students in elementary schools—or better."[17] At one point, the Ontario government planned to install a computer for every child in the school system, but this seems to have been abandoned because of budget restraints—for the time being, at least. (A Ministry of Education discussion document, which was leaked to the CBC in October 1997, indicated that the then-minister had a vision of education in which, once they have learned to read and write, students learn primarily from their Internet-connected computers.)

British educators have also been grappling with the need to encourage computer literacy in the face of considerable public pressure to expose children to technology in schools. In the 1980s, the Department of Education and Science (DES) introduced a centrally planned scheme to enhance educational computing, and the Department of Trade and Industry (DTI) offered schools a subsidy of

50 percent on their first acquisition of computers.[18] Much of the DES funding under the scheme went on the purchase of hardware. Critics charged that the policy had not grown out of the demands or needs of pupils or teachers and that consequently little consideration had been given to educational objectives. And although the DTI intervention promoted computer awareness among students and teachers, it was widely dismissed as "rushed, ill thought out and coercive."[19]

Even so, the number of computers in British schools has risen as fast as anywhere else. In 1988, a DES survey found that there was one computer for every sixty-seven students in primary schools and one for every thirty-two students in secondary schools. Six years later, the number of computers had more than tripled and the computer-student ratio had dropped to one to eighteen in primary schools and one to ten in secondary schools.[20]

Government enthusiasm has been more than matched by the media. Newspapers across North America are devoting increasing space to high-tech advertising, and many have sections devoted to computer technology, such as the "Fast Forward" section of *The Toronto Star.* Family magazines also contain all sorts of advertisements for children's software and computers, and in those publications that are entirely devoted to home computer use (such as *Family PC* and *Home PC*), the number of such ads is very much higher.

This advertising blitz has not been balanced by critical reporting on computer technology. Rather, the media have encouraged the widespread perception that mastery of computer technology is a matter of both personal and national survival. "While there is no law saying people must become computer literate, there is a growing social and economic stigma attached to those who refuse to ride the digital rocket into cyberspace," warned an article in *The Toronto Star* in 1994. "While government, education, union and industry spokespersons may squabble over how we should become a more computer-literate society, they agree we need to become one if we are to compete successfully in the information-based global economy."[21]

It is no exaggeration to say that advanced technology has become both an icon and a defining characteristic of North American society (in contrast to Europe, where technophilia is less pronounced). The preferred solution to problems and challenges is the high-tech solution. Educators are not exempt from this technocentric approach, and they have drawn much of their inspiration from research carried out by the U.S. military.

This is not as surprising as it might first appear. The U.S. military has long been in the forefront of research into applications of technology for the training of military personnel.[22] Douglas Noble points out in his book *The Classroom Arsenal* that U.S. military expenditures on educational technology research far exceed what civilian agencies spend. "Each year, for example, the military spends as much on educational technology research and development as the Department (formerly Office) of Education has spent in a quarter century."[23]

When computer-based education was introduced into schools, much of the military mind-set came with it. Computers were seen as an efficient way for children to learn basic skills, using drill-and-practice programs that still account for a large proportion of school computer use. The military's need for swift information processing and decision-making (originally a matter of whether or not one had seen an enemy aircraft on a radar screen) lies behind the emphasis on using computer programs to develop problem-solving and decision-making skills—skills that are sometimes assessed purely in terms of successful computer use, as if this were the only context that mattered.

There are those who say that the computer is just a tool, which can be used in good ways and bad ways. But this view ignores the fact that, like any other tool, computers are not neutral in their effect on the people who use them. They create their own conditions for exploiting their use. (A notable example, in the case of a very different technology, is the way in which widespread ownership of automobiles made possible the development of the suburban sprawl that surrounds North American cities.) Because computers are extremely powerful and adaptable tools, they can affect a particularly wide range of human activities. And, as in society as a whole, the willingness to embrace computer technology in schools has consequences that extend well beyond the mere fact of its use: when much of students' learning takes place at a computer screen, many other things change.

In many ways, computer technology is reenacting the revolution brought about by the earlier technology of print, which has itself had a profound effect on human societies. Being able to read and write things down changed the way people could think about things, because written language could be referred to again and again, and could be communicated long after it was first expressed. Literacy, as has often been pointed out, is not just a matter of acquiring the ability to read and write. Mastering the technology of print brings about a new mentality, a new way of considering things.

Computer technology has a similar effect. When children learn to use a computer, they are not just learning a skill. They are changing the relationship between themselves and the world around them. The way in which information is accessed, the manner of its presentation, the scope for its manipulation—all these factors alter children's perceptions of knowing and doing.

Computer use changes perceptions in a radically different way from print, one that is in many respects diametrically opposed to the effects of the older technology. Unlike print, which encourages reflection and a careful consideration of various points of view, computer software urges immediate action. Words and images on-screen invite constant change or substitution—this is, after all, one of the things the computer and the software it runs are designed to do. And the faster you can manipulate what you see on the screen, the more control you appear to have over the technology you are using. Since a sense of being in control is generally desirable, there is a tendency for the process to accelerate as greater confidence is gained. Speed and control are emphasized at the expense of thoughtfulness and understanding.

The sheer volume of information available through computer technology encourages this kind of quick-fire response. There is just too much to see, or at least too many possibilities to explore. Thus, a situation emerges in which a high-speed search for information, followed by rapid review, replaces a slower, more deliberate build-up of knowledge and the formation of ideas.

Is this type of learning good for the healthy development of young minds?

Overwhelmingly a visual medium, computers deal in images, not actual things. Young children, on the other hand, need to be oriented to the world around them, with its sights, sounds, smells, tastes, and textures. Many adults think that something wonderful has happened when their three- or four-year-old succeeds in making a few words appear on a computer screen. But something equally wonderful is happening when that child takes pleasure in smelling a flower, makes a tower out of building blocks (and knocks it down again), or has conversations with a teddy bear. Computers cannot provide these kinds of sensory experiences. Nor can they cultivate the emotional and intellectual bonds that develop between children and those who help them learn. Computers might be more efficient in conveying facts and figures and in presenting drills, but they cannot match a good teacher's ability to inspire interest and excitement in learning. They cannot speak with passion and commitment about ideas. Moreover, although a computer program may post a word or two of praise when a child gives a correct answer, the computer doesn't *care* whether the answer is right or not. It knows when a child has made a mistake, but it is not interested in *why* the mistake has been made. It has no feelings; it's only a machine. Any form of encouragement it gives is merely a pale imitation of the real thing.

It is also extremely doubtful whether computer software helps to create an environment in which young children can fully develop their powers of speech. In order to learn language, children need to talk with other people, in particular their parents and other family members. To do this successfully, they must listen attentively to what is said to them and gauge the effect of what they themselves have said to see whether it matches their intentions. At a certain point, they learn to internalize oral language as a means of working out what their intentions are before expressing them in speech. This internalization of speech, which enables us to "hear" the content of our conscious minds, is the prelude to the ability to engage in rational thought.

Most computer software, which like television provides a rapid succession of powerful visual images, militates against just these kinds of mental activities. The constant stream of images that appears on the screen crowds out thoughts and reflections and undermines the ability to concentrate on quieter, more subtle experiences. Electronic technology does not allow breathing space for the mind. Instead, it induces a kind of mental congestion. With television, this results in intellectual apathy, while computer use can easily lead to a compulsive, though increasingly unproductive, persistence. It is very easy to stare at a computer screen and play around with commands without doing anything very constructive.

This tendency, which has been observed in a number of studies of classroom computer use, is at odds with the widely made claim that computers encourage interactive rather than passive learning. Although when using a computer you must constantly "push the buttons" in order to make any progress, your thoughts might not be any more active than when reading. In a recent article, David A. Dockterman, vice-president and editor-in-chief at Tom Snyder Productions, a software production company, questioned the assumptions often made about interactive technology.

> Are the books students read always less interactive than the computer programs they use? Of course not. What's so special about technology anyway? A computer may be more interactive than a television in that you have more control over its use, but both may provoke either dreamless sleep or dynamic discussion.
>
> The point is this: As each new marvel of technology comes knocking on your classroom door, look beyond the glitz and glitter. It's not how many buttons students can push, but whether we can use the technology to spark thoughtfulness and interaction. Does it get students to talk to one another? Does it generate a conversation within each student's own head?[24]

The current adulation of computer technology reflects the ethos of our increasingly frantic times. The pace of life is faster than ever before, largely thanks to computers, and, in the current view, it is only through more extensive use of this same technology that we will be able to keep up. Children are not being spared the effects of the accelerating treadmill we have constructed for ourselves. In schools, if not in homes, we appear to be creating an environment that mirrors the fast-paced adult world, in which time, productivity, and instant communication are of the essence. Yet there is surely an argument to be made that schooling, particularly in the elementary grades, should provide a refuge from the world of "getting and spending" and allow children time to think and wonder and get to know themselves and the real world they live in. This is not just a matter of indulging young personalities before the serious task of joining the world online begins. Early childhood experiences have a profound and far-reaching effect on later development. Young children are already learning an enormous amount in a relatively short time. To subject them to an additional barrage of brightly colored stimuli is like trying to plug too many electrical appliances into a single outlet. Eventually, something has to give.

One significant casualty could be the ability to develop the full potential of language as a means of regulating thought. In her book *Endangered Minds: Why Our Children Don't Think*, Jane Healy writes, "I am convinced that a major reason so many students today have difficulty with problem solving, abstract reasoning, and writing coherently is that they have insufficiently developed mechanisms of inner speech." On the other hand, "Children who use inner speech effectively can remember information and events better. They are better at problem-solving because they can 'talk through' steps, evaluate alternatives, and speculate about possible outcomes."[25] In other words, the development of inner speech is directly related to the ability to think.

Learning how to think is such a basic, and yet all-important ability that it's easy to forget that it does not occur all by itself. Teaching a child how to think—how to use his or her inner voice—takes time and concentration on the part of the learner. It won't be any easier if the sound of this voice is drowned out by wave after wave of electronic noise. Ironically, the very technology that so many champion as a means of enhancing students' thinking may be responsible for exactly the opposite result.

It is possible, of course, that entirely new ways of thinking will emerge, ways that are more in tune with the technological future we are so single-mindedly constructing for our children. But this is speculation. The long-term effects of computer use are still unknown, and whether these effects will be beneficial remains much in doubt. Meanwhile, as we listen to the claims that computer technology can really make a difference, it's worth looking back on similar technological experiments that were conducted in our schools in the past.

Computers are not the first technology to enter North American classrooms, promising increased productivity and intellectual enrichment. Earlier in this century, movies, radios, lantern slides, tape-recorders, overhead projectors, reading kits, language laboratories, and televisions were all touted as promising teacher aids. Enthusiastically embraced by educational reformers, they were sparingly used and soon found to be ineffective by the teachers upon whom they had been foisted. In due course they were relegated to storage closets throughout the nation's schools, dust-gathering footnotes in the history of education.[26]

Beginning in the 1920s, radio was first licensed for commercial and educational stations, and a New York City high school became the first public school to use radio as an educational aid. "The central and dominant aim of education by radio," said reformer Benjamin Darrow, "is to bring the world to the classroom, to make universally available the services of the finest teachers, the inspiration of the greatest leaders and unfolding world events which through the radio may come as a vibrant and challenging textbook of the air." As Larry Cuban documents in *Teachers and Machines*, his provocative summary of the history of machines in the classroom, many major North American cities broadcast educational programs for school children on a host of topics ranging from automobiles to farming and science. Parents dutifully raised funds to buy receivers, and school superintendents pressured teachers to incorporate radio broadcasts into their teaching. Surveys were undertaken to count the number of radio sets and to gauge the number of listeners. Time and motion studies were done to prove that radio was a more effective learning medium than textbooks. School districts, state departments of education, and universities produced radio shows for classroom use.[27]

In spite of the best efforts of radio enthusiasts at every level of government, radio simply did not take hold in the classroom. By 1943, a six-year, federally funded study to evaluate broadcasts in schools was completed. It concluded that "radio has not been accepted as a full-fledged member of the educational family."[28] By the 1950s, research on this technology, along with the initial enthusiasm, had pretty well dried up.

The next technological breakthrough came with television. Beginning in the early 1950s and continuing throughout the '60s, television was used experimentally in classrooms. Electrical wiring was fished through walls, extra fuse boxes were installed, production studios were built, and clusters of television sets were put out on metal stands. In the United States, the Ford Foundation set aside substantial amounts of money for grants to assist schools in the purchase of this technology. Indeed, the Ford Foundation seemed convinced of the advantages of television use. "Students in today's classrooms can be eyewitnesses to history in the making.... They can see and hear the outstanding scholars of our age. They can have access to the great museums of art, history, and nature. A whole treasure-trove of new and stimulating experiences that were beyond the reach of yesterday's students can be brought into the classroom for today's students."[29] This is very much what people are saying about the educational advantages of computer technology today.

Despite meticulous and costly planning and design, evaluations of the impact of television indicate that teachers continued to use the technology sparingly and that it had little effect on students' learning. Standardized achievement tests were administered to compare the effectiveness of televised lessons and conventional instruction used by classroom teachers. The findings indicated that children did not learn more from the television than they did from their teachers.[30]

If television proved unsatisfactory as an instructional tool, at least the flirtation with it was mercifully brief. Children are occasionally to be found sitting cross-legged in front of a TV screen in school, but usually only when their teachers find a documentary of some relevance to the classroom, or for the purpose of giving the students a leisurely break for a movie. A survey of television use undertaken for the Corporation for Public Broadcasting in the United States found that students at all grade levels averaged about one and one-half hours per week watching video material in school. Elementary students are estimated to spend about one hour per week watching videos in school.[31]

Will the current obsession with computer use in schools come to a similarly disillusioned end? When *Time* magazine featured a computer on the cover of the May 3, 1982 edition as the editors' choice for "Man of the Year," it also included a special section called "Here Come the Microkids," heralding the start of "the information revolution." The technology needed to accomplish this revolution, however, proved to be too slow, too expensive, and too complicated to operate to make much of an impression on the school system. Now, more than fifteen years later, with the information revolution in full swing, with faster, cheaper, and (supposedly) user-friendly technology, and with billions of dollars already spent on educational hardware and software, it's worth bearing in mind that, as far as our schools are concerned, the revolution is far from being achieved.[32] Indeed, with computer technology developing so rapidly, it is unlikely ever to be achieved.

Nevertheless, millions of parents are intent on preparing their children for electronic education. Approximately one third of North American households now has a computer, and many of these have signed on to the Internet. Parents rush to buy their toddlers software and sign up preschoolers for computer camps, which sprout like mushrooms in a damp spring. It is the rare school nowadays whose students do not have some acquaintance with computers. Parents seek out schools that promise to expose their children to computers before they can write their names, read a traffic sign, or tie their own shoelaces. Life for these "silicon kids," as they are so often called, is unfolding in a markedly different way than it did for their parents. If the present trends continue, computers will be even more influential in shaping children than television. Yet there has been a curious suspension of disbelief where the computer is concerned. Few appear to consider that computers could prove to be just as wasteful of childhood as television, and just as harmful to a child's overall development.

The average North American child spends an average of twenty-five to thirty hours per week in front of the television (at least as much time as he or she spends in school). Most parents concede that this is a far from ideal situation: few seriously believe that television sharpens the intellect, stimulates the imagination, or even depicts a legitimate view of the world. But many people now work longer hours each week than they did a decade ago. Consequently more children spend time alone at home with television, simply because their parents are not around to supervise them. As home computers become more common, they will increasingly challenge television's status as "the electronic babysitter."

Before the computer craze set in, children who did little but watch television at home could at least count on spending six or seven hours a day nurtured and supervised by their teacher, who would provide a variety of activities which they were not likely to get otherwise. This served as an antidote to an excess of electronic stimulation at home. But if computers are integrated into classrooms, and students work at computers for several hours per day, this balance could be undermined.

Recent trends in education are not encouraging in this respect. The time devoted to classroom computer use has *increased* over the years. Consider, for example, a report prepared for the Ontario Ministry of Education in 1988, which stated that "the ultimate goal is for every student to have access to 30 minutes of computer time daily."[33] While this goal has still to be met in many Ontario elementary schools, those schools that have been able to embrace computer technology have far outstripped the report's expectations. At the River Oaks Public School near Toronto, Ontario, a showcase high-tech school, the view is that students should use computers whenever they find them to be the most effective means of getting a task done. Students at this school may spend anywhere from 35 to 70 percent of their time working at computers (the figure varies depending on whom one talks to).[34]

Immense effort has gone into figuring out how best to include computers in the school curriculum. But just because computers *can* be used in schools is not a good enough reason for deciding that they *should*. In the absence of any precise educational goals, computerizing classrooms is merely an excuse to use expensive new toys.

These toys will not remain new for very long, and the computer skills learned by children today may well be irrelevant by the time they enter the workforce. It is also by no means certain how, in a broader sense, the world will be working by the time our children are grown up. The current preoccupation with computer technology is sustained by a vision of the future that might never materialize. The changes already being wrought by technology are so far-reaching that the next generation may well be confronting challenges of a completely different order. Are we really doing our children a favor by encouraging them to develop a computer-focused mind-set at an early age? This might well close them off from options that would otherwise be open to them. The advance of computer technology, surely one of the great (if not the greatest) success stories of the late twentieth century, is nonetheless threatening to destroy our sense of balance in the way we define and evaluate our experience of life.

What we are witnessing is a loss of nerve in the face of the growing influence of computers in our lives: the future, we are told, is already here, and there is nothing we can do to change it. But it is only by doing nothing to change current attitudes that we will allow the most depressing predictions of twenty-first-century life to come true. Moreover, there are compelling reasons why, for the sake of our children, these attitudes must be challenged.

2

White Knight or White Elephant? The Real Costs of Computerizing Education

When students are seen as not sufficiently competent, it is likely to be computers that the school purchases rather than extra teacher's time and extra human help.

Ursula Franklin[1]

Try not to be intimidated by people who claim that children will be left behind or ill prepared for the computer age unless they are exposed to the computer early on. People who say such things are invariably trying to sell you something.

Aaron Falbel[2]

Across much of the industrialized world, this is a time of fiscal restraint. Governments at all levels are cutting back on spending in an attempt to reduce deficits. This belt-tightening has affected virtually all areas of government expenditure, and education budgets have borne their share of the pain. At the same time, however, the rush to computerize classrooms has continued unabated. Despite the huge sums of money involved, there is a widespread belief that schools must embrace the new technologies or see their students fall behind in the increasingly competitive scramble for jobs and prosperity. Indeed, in many ways, computers are seen as white knights who will rescue schoolchildren from the dragons of boredom and mediocrity. But will these glittery chargers deliver? Is the money allocated to them well spent? In order to answer these questions, there needs to be a realistic assessment of the cost of computerization and its impact on other areas of education spending.

In making such an assessment, we should not be fooled by the apparent largesse of the computer companies that have offered to pay at least some of these costs themselves. Equipping a school with computers, printers, peripherals, and software is a far more costly proposition than providing students with pencils, paper, and textbooks, but there is a danger in relying on corporate funding for high-tech equipment. The goals of corporations are different from those of public education systems. The mandate of our schools is to educate our children. The overriding aim of corporations is to make money for their shareholders. We regard schools as permanent institutions in our society because the need for education remains a constant. In contrast, corporations, if they are to succeed, have to be quick-footed opportunists. Supplying schools with their products and technical expertise may be a means of generating future sales, but it is unlikely that corporations will be prepared to make the kind of long-term commitment that we expect from our schools. And when a company pulls out, the effects can be painful.

This is precisely what happened at the Open Charter School in Los Angeles. From 1987 to 1992, this elementary school, set in a middle-class section of the city, was used by Apple Computer as a research-and-development site for new educational software. Under the auspices of Apple's Alan Kay, the school undertook what was touted as the most innovative educational project of its kind—the Vivarium Project.

Described by Kay as teaching children to "put intelligence into the heads of animals," the Vivarium Project involved students from kindergarten through grade five in constructing an imaginary sea creature. After researching the behavior and habitats of real sea animals, children at the Open School pooled their research with students in San Jose, California, and Erie, Pennsylvania. In a number of papers that he wrote at the time, Kay suggested that the way to interest children in biology and environmental issues was to allow them to design "living things." These early forays into artificial intelligence could, he said, teach children a great deal about animal behavior. The end result was the design of a two-dimensional electronic sea creature, which eventually took up residence on the Internet.

Its small size (380 students) and status as a charter school made the Open School an ideal choice as an R-and-D site for Apple. Founded in 1977, the oldest charter school in Los Angeles, it is run by a board of directors composed of teachers and parents. The teachers are members of the union, but they are chosen by a committee made up of the principal, parents, and teachers. This structure allowed the school to make autonomous decisions about its relationship with Apple.

A teacher with eighteen years' experience teaching grades three, four, and five at the Open School, Betty Jo Allen-Conn was unreservedly enthusiastic when Apple approached the school. She had already tried to educate herself concerning the benefits of computer technology for her students: "I knew the twenty-first century was coming and we had a responsibility to make sure the kids were up on it. So I took classes in Logo and word-processing."

Although the cost of setting up the project was considerable, Apple spared no expense. Allen-Conn was one of twelve teachers who spent months taking training courses with Apple personnel. They each received a bonus of $12,000, to compensate them for giving up their holiday time for these courses. At the beginning of the project, Apple flew them up to the Exploratorium, a science center in San Francisco, to experience hands-on science activities that would be both fun and inspiring, because "Apple wanted us to see how easy science is."

The company also paid to hire four extra staff, an expense amounting to $250,000 for each of the five years the project ran. In this way, the school acquired an art teacher, a music teacher, a physical education instructor, and a gardening consultant. The extra classes they provided allowed the regular classroom teachers an extra two or three hours per week of preparation time to upgrade their computer skills and develop lesson plans maximizing computer use. This time was allotted to them in the course of the school day.

Apple also donated all the hardware and software. Altogether there were 190 computers for student use, or one computer for every two students. Apple picked up the tab for ongoing technical support, as well as the cost of maintaining and repairing the equipment. The teachers received free computers and printers, which were upgraded twice during the life of the project to ensure that they remained state-of-the-art. Apple has found that it works well to begin by giving teachers their own personal computers, so they become both comfortable and adept with the technology and enthusiastic about using it in the classroom.

All in all, the Vivarium Project was a costly one. However, Apple's involvement ensured that it was implemented under the most supportive circumstances—a large corporate donation, ongoing training and technical support, and the backup of the energetic Alan Kay.

From the teachers' point of view, the experience was a positive one. They found their training stimulating, and they entered into their new courses with enthusiasm. The administration was pleased with the results: every child in the school was exposed to leading-edge technology, and parents felt their children were acquiring skills that would prepare them for the future job market.

When Apple completed its research, the project wound up, and after 1992 it fell to the school's parent group to find the money to maintain the equipment. Now that Apple was no longer there to take care of them, the costs of computer-based learning proved to be much larger than anyone had imagined.

When I visited the school in 1996, nine years after the Vivarium Project was launched, the room that had once been the project's primary site was a repair shop for computers that had broken down or been abused: one monitor had a burn mark on the screen and looked as though its useful days were at an end. The only sign of life was a teacher using a blackboard to tutor three special-education students. The shining white knights had become a collection of battered old white elephants.

"Our equipment is no longer state-of-the-art," said Allen-Conn. "It is falling apart, so to speak." The principal, Dr. Grace Arnold, agreed: "Repair is the biggest issue." Most of the computers and printers at the

Open Charter School date from the early days of Apple's research effort, and keep running only thanks to the constant repair work of the teachers. Before it left the school, Apple provided some final training courses in the repair and maintenance of aging equipment, and it continues to give a discount on replacement parts. Because of the number of teachers who are qualified Apple technicians, the Open Charter School is in fact a certified Apple repair center.

Each week, each member of the team of six teachers (half the teaching staff) spends four hours on repairs—twenty-four hours altogether, taken from their after-school time. Allen-Conn conceded it was hard at the end of a long school day "to be laboring over computer equipment counting screws, rewiring faulty connections or cleaning screens," and called it "a mind-boggling job."

"I don't feel very happy about this," said Dr. Arnold. "I would prefer that [the teachers] would be spending their time in curriculum and conceptual development rather than on their hands and knees on labor." Yet she noted that if the teachers didn't put in the extra hours, the school couldn't afford to continue using the technology.

The school's board of directors hopes to be able to raise money to replace the equipment sometime in the future. At present, however, its efforts are directed towards raising money for the extra teaching help they got used to when Apple was paying for it.

The experience of the Open Charter School is not unusual. Schools that accept technology from a corporation, either as a one-time grant or as part of an ongoing research project, are often caught short of funds when the corporation withdraws its support and the equipment starts to wear out. Schools that make computer purchases with a community or government grant frequently run into the same trouble.

One of the hardest lessons learned at the Open Charter School was that computer systems need continual maintenance and repair. When a company in the private sector sets up a new computer system, it allocates fully 30 percent of the original purchase price annually towards technical support and maintenance of the equipment. George Moon is vice-president of engineering for MapInfo, a multinational computer software company based in Troy, New York, and a major provider of computer mapping software. A father of two, Moon attended a parent meeting at his children's school to discuss the funding needed to purchase new computers, printers, and up-to-date software. The school was trying to raise $300,000 for this purpose, but he was concerned to discover the committee had budgeted nothing for ongoing technical support; nor had it budgeted for the cost of replacing worn-out equipment, something the corporate sector routinely takes into account. "It's not a one-time expense," said Moon. "You have to plan ahead to replace equipment because it goes out of date so quickly." In Moon's experience, businesses replace their computer equipment every three years—some every two years. Schools, however, can rarely do the kind of long-range financial planning necessary for such costly purchases, since it is often the case that the funding for computer technology comes from short-term grant allocations.

School boards, administrators, and parents are, in fact, often unaware that the initial cost of software and hardware is just the beginning. One-time grants from state or provincial governments, local municipalities, or community foundations typically range from $10,000 to $250,000 and cover the cost of purchasing computers, printers, and software. Once the maintenance contract runs out (the industry standard is one year), the school board or parent association must secure additional funds to keep the equipment operating. As with a car, the older the equipment, the more expensive it is to keep in working order. Older machines are also sometimes impossible to repair when they break down because replacement parts just aren't available.

Since new software is designed to be compatible with the latest hardware—computer terminals and printers—the useful life of the average computer is short. In order to be current, hardware needs to be upgraded approximately every five years. Yet a large proportion of the computers in North American classrooms are fifteen rather than five years old. In 1992, for example, half of the computers used in elementary and secondary schools in the United States were Apple II models, unable to run the latest software then being developed.[3] Many

Canadian schools still use the old Commodore 64s manufactured in the late 1970s and early 1980s, which cannot run any of the current software at all.

The constant need to maintain and upgrade computer hardware and acquire the latest software is having an enormous impact on school technology expenditures. If school districts are to keep up with developments in computer technology, they must continue spending. That they certainly are doing. Schools in the United States have been buying some 300,000 to 500,000 computers per year at an annual cost of up to $500 million or more.[4] Spending on software has been even higher. The Software Publishers Association estimates that American schools each spent on average $11,000 on software over the 1993-94 school year.[5] With approximately 80,000 public schools in the United States, this works out at a total of around $880 million for a single year. According to a survey carried out by Quality Education Data, a Denver-based research company, spending by U.S. school districts on educational technology is estimated at $5.2 billion in the 1997-98 school year, up from $4.3 billion the year before.[6] In the 1991-92 school year, spending was $2.1 billion.

These figures, however, pale to insignificance when compared with the amounts that would be spent if plans for universal access to computers in schools were to be implemented. In 1995, the now-defunct U.S. Office of Technology Assessment estimated the one-time installation costs of having "one personal computer per student desktop, with full, ubiquitous connection to the Internet" at anywhere from $66 billion to $145.5 billion. (Total U.S. educational expenditures in 1992-93 were $280 billion.) On top of this, there would be between $4.5 billion and $11 billion in annual operating costs (including annual training and support for teachers).[7] And this is before the cost of replacing machines is taken into account.

In California alone, according to state school officials, the cost of meeting school technology needs could run as high as $7 billion between 1997 and 2000, and this figure is $4 billion less than the spending recommended by a task force that reported in 1996. So far, Governor Pete Wilson has responded with a proposal for a four-year school technology plan which would provide up to $500 million in state aid, to be matched by local government spending.[8]

Other states are embarking on a similar course. A bill tabled in the Massachusetts legislature provides funding for computer technology in the state's public schools. The bill would equalize payments among rich and poor school districts and would make available approximately $2,000 per child to equip schools with the latest hardware and software and to enable schools to gain access to the Internet.

School technology spending has also been proceeding apace in Canada. British Columbia spent $40 million between 1992 and 1995 to upgrade its systems, and plans to spend another $60 million by the turn of the century. Ontario spent upwards of $150 million over the same three-year period. (It is very difficult to get exact figures on the amount of money spent on technology, since so many schools receive corporate gifts to get them started.) These expenditures cover new computers, printers, and software; they do not include the yearly maintenance costs that will be required if the equipment is to be kept in good working order.

Spending on school computers has been increasing rapidly in Britain, too. According to the Department for Education, the amount spent on "information technology equipment" rose from just under £30 million in 1987-88 to over £197 million in 1993-94. Spending for primary schools increased over ten times during this period and accounted for more than 50 percent of the 1993-94 total. Nearly 30 percent of the funding for primary school computers, however, came from parent-teacher associations rather than from regular school budgets or central government grants.[9]

Installation, maintenance, and upgrading costs are not the only concern. If a recent trend continues, schools may find it increasingly expensive just to keep the equipment on-site. According to a June 1996 article in *Education Week*, computer theft from schools is becoming a serious problem, and in some cases it appears that thieves have been using students for inside information. In Sacramento County's San Juan school district, with 48,000 students, more than $150,000 worth of computers was stolen during the 1995-96 school year. As a result, schools are having to spend money on computer security. In Dade County, Florida, most of the district's computers are "locked in place, at a cost of $100 per machine." To protect a new shipment of computers, the Canterbury Magnet and Elementary School in Arleta, California, spent more than $15,000 to install security grilles on the school's windows, "money that would otherwise have been spent on instruction."[10]

Among operating costs, Internet use, which is now widespread in schools, represents an increasingly significant factor. In the United States, many public school teachers currently gain free access by logging on to a university computer center, where costs are assumed by a government agency or private funder. Those who come from small, rural school districts are unlikely to have this option and run up long-distance phone charges. Two teachers from rural New York State who attended a 1994 graduate seminar on telecommunications commented that, in addition to the difficulty of finding the time, cost was a major factor in restricting their Internet use. One "had hoped to be able to use the Internet much more than I have so far" and was "unhappy that we must pay such huge phone bills to do what many other people are doing virtually free." The other regretted that, "When I do manage to get on, the old dollar signs keep spinning by so I always feel rushed."[11] Schools that provide access to the Internet from multiple computer terminals could, according to one estimate, face operating fees of up to $2,000 per month.[12]

The U.S. Telecommunications Act of 1996 contains "universal service" provisions under which schools and libraries are guaranteed access to telecommunications services at "affordable rates." But the United States Telephone Association (USTA) argues that "the universal-service funding mechanism should be limited to funding the provision of telecommunications services only" and that other costs "such as teacher training, software, and equipment, must be determined and recovered separately by the educational institution and the community." In other words, the phone companies should do no more than provide schools with basic telephone services at reasonable rates.[13]

As the USTA recognizes, in addition to affordable access, teachers need the knowledge that will enable them to use the Internet effectively.

This will involve more than a short introductory course. The Internet is constantly changing. Cleborne D. Maddux, of the University of Nevada, Reno, observed in a 1994 article that changes were occurring so quickly that the instructions he prepared for his students at the beginning of a semester were seldom of any use by the end. In fact, sometimes they were "worthless after only days or hours!"[14] Since then, the rate of change has become, if anything, even more hectic, making ongoing technical support and teacher training even more essential if schools are to make good use of electronic communications.

Clearly there is no point in having a lot of expensive computer technology in our schools if teachers do not know how to use it effectively. Computers sitting idle or being used for trivial purposes represent a wasted resource. Yet many teachers have little or no experience of computers, and those who *are* familiar with the technology need time to explore the best ways of using it with their students. Even when they have received training, teachers still regularly need to upgrade their knowledge and skills to keep pace with new developments. There are, therefore, costs involved in teacher training and preparation time, and in creating the right conditions for students to work with computers. According to some estimates, these costs should far surpass the amount spent on the technology itself.

Henry Jay Becker, of the University of California at Irvine, is an educational researcher who has made a detailed study of the real cost of computerizing schools, in research spanning some twenty years. He calculates that for an average-sized school of 800 students it would cost $1,375 per pupil per year, or $1.1 million per school, to cover only the personnel-related costs for providing a meaningful technology program. This is more than double the corresponding cost of hardware and software, which Becker estimates at $556 per pupil per year. The largest items included in these personnel costs (but almost entirely lacking from school district estimates) are funds for teacher training, greater access to school computers for lesson preparation and other professional use, and the creation of smaller classes.[15]

Bob Pearlman represents the Boston Teachers' Federation and has served as director of research in the field of educational technology for the American Teachers' Federation. He also thinks that much more money is needed to train teachers in the educational use of computer technology, and he generally supports Becker's estimates. Pearlman considers that more than 50 percent of the technology budget (Becker recommends 70 percent) should be set aside for teacher training, but knows that in reality this is never done. Both Pearlman and Becker agree that to make this technology meaningful in an educational setting, the costs will be enormous.

Recent examples from California illustrate the relative neglect of personnel costs in technology budgets. The California Department of Education recently calculated that the cost of placing a very modest amount of computer technology in state schools would add up to $3 billion. This was for a low-end system: two computers and a printer per classroom, related software, and *one-time* teacher training, which would amount to $375,000 per school.

As an example of a high-end system, costing up to three times more, the New Haven Unified School District in California plans to spend $27 million to equip every classroom in its eleven schools with an average of seven computers per classroom. This amount covers items like $9 million for fiber-optic cabling, $800,000 for computers and printers, $3.1 million for electrical upgrades, $300,000 for video distribution systems, $100,000 for telephone upgrades, $1.2 million for fiber-optic cabling between district headquarters and the school, $1 million for document management systems, and $750,000 for video centers. *This does not, however, cover the cost of teacher training.* In order to find time for teachers' in-service training, the district got permission to start classes one and a half hours late each Wednesday, a situation that will continue for the first four months. So the additional costs will simply come out of the time for student instruction. No funds have been set aside for ongoing teacher training or for a permanent maintenance budget. (Similar oversights have occurred in Canada. Manitoba recently upgraded computers in its schools, but neglected to budget for either teacher training or ongoing technical support.)

No one disputes the high costs of teacher training in order to make the use of computer technology a meaningful experience, yet few school districts or boards in North America are taking the steps to ensure that teachers receive appropriate training. One federal U.S. study showed that only 15 percent of the budget for educational technology was going towards teacher training. In Canada, British Columbia has earmarked $20 million out of its $100 million technology budget for teacher training, but the director of technology for that province, Barry Carbol, concedes that this is misleading. "What you will find," he said, "is that the allocation for teachers' professional development, the bulk of it, really isn't there—the teachers or their districts have made plans to use it." Most of the allocated reserve for teacher training has in fact been spent on software and hardware.

If teachers do not receive adequate and ongoing training, money spent on computer technology will largely be wasted. There are many stories of equipment being purchased, and then being used only by one or two teachers. Very often, in fact, a school buys computers because a few teachers or an administrator became interested in using them. An informal kind of training may then take place in which the "experts" share their knowledge with both students and fellow teachers. However, when these expert users leave the school, it is not uncommon for the technology program to flounder, because they have not been able to engender the same enthusiasm or commitment among their colleagues. One elementary school in Winnipeg, singled out in the media as an exemplary computer-using school, didn't have a single computer turned on the day I visited. The computer coordinator had moved to another job, and there was no one to continue the program. As a result, the costly equipment was basically sitting idle.

Teacher training will not be effective if it is confined to a one-time introductory course. Apple Computer has discovered that it takes an average of five to six years for teachers to change their method of teaching so that they are using the computers in a way that benefits students. This might well explain why, in a national U.S. survey, the prestigious Bank Street School of Education in New York concluded that only 5 percent of those teachers using computer technology in American public schools could be counted as "exemplary" users.

The Bank Street study found that teachers who were using the technology wisely—for instance, helping their students produce a yearbook or newspaper, instead of allowing them to use computers for game-playing activities—were those who had received considerable training and who were supported by both their school and their district in their use of computer technology. They differed from other computer-using teachers in that they were much more likely to have had a liberal arts background, as opposed to a degree in education, computer studies, or social sciences. The single most important factor, however, was class size. Teachers with the best record of meaningful use of computer technology had, on average, classes of twenty students— 20 percent smaller than the overall average class size.

These findings further underscore educational research by Becker and others which indicates that class sizes must be kept smaller than average in order for students to derive the maximum benefit from the technology. This contravenes the widespread belief that by increasing the number of computers in the classroom, the teacher will be able to teach more students. Concurrent with this kind of thinking is the notion that once students are given computers, they will somehow become less dependent upon the classroom teacher for learning. In fact, introducing a computer into the classroom, particularly for schools that are connected to the Internet, will make the role of the teacher, and thus adequate teacher training as well, more essential than ever.

It's clear that school technology costs are not going to go away, and will not even significantly decline, once computer systems are in place. The question therefore arises: If schools are to accommodate large expenditures on computer technology, which other areas of their budgets will be reduced?

The first casualty might well be the condition of school buildings. In its 1995 report on school technology, the U.S. Office of Technology Assessment pointed out that "school districts are facing huge costs just to bring their aging, dilapidated school buildings to where they meet basic standards. The General Accounting Office [GAO] reports that

$112 billion is required for the repairs, renovations, and modernization required to restore the nation's 80,000 public schools to good condition and to comply with federal mandates related to accessibility and safety regulations, for major building features such as plumbing and environmental conditions such as ventilation, heating, lighting, or physical security."[16] In particular, a 1995 study by the GAO found that almost half of U.S. public schools had inadequate electrical wiring for computer and communications technology.[17]

Compounding this problem is the fact that the use of computer technology requires more classroom space than traditional teaching approaches. In 1970, an average elementary school provided 62 square feet (5.76 m^2) per student. In 1995, the average space per student was 111 square feet (10.32 m^2), according to an annual report by *American School and University* magazine. One reason for this increase was increased use of technology. In the view of many school planners, "the size of the standard classroom needs to increase another 25 percent to incorporate new technology into everyday instruction."[18]

Even where schools have been designed and built with computers in mind, and have received corporate funding, technology expenditures can have a noticeable effect on other areas of a school's budget.

For more than five years, the River Oaks Public School in Oakville, Ontario, has considered itself a model technology school, boasting one computer for every three students. It is frequently featured in the media as a leader in the educational use of computers. Like the Open Charter School in Los Angeles, River Oaks has taken advantage of heavy corporate sponsorship. Its first computers were donated by Apple, and discounts on parts and services have been provided by that company, as well as by other corporate sponsors like Northern Telecom, Sony, and Husqvarna (the last providing computerized sewing machines). Currently it is testing out some new educational software and so is obtaining the software and some technical support while doing so.

Even with the discounts on expensive high-tech equipment, River Oaks, like most public schools in Canada, must pay for the support and maintenance of its computer technology out of its general operating budget. The school principal, Gerry Smith, has suggested that in order to afford the technology there is no alternative but to cut back on more traditional materials. This means that the school's budget for textbooks has steadily decreased, while computer technology has taken an ever larger share. With the exception of mathematics texts, the school has all but dispensed with textbooks. River Oaks has also cut its budget for library books and magazines. Recently the school has begun to seek out new ways of fundraising, since its computers are now more than five years old and in need of replacement.

If schools don't find new money to support the equipment now sitting in their classrooms, they will likely face some hard choices in the future—either scrap their computer programs, or cut other areas of the curriculum to pay for them.

Arts programs seem to be particularly at risk. At least one Toronto school has already scrapped its entire music program in order to channel the funds into a technology program, and the same thing has happened in the Lambton County Board of Education in southwestern Ontario.[19] The Hamilton (Ontario) Board of Education cut its music coordinator and reduced delivery of its music programs, while still keeping substantial funds available for computer technology.

It's the same story in the United States. The cover article of the July 1997 issue of the *Atlantic Monthly* cited three instances in which arts activities had been displaced or curtailed because of technology spending. "The Kittridge Street Elementary School, in Los Angeles, killed its music program [in 1996] to hire a technology coordinator; in Mansfield, Massachusetts, administrators dropped proposed teaching positions in art, music, and physical education, and then spent $330,000 on computers; in one Virginia school the art room was turned into a computer laboratory."[20] And *The New York Times* recently reported that a school district in Des Moines had eliminated 104 school jobs, including teachers' and teachers' aides positions, while obtaining $2 million in state funding that was earmarked for technology purchases.[21]

A particularly worrying problem that has arisen as a result of spending on computer technology is the decline in school budgets for library materials—books and periodicals. Like many school boards across Canada, the Calgary Board of Education cut its library budget for 1996: library expenditures decreased by 15 percent, while the technology budget went up by 30 percent. Cuts to libraries are justified by administrators on the grounds that books can soon be dispensed with and that students can get all the information they need from electronic encyclopedias and the Internet. There is also a belief that computers will change the role of teachers and librarians (or in many cases teacher-librarians) by enabling children to learn more independently.

Experienced teacher-librarians are now being put into the position of having to learn technical skills that are better performed by someone who has been hired expressly for this purpose. In other words, highly trained teachers and especially teacher-librarians are having their jobs turned into technical occupations. Moreover, teachers who are taking over these technical tasks are no longer available to students in a real teaching capacity, so students are losing out on the time they could be spending with knowledgeable teachers. When teachers are spending time dealing with malfunctioning equipment instead of tending to the needs of their students, the real costs of using computer technology must be seen as very high indeed.

School administrators are also under considerable pressure. Computer technology has proven to be so expensive that many schools have had to put a great deal of time and energy into fundraising efforts. The Peakview Elementary School in Aurora, Colorado, for instance, has taken a novel approach to funding its computer program. Like the Open Charter School, Peakview was given new computers by Apple and supplied with technical support for a couple of years. But since the initial acquisition of equipment, Peakview has had to undertake the cost of maintaining and replacing the equipment itself. In order to continue to pay for technical upgrades, the school's administration evolved the idea of giving computer workshops. These workshops now attract teachers and administrators from all over the United States.

Peakview is a year-round school, where forty-five-day terms are followed by a two-week break. The workshops are held four times a year, during break time, and cost $285 each for an average of about fifty participants. Virtually all of the money is profit. Apple Computer continues to play a role in the workshops, occasionally offering technical expertise, but mainly by paying for the cost of the participants' meals. (This is a good deal for Apple: the company stands to benefit from future purchases, since all the instruction is done on its equipment.) Peakview's technology coordinator leads the sessions.

The workshops net about $50,000 a year, to which the school adds about $10,000 from its central grant. Peakview's home and school association contributes an additional $10,000 to $15,000 from general fundraising efforts. This does not, however, include the $50,000 salary of the full-time technology coordinator, a position the school administration considers essential to keep up with staff training, review software, and make purchasing decisions. The school has also added a part-time technology assistant whose salary is about $25,000. Factoring in these salaries, Peakview spends over $135,000 every year just to keep its program running.

Peakview also makes other accommodations in order to cover the costs of its technology program. In order to be able to have a technology coordinator and a part-time assistant, it increased class sizes in every grade. This means that the school now makes do with one fewer regular classroom teacher. The lower grades average about twenty-five students per class (fewer in the kindergarten), while grades four, five, and six average about thirty students. As well, the school's art teacher has had to change her method of art instruction because her class sizes have grown to the point that doing large group projects (like creating a mural of a New York City street or an installation of a life-size humpback whale) have become much more difficult.

Peakview's unique solution to the problem of funding computer technology is not available to most schools. It is clear that schools that decide to go the high-tech route will have to turn more and more to corporate sponsorship, and to special fundraising activities. Yet it would require a radical change of the Canadian educational system to allow individual schools to begin to market the skills of their teaching staffs in the way that Peakview has. "We would object," says Jan Eastmen, president of the Canadian Teachers' Federation, "to using scarce teacher energy to give courses to pay for education resources that are underfunded. It is akin to asking doctors and nurses to give courses on nutrition in order to buy medical equipment. And it is a sad statement about the funding going to education." Currently, many school boards in Canada are requiring teachers to upgrade their computer skills on their own time and are expecting them to pay out of their own pocket for their training.

It is no surprise that corporate donations, of both expertise and equipment, have reached unprecedented levels. This situation is likely to continue, since such donations can usually be written off as corporate tax breaks. When Steven Jobs was chairman of Apple Computer, he, among others, managed to lobby the California legislature into giving a 25 percent tax credit for corporate donations to schools. What amounted to a tax saving for Apple was also a form of advertising, since it gave Apple an opportunity to capitalize on the school market and thus helped ensure customer loyalty. The fact that the company was saving on its taxes meant less money for the state, and this at a time when spending on education in California was at its lowest point in more than a decade.

Canada, too, gives tax breaks to corporations for donating high-tech equipment (though they are not yet as generous as those available in some American states). These donations have been a source of some irritation to teachers and administrators, since the equipment is often out-of-date or close to obsolescence when a school district receives it, so the school is liable for repairs and is training on old equipment. Many schools may therefore be better off not accepting the equipment at all.

Partnerships with the corporate sector, while providing fiscally strapped schools with free or subsidized technology and a certain amount of technical support, have given teachers' unions and school districts a number of qualms. Corporations donate equipment and expertise to schools in order to increase the profile of the company and in so doing build customer loyalty for their product. Software developers also benefit from observing children and how they use the software in the quest to perfect new applications. Children can be employed in a variety of ways, from debugging programs to assessing the degree of user-friendliness, to figuring out new uses for the programs. While this may benefit the corporation conducting the research, it isn't at all clear that the students, or their teachers, are engaged in activities that have meaningful educational content. Although it is not a cost that shows up on a balance sheet, time spent in pursuit of activities of dubious educational value amounts to a high cost to pay for the introduction of computer technology in the elementary school years.

Plans are under way all across Canada and the United States to put schools on the Internet and to connect classrooms around the globe. In the United States, one reporter has likened the cost to the creation of another Pentagon, with ultimately billions and billions of dollars being spent to wire the country. But trying to grasp the full costs of this technology will be very difficult. The cost of training teachers, of acquiring and upgrading systems, of the lost tax base due to corporate write-offs is only part of the equation. For a full reckoning, the costs of computer technology must also be measured in terms of the other kinds of learning it displaces. If access to libraries and printed materials is limited, if class sizes balloon, if music programs are canceled and art programs scaled back in order to pay for this costly technology, then we must begin to ask questions about what we are losing.

The first attempt to computerize classrooms in the 1970s is considered to have been largely a failure for several reasons, one of the chief ones being that so little attention was paid to teacher training. There is a danger that the same error is being made all over again. In its 1995 report on teachers and technology, the U.S. Office of Technology Assessment concluded that, because teacher training had been generally ignored, the approximately $4 billion schools spent each year in the United States on computers, software, and other technologies had brought few benefits to classroom instruction. (Less than half of this amount was spent on textbooks in the same period.) "There is a consensus," writes American education activist Douglas Noble, "that except for a few futuristic demonstration projects, all of this money and hardware has had an insignificant effect on educational practice in the nation's schools."[22]

Apple Computer concurs with these findings. As early as September 1992, an article in the Apple/Macintosh magazine *Macworld* described the reality of computer use in schools in this way: "Antiquated computers; unused computers; computers used for games and not for teaching; schools and teachers unprepared to use computers that they own; mismanaged or misdirected policies; and unknown hundreds of millions of dollars spent over the last decade for little return."[23]

Computer-based education is an expensive proposition. Even supposing we could afford to computerize every classroom, we have not determined whether this would be money well spent. If our aim is to ensure that our children get the best education possible, we need to ask: What are the optimal conditions for children to become competent learners and thinkers? What kinds of experiences do children benefit most from in the early years of schooling? How do we create a system of education that is best suited to the developmental needs of the child? The answers to these questions—not an unexamined desire to expose children early to technology—should guide us.

3

The Disembodied Brain

I lay it down as an educational axiom that in teaching you will come to grief as soon as you forget that your pupils have bodies.

Alfred North Whitehead[1]

One of the most seductive arguments for the early introduction of computers into the lives of children is the claim that this technology will sharpen their intellectual skills and accelerate their intellectual development. Put simply, the belief is that computer use will make children more effective thinkers and will enable them to engage in abstract, adult kinds of thinking at an earlier age.

A number of cognitive scientists hold the view that the brain is a computer and the mind is the program it runs on.[2] This image commonly surfaces in everyday speech, in schools as much as anywhere else. One morning, while visiting an elementary school, I overheard the sweet, piping voices of a children's choir. Entering the gymnasium, I saw six- and seven-year-olds learning the music for a new song. The music teacher asked them if they had memorized the lyrics. "Have you put the words into your computer?" she asked twice, tapping the side of her head for emphasis.

Using the brain-as-computer metaphor in everyday speech may not, in itself, be a matter for serious concern, but it can be seen as a symptom of a more dangerous trend: the increasing tendency to equate intellectual ability with the mastery of technical skills. Skills involving computer technology are especially admired, since computers are regarded as being at the leading edge of technological advance. Intelligence is thus associated with a kind of technical mimicry in which the brain works in sync with the step-by-step procedures of the machine, while human memory becomes just another data bank.

This deification of technical reasoning—the primacy given to the ability to understand technical functions—has eroded a more expansive view of what it means to become educated. A liberal arts education, for instance, consists of far more than the acquisition of information and skills; the word "education" derives from the Latin *educare*, which means to lead out. Socrates believed that the role of a teacher was to draw out of a pupil the awareness, insight, and knowledge that would dispel ignorance and lead to clarity of thought. In other words, education entails the development of a certain frame of mind, one that in the past has included the idea of meditative thinking based upon self-knowledge and careful observation of the world. (The German philosopher Martin Heidegger, for instance, distinguished between two types of thinking, meditative and calculative, the latter being concerned with the solving of specific problems without regard for their wider implications.) This is a far cry from molding young minds to fit technical criteria.

As mentioned earlier, the idea of using computers to teach children to become better thinkers originated with Seymour Papert. Papert believed that the computer would "blow up the school," revolutionize education, and reshape the minds of children. The incendiary material for this proposed revolution came in the form of a uniquely accessible computer programming language. Influenced by the Swiss developmental psychologist and philosopher Jean Piaget, with whom he studied, Papert claimed to have combined Piaget's complex theories of child development with his own work in the field of artificial intelligence. This apparent fusion led to the creation of Logo, which Papert hoped would systematize the use of computers in learning, beginning in kindergarten, if not earlier.

Papert is not unique in his assertion that the models or tools a child is given will ultimately shape how and what that child can learn. He belongs to a long line of behavioral theorists, from B. F. Skinner to the more recent, and more extreme, Glenn Doman of the Better Baby Institute in Philadelphia. (Doman has persuaded generations of parents to shine bright lights into the eyes of newborns, dangle geometric shapes over babies' cribs, and teach two-year-olds to read using scarlet-colored flashcards—each of these being techniques for speeding up the development of what Doman believes are dormant cognitive abilities.) What makes Papert different is his overwhelming reliance on a single technology.

Papert's faith in the computer as a learning medium is linked to his fascination with gearboxes when a very young child. "Before I was two years old I had developed an intense involvement with automobiles. The names of car parts made up a very substantial portion of my vocabulary: I was particularly proud of knowing about the parts of the transmission system, the gearbox, and most especially the differential. It was, of course, many years before I understood how gears work; but once I did, playing with gears became a favorite pastime."[3]

It was through Papert's early experience of playing with gears that mathematical ideas entered his life. Gears proved an effective learning tool for a number of reasons. They were part of the natural "landscape" around him, objects that he could discover on his own. They were also part of the adult world to which he wanted to belong, and thus a means of relating to adults. In addition, he could use his knowledge of body movement to think about the way gears worked, and in so doing come to grips with the mathematics involved. Far from being just a physical object, by acting as a launch pad for abstract thought, the differential gear was transformed into what Papert called an "object-to-think-with."

For Papert, the differential gear was thus a learning tool of prime importance. Gears, however, have a rather specialized appeal. Few children are likely to derive significant mathematical insights from playing with the innards of an automobile. Papert had to wait until he went to M.I.T. to discover what seemed to be the ultimate, universal "object-to-think-with": the computer. Papert's thesis, then, as he himself succinctly states, is: "What the gears cannot do the computer might."[4]

And what might learning to use computers do for children? Nothing less, in Papert's view, than change the way they learn everything else. Many people have interpreted this to mean that the computer can be used to teach absolutely anything.

It's clear that Papert became as fascinated by computers as an adult as he was by gears when a child. Describing his work with Marvin Minsky and Warren McCulloch at M.I.T., he says that he was "playing like a child and experiencing a volcanic explosion of creativity." If this could happen to him, he wondered, "Why couldn't the computer give a child the same kind of experience? Why couldn't a child play like me?"[5] Papert was so enthusiastic about the computer's potential to educate children that he dubbed it "The Children's Machine" (also the title of his second book).

The model on which Papert bases his approach to learning is the way in which a child learns to talk. Speech is part of the child's natural landscape, and children learn to talk "naturally" as they listen to and communicate with their parents and other members of their family. Speech is not forced on children or drilled into them; they seize the opportunity to talk because it makes sense to do so. Make computers a part of the child's natural environment, Papert argues, and the child will seize the opportunities they offer to explore and learn. It's Papert's belief that such spontaneous learning will make much formal education unnecessary. "I believe that the computer presence will enable us to so modify the learning environment outside the classrooms that much if not all the knowledge schools presently try to teach with such pain and expense and such limited success will be learned, as the child learns to talk, painlessly, successfully, and without organized instruction."[6]

Infectious as Papert's enthusiasm may be, one must ask whether his emphasis on computer-based learning is an appropriate response to the needs of the vast majority of students. There are dangers in basing child-development and educational theories on the experiences of an exceptional or gifted child, as Papert evidently was, particularly when that child had a rather unusual fixation. Gifted children often have difficulty functioning in a regular classroom because they learn more quickly, in markedly different ways, and often with less instruction than other children. Logo was intended as a universal gateway to a new form of learning, but in reality it has thrown up a number of formidable roadblocks.

Decades of research into the effectiveness of Logo have shown that, for the majority of children, the process of learning how to program is anything but effortless. The evidence from conferences, reports, and literally hundreds of research studies also shows that Logo does not appear to enhance children's thinking or problem-solving skills. For many children, the experience of using Logo is simply bewildering.

Papert has always opposed the use of the computer as a drill-and-practice machine. Instead, he favors a discovery-learning approach, in which students are largely free to experiment with Logo on their own. The problem is that this style of learning encourages a trial-and-error approach which makes it difficult for children to develop an understanding of the programming language. Although this might eventually give students a knowledge of various commands, they are unlikely to develop sufficient competence in the program for them to engage in the kind of learning Papert envisaged. Contrary to the assertions that have been made for Logo, the program isn't simple enough that children can master it in the way its creator intended.

In order to learn to create even the simplest geometric shapes on the screen, for instance, children must first learn to conceptualize movement in terms of direction and distance, and do so from the turtle's (a triangular cursor) point of view rather than their own. Only then will they be able to work out the appropriate numerical codes to key in. Producing a square on the screen, for instance, requires that children learn the following sequence of commands: "FORWARD 100, RIGHT 90, FORWARD 100, RIGHT 90, FORWARD 100, RIGHT 90, FORWARD 100" (with a final "RIGHT 90" to have the turtle facing the same way as when it started). If the turtle starts at the lower left-hand side of the screen and is pointing upwards, the first "FORWARD 100" will create a line that goes from the bottom to the top of the screen; "RIGHT 90" will turn the turtle 90 degrees to the right; the next "FORWARD 100" will create a line at right angles to the first, going from left to right across the top of the screen; and so on. "FORWARD 100," which to a child might indicate movement in one direction only, in fact moves the turtle both up and down, and left and right; similarly, "RIGHT 90" turns the turtle left as well as right (to complete the square, you need a line going left along the bottom of the screen), although from its own perspective the turtle in fact makes a right turn each time. Many young children will find the relationship between these commands and the resulting actions confusing. This is because they are still coping with the concepts of left and right, up and down as they experience them directly themselves. Yet, to be able to use Logo, children must be able to transfer these concepts to an object whose sense of direction is independent of their own.

It is not until grade five that children are expected to be able to use mathematical language to describe geometric concepts. Most children are not expected to understand key concepts in transformational geometry using concrete materials and drawings until they are about ten years of age.[7] If children are not developmentally ready to cope with the concepts involved, they will find working with Logo a difficult and frustrating experience. This was the case in a year-long study of second-graders in Ontario. Many children in this study needed extensive guidance from their teacher throughout the duration of the project. Leaving them to work on their own simply slowed them down to the point where they became bored and suffered from a sense of their incompetence. These children soon gave up trying to solve a particular problem and played around aimlessly, waiting for their turn at the computer to be over. Although the children were approximately the same age, they varied considerably in ability, and this made it difficult for the teacher to provide appropriate support to the class as a whole.[8]

Researchers at the University of Stirling in Scotland, who had been working with older children aged nine to eleven, drew similar conclusions. They found that it was simply not feasible to allow children to find their own way through what they termed "this web of complexity." Allowing children to construct their own problems and solve them by testing hypotheses was a desirable goal, but in this case it was outweighed by the "real difficulties" that arose.[9]

Non-structured work with Logo places enormous demands on teachers' time, and this fact alone makes its inclusion in the daily curriculum problematic on strictly practical grounds. Moreover, without continual guidance and assistance, children are likely to approach Logo in a haphazard way that will do little to enhance their cognitive development. Logo may, in theory, provide opportunities for them to think about how to solve problems, but in practice there is no guarantee that children won't use the turtle simply to fool around or play games. Many, it seems, have no understanding of how a computer works and fail to grasp the point of the exercise. Two Manhattan teachers who set out to use Logo with their fourth-, fifth-, and sixth-grade students discovered that the children did not have any realistic idea of what they could do with the program and couldn't figure out the steps involved in solving their problems.[10]

On the other hand, although children appear to learn Logo more readily with a teacher to guide them each step of the way, a more structured approach can lead to a narrow focus on Logo as a programming language rather than a means of developing cognitive skills. (This is in fact what happened with the Manhattan teachers mentioned above.[11]) It seems that there is a kind of Catch-22 at work here. The broad effects claimed for Logo require a certain competence in programming, but an emphasis on programming tends to displace the discovery-learning through which these broad effects are supposed to be achieved.

Teaching children to think logically or procedurally might prove to be more complex and elusive than Logo educators have considered. As Theodore Roszak, author of *The Cult of Information*, points out, "students have to be lured into it cleverly and then work at it with great persistence." Yet all the persistence in the world will yield little result if the child herself is unwilling or unable to absorb this kind of thinking. "Has it ever occurred to Logo educators that there may be a reason for the seeming strain of the exercise? It may be because the mind does not always and spontaneously solve problems in that way, especially the young and growing mind. Children may be much more absorbed at feeling their way through the major contours of mental life.... Envisioning things as meaningful wholes, choosing among them: this may be the first order of intellectual business for children. Careful, logical plotting of procedures may be premature for them, and so a distraction."[12]

There is, in fact, no consistent evidence that children learn to think in a logical or sequential way, and thus develop problem-solving skills, as a result of programming in Logo, or that they can then apply these skills in other situations. Problem-solving skills can be taught, but learning skills in one context does not necessarily mean children will be able to transfer them to another subject or situation, especially if it is an unfamiliar one. Yet without the transfer of problem-solving skills, where is the intellectual boost that Logo was designed to give?

Basically, there are two ways in which the transfer of skills can occur.[13] One occurs when a skill is practiced in a variety of situations to the point that it becomes completely automatic, like learning to ride a bicycle. We simply transfer the skill to similar situations without having to think about it. The other type of transfer involves a conscious awareness that skills learned in one context can usefully be applied in another. This implies, of course, that we know very well what we are doing. We make a deliberate rather than an automatic response. Children who learn to read music in order to play the piano can easily transfer the concepts of musical notation to learning to play the flute or reading choral music. Mathematics, which requires an understanding of numerical patterns, is another good example. Children can learn to add, subtract, multiply, and divide using blocks, shells, or beads, or their fingers and toes. Once these patterns are understood and memorized, they can be applied in all sorts of other contexts, like counting change at the corner store or measuring correctly when baking. Transferring the concepts Logo is designed to teach would mean that children would be able to describe in words, or reproduce by hand, what was meant by a rectangle, triangle, or circle.

Is either form of transfer likely to occur with problem-solving skills learned through programming in elementary schools? Most of the evidence points to the answer no. In order to develop the necessary knowledge and skills, students would have to spend far more time programming than most schools would ever contemplate, and would need considerable guidance from teachers with a good understanding of programming.

There may be a better case for arguing that, if there is any real benefit in programming, it comes from the kind of cooperative effort involved when several children are sharing a computer. A number of studies have noted that children working together at a computer tend to socialize more and ask each other questions more often than when working at more traditional classroom activities (although collaboration can often lead to conflict since only one child at a time can be in charge of the keyboard). Some researchers have gone so far as to suggest that this kind of interaction among children is as important as anything that happens between the children and the computer.[14] But this raises the question of whether there aren't other activities that could encourage socializing and questioning without having to resort to the computer in the first place.

Meanwhile, Logo and its spinoffs continue to be widely used in schools, and few teachers are entirely clear why they are using them or indeed what they hope their students will accomplish. Observing a group of eight- and nine-year-olds working with Logo in a California classroom, I saw how painstaking it was for them to key in the correct commands in order to direct the computer to copy various geometric shapes, which were etched on transparencies and affixed to their computer screens. The forty-five-minute exercise seemed both laborious and tedious.

"Is it part of their geometry class?" I asked their teacher.

"No."

"Part of their math class, then?"

"No," she responded. "It teaches them to think procedurally."

"What skills do they take away from this?" I persisted.

"Studies have shown," she informed me, "that the skills are not transferable."

Even if students are able to exploit the creative potential of Logo, it remains questionable whether Logo or programs like it actually promote cognitive development. It might simply be that such programs presuppose a level of mental development at least as high as that which they purport to encourage. As child psychologist David Elkind suggests, "a child who really understands programming is at a sufficiently high level of mental development that learning programming is not really going to promote additional mental development."[15] It has been suggested, for example, that children won't really benefit from using Logo until they are about twelve years old, the age at which they develop the ability to deal with abstract concepts.[16] It would appear that this ability precedes the beneficial use of Logo rather than the other way round.

Piaget referred to the early stage of childhood as the "concrete" or "operational" stage of development. "Concrete" thinking is well developed by the time the child is six or seven years old. Up to this age, and for some years afterwards, children learn a great deal through their bodies by manipulating objects in the world around them. It is a time when children learn to count using blocks, marbles, or their fingers. What Piaget called "formal" thinking develops around twelve years of age, although many children are well on their way to it several years before. This is a period when children begin to engage in abstract or symbolic thinking, and it marks the transition to adult modes of thought.

It is here that Papert departs significantly from Piagetian psychology. Piaget and others assume a slow, continuous growth with certain spurts which, in the normal course of events, occur naturally at key stages of development. There is thus a natural pattern of development that should be allowed to unfold at its own pace. It follows that certain types of learning are appropriate for children of certain ages. Papert, on the other hand, believes that computers can speed up the process of cognitive development, shifting the boundary between concrete and formal and allowing children to make the passage to adult thinking at a much earlier age than was previously considered possible.[17]

This faster, smarter philosophy lies at the heart of computer-based learning. Its aim is to catapult children into the adult world as quickly as possible. Through the wonders of computer technology, young minds will be able to leapfrog over the tedious obstacles of childhood learning and become full members of the cyber-culture their elders are so eagerly embracing. Viewed from this perspective, the computer, far from being "the children's machine," is very much part of an adult agenda.

This approach to learning ignores both the fact that children have bodies and the nature of the relationship between their physical and cognitive development. Using a computer precludes the use of the full range of sensorimotor skills and inhibits children's physical exploration of their environment. Advocates of computer use for young children overlook the consequences of such a sedentary form of learning, which relies almost entirely on a single (that is, visual) sense.

At the moment, we can only speculate as to what these consequences might be in terms of children's cognitive development. Our understanding of cognitive processes remains very rudimentary and, in many instances, highly conjectural. The little we know about the brain is dwarfed by the amount we do not know. What we do know is that sensory stimulation and physical development are critical to the cognitive development of children, and that this relationship exists from the moment of birth. Infants first bond with their mothers through their sense of smell. Almost immediately after an infant smells its mother's body for the first time, networks begin to form in its brain.[18] Moreover, there are certain critical stages or windows of opportunity for cognitive development which, if missed, cannot be recovered later. An infant who is placed on its mother's stomach within minutes after birth will learn to crawl towards the nipple; an infant who is removed from its mother, even for a short time, will not learn to do so. The delicate relationship between mother and child can be disturbed in ways that are not fully understood.

The bonding that occurs between parent and child has profound implications for the child's physical and cognitive development. Babies, especially those prematurely born, grow faster and are healthier when they are held and cuddled. Touching babies activates their sensory systems, and they become more alert and attuned to the world. Securely bonded, well-fed children are naturally more able to learn from their surroundings.

As infants grow into toddlers, it becomes even clearer that children's cognitive and physical development are inextricably linked. Maria Montessori noted that observations of children all over the world confirm that a child's mind develops as a result of physical movement. Language development increases alongside the child's use of those muscles that are needed to form sounds and words. "Movement helps the development of mind," she wrote, "and this finds renewed expression in further movement and activity. It follows that we are dealing with a cycle, because mind and movement are parts of the same entity. The senses also take part, and the child who has less opportunity for sensorial activity remains at a lower mental level."[19]

Continued observation of children has deepened our understanding of these intricate links. The action of finger-pointing, which is unique to human babies, has recently been closely correlated with language acquisition. Babies who start to point early in life acquire words more readily than babies who do not point. Some babies begin to speak before they learn to point, but learning to point speeds up the process of language acquisition by drawing objects to the attention of adults who can then name the objects. Pointing thus initiates conversation between adult and child, which is of crucial importance in the development of the child's oral language. One baby can also learn to point by watching another do so. The fact that babies point at things they want to have identified for them suggests a strong connection in the nervous system between those areas of the brain that control pointing and those involved in speech. The physical coordination necessary to see, hear, and point seems to stimulate the mind.[20]

It is during infancy and childhood, up to the age of about twelve, that the most critical structural organization of the brain takes place. This is when the brain is most actively learning from its environment. It shapes itself according to the sensations it experiences and can reorganize itself extremely quickly in response to changes in stimulation and environment. The first three years are especially important, since it is during this time that the foundations for thinking, language, vision, and other attributes are established. But the "windows of opportunity" that permit information to reach the brain and cause changes in its structure are open for only a brief time at various stages of a child's development. When these windows close, the brain loses much of its ability to remold itself. Its basic structure has now been determined.[21]

Certain kinds of sensory experience need therefore to occur during the right period of development if the brain is to take advantage of them. As we well know, it is much easier to start learning music or a foreign language as a young child than as an adult. On the other hand, if deprived of the right kind of stimulation, some neural pathways in the brain will simply die off and, once gone, will not regenerate. For example, visual stimulation at birth is of vital importance. Without it, the brain cells designed to interpret vision will either wither away or be diverted to other tasks. If this happens, eyes that are perfectly healthy will never be able to see. For this reason, infants born with cataracts now have them removed as soon as possible after birth, since delaying surgery could leave them permanently blind. As well, children who have amblyopia (lazy eye) must have their strong eye patched in order to allow the weak one to develop the appropriate neural connections in the brain. Without enough sensory stimulation, the brain will shut off vision to the poor eye.

Children in elementary schools who spend hours a day on the computer face similar, if less extreme, risks since they might be losing out on essential sensory experiences. If the brain needs to be activated by using the whole body, what centers in the brain will be undernourished by a lack of tactile or sensorimotor stimulation? Computer programs can be mentally stimulating in some respects, but they offer little in terms of overall sensory experience. Placing a child in front of a computer is more physically restricting than placing a child at a desk and expecting him to stay there. The eye's focal range is fixed at one distance for long periods of time, something that does not occur when reading or looking at the blackboard. (This is discussed in more detail in chapter 9.)

The risks are all the more real when children begin using computers at a very young age. Software aimed at toddlers and preschoolers appears to be a growing market. Of the ten best-selling CD-ROM titles in the United States in 1995, four were considered suitable for children aged three, and one was advertised for users as young as eighteen months old. With the National Association for the Education of Young Children approving computer activities for children of three and four years old, we can expect this trend to continue.[22]

The argument put forward to justify computer use at such an early age is that these very young children can learn to operate simple programs. Children aged two and three can, for example, use a computer simulation to sort objects into categories with no more difficulty than using real-world objects, and their ability to do so has been seen as proof that such simulations are not too abstract for them.[23] But it's by no means certain that working with a computer program offers any *additional* benefits compared with activities involving real-world materials; on the contrary, there may well be significant drawbacks.

Early-childhood educators have long recognized that the younger the child the more he or she requires a range of physically diverse, "hands-on" activities. Using computers during their preschool years, which many of them do, deprives children of more stimulating kinds of learning. In their book *Engaging Children's Minds*, Lilian Katz and Sylvia Chard argue that "just because children *can* do something when they are young does not mean that they *should* do it." Certain activities, for example, can be within a child's capability but may have an adverse long-term effect if engaged in frequently. It is particularly important to distinguish between what young children can do and what they should do "because most children appear willing, if not eager, to do what is asked of them." But, say Katz and Chard, "children's willingness and enjoyment are misleading criteria for judging the value of an activity."[24]

The narrow sensory range of computer-based learning should be a concern, especially in terms of its cumulative, long-term effects. Far from opening up a world of learning, as is often claimed, computers tend to restrict the arena in which children's learning takes place, emphasizing the development of abstract skills at the expense of concrete modes of learning. But the brain is, after all, part of our bodies, and the mind receives information through all our senses. Some children who do not learn to read easily, for instance, are simply not strong visual learners and learn sound-word correlations more readily when they paint the words, hear them spoken, or practice writing in sand. In an experiment in California, researchers discovered that young children become better spellers if they first say each word and letter before they spell it, and then repeat each letter as they write it. This method, called "Simultaneous Oral Spelling," was found to be a better method of teaching spelling to grade-one children than simply typing letters onto a computer screen. The *combination* of seeing, hearing, and writing the words by hand seems to enable children to learn and remember the correct spellings.[25]

Physical forms of learning are especially important for young children, who are still discovering much of the world about them through bodily contact with it. There is an interesting parallel here with other animal species. As John A. Livingston has described in his book *The Rogue Primate*, domesticated animals like chickens or cattle have much diminished sensory capabilities compared with their wild counterparts. In the domesticated animal, "scent, hearing, vision and tactility are in varying degrees crippled. From the outset of its life the animal is poor at processing even the meagre sensory information available in its simple, monotonous environment." Children today are already growing up with a much reduced potential to develop sensory acuity because of the monotony of their environments. Watching television, playing with computers, and spending large amounts of time indoors all contribute to a lack of sensorimotor stimulation. Like domesticated animals, children do not experience the full potential of their physical selves.[26]

One critic of Logo has described its learning environment as having "no smells or tastes, no wind or birdsong (unless the computer is programmed to produce electronic tweets), no connection with soil, water, sunlight, warmth, no real ecology (although primitive interactions with a computerized caterpillar might be arranged)." It is "almost autistic" in the enclosed relationship it develops between the child and what appears on the screen, and it offers far less variety of stimulation than children's playground games.[27] The comparison with play is instructive. As well as helping to develop body coordination through physical movement, many children's games demand a high degree of visual and auditory concentration, qualities that are invaluable in the classroom, where academic failure is often associated with an inability to pay attention. They also help children discover what is and is not possible in terms of their physical capabilities and their interactions with others. Learning through direct physical experience cannot be reproduced on a computer screen.

Early-childhood educators like Maria Montessori and David Weikart, to name just two, were instrumental in changing the monotonous classroom environments in which young children were expected to learn. It is thanks to their research into child development that classrooms lost their spartan feel: wooden desks and chairs were replaced with cushions and carpets for reading corners; water-tables, building blocks, dress-up corners, live animals (like hamsters or white mice), and window boxes with growing plants became standard features in elementary schools.

Papert has argued that computers enable children to undertake more complex projects than they normally can in the physical world. Children often imagine things they would like to make or do, but when they try to put their ideas into practice they are frustrated by "the unintelligible limitations of matter and people." With a computer program, these limitations can be safely encountered. As a result, children can acquire "a feel for complexity."[28] Complexity, however, is not confined to computer activities. "Matter" and "people" offer not only the sensorimotor challenges which are so important to children but the rich social and emotional interactions that are not part of life on the screen.

Graphics programs, for example, enable children to produce pictures more sophisticated-looking than those they create with paint or crayons, but they deny them the spontaneous, tactile experience that is essential to art. Computer graphics give nothing of the concrete experience that comes from mixing your own paints, and watching as yellow and blue blend into green. Precision within clearly defined limits is gained at the expense of subtlety and spontaneity. On-screen there is no need to live with messy imperfections or worry about spoiling what you have already done. If you make a mistake, you have only to choose "undo" or "cancel" and the error will disappear.[29] But in art, as in many other activities, "mistakes" often create opportunities for learning. This is rarely true of most software environments.

The fact that computers enable children to present their work in a professional format is not necessarily an advantage to them. What they may lose is ownership of their individual creativity. In many ways, a flawless computer printout depersonalizes children's work. Some judge work as more successful if it has a computer-generated neatness, like those who prefer a word-processed page to the imperfections of their students' handwriting. The heart of artistic expression, however, lies in originality. Computer-generated material gives less scope for personal creativity, because a child must work within the constraints of the computer program. The result, in the view of Toronto artist Konrad Bonk, is depersonalized art "unsoiled by the human hand."

Karl Pribram, a leading brain researcher at the University of Virginia, has suggested that computers will not spawn any genuine creativity until the user can design the program. Pribram is also of the opinion that a wide range of activities should be given to children in elementary school, including visual art, hands-on science, music, and languages.

Some schools do emphasize the importance of original creative work. Waldorf schools, which now represent the fastest-growing educational movement in the United States, offer tremendous scope for and encouragement to individual creativity. For instance, the main lesson books produced by children in a Waldorf school are remarkable because they are so personal. Each book reflects the style of its creator and no two are ever alike. Such highly original books are, in a very real sense, the handiwork of the students concerned; one can see the amount of work, both physical and mental, that has gone into the making of them. Because each book is unique, it encourages children to stay connected to and take ownership of their work and their learning. And like adults, children are more highly motivated when they feel an emotional and physical connection to what they do. At a Waldorf school, computers are eschewed until high school in order to give a child as much scope for the creative arts as possible. Nurturing a rich imaginative life in childhood, Waldorf educators say, is the key to a successful social, emotional, and intellectual adulthood.

The physical effort and control required in working with concrete materials can at times make learning seem slow, but it appears to pay off in the long run. Researchers investigating the role of sensorimotor-perceptual skills in children's cognitive development were surprised to discover that certain kinds of activities—like putting pegs into holes, solving pencil-and-paper mazes, and copying geometric shapes—were related to academic achievement not only for five-year-olds but also for older children up to thirteen years of age.[30]

Underlying the importance of learning through physical sensations and the use of physical materials is the fact that children are first and foremost creatures of sense. As the noted naturalist Diane Ackerman has written, "There is no way in which to understand the world without first detecting it through the radar-net of the senses. What is beyond our senses we cannot know. Our senses define the edge of consciousness."[31] Making "sense" of the world means using the senses to find meaning and sustenance in our environment. At birth, babies emerge from the Eden of the womb into a tumultuous world of new sensations in which they must try to find their bearings. It is from this tangle of sensations that infants slowly build up an understanding of their world, a process that continues in early childhood.

Though it is often claimed that computers offer a rich, active learning environment, the fact is that much of the software aimed at children does little more than bombard them with a lot of visual information within carefully designed parameters—just like children's television programs. Developmental theorists argue that because some children now get more information from visual images than from talking with other people, their brains are simply not being trained to understand oral language and retain what has been said. In *Endangered Minds: Why Our Children Don't Think,* Jane Healy suggests that overemphasizing the visual sense deprives children of the opportunity to acquire listening skills, which are crucial to overall cognitive development. "Children with poor auditory skills—whatever the reason—have a difficult time learning to read, spelling accurately, remembering what they read long enough to understand it, or retaining the internal sound of a sentence they want to write down."[32]

Language skills are built up from listening to stories and rhymes and from having meaningful conversations with parents, siblings, and caregivers. When children talk with others, the conversation proceeds at a pace that enables the children to follow what is said. It also concerns things of direct interest to them. Words that accompany the images of electronic media have none of this immediacy, and the succession of images is so rapid that children either cannot or choose not to pay attention to what they are hearing. They may hear, but they don't listen. Children who don't learn to listen can easily develop habits that let them avoid exercising—and thus building—important auditory-processing connections in the brain. As Healy argues, "*habits of the mind soon become structures of the brain....* The very act of remembering lays down physical tracks in the brain, but children can quite easily avoid having to build these systems."[33]

Too much electronic stimulation, whether from computers or television, is possibly contributing to the rise in the incidence of learning disabilities such as auditory-processing problems and attention deficit disorder. Many teachers believe that the listening skills of children in schools today are much worse than those of previous generations, and many teachers report that children who watch television or play a lot of video games are much harder to teach, because they have trouble paying attention.

Children are also becoming less physically coordinated because of their increasingly sedentary habits. In research spanning several decades, child development expert Phyllis Weikart has found that children engage in less physical activity than they used to—about 75 percent less than they did at the turn of the century. Largely because of the time pressures on parents, children are not given enough time or space to allow them to have the necessary experiences that are optimal for their growth. "Children are not encouraged to spend as much time crawling, or exploring their physical environment as they once were. We have children who are not growing up with adequate coordination. As a result there is much more clumsiness in children." And in teenagers, too. In her program with adolescent girls, Weikart has observed a steady decline in certain key skills. Teenagers are much clumsier physically than they were just twenty years ago, a fact she attributes to lack of key physical experience in the early years.

This clumsiness, Weikart believes, indicates a corresponding cognitive underdevelopment. "The body is the primary learning centre for the child. We give inadequate attention to the body, so we are not building the learning foundation in developmentally appropriate ways." As psychiatrists and health care practitioners are well aware, physical clumsiness is often linked to learning disorders.

As well, insufficient attention is paid to the kinds of activities that are appropriate to the child's development. For instance, a child needs to work with fine-motor skills before the gross-motor skills are in place. Weikart's research indicates that the ability to keep a steady beat—simply clapping hands rhythmically—figures prominently in cognitive development. Children who cannot keep a steady beat have great difficulty reading. This basic sense of time is learned through early experiences of being rocked or sung to or from listening to rhymes and stories—all experiences dependent upon intimate contact with an adult. By pressing abstract thinking upon children prematurely, we could be ignoring many such subtle links between physical coordination and intellectual and emotional development.

One fine-motor activity that is intimately connected with computer use is keyboarding, a skill that children are being encouraged to learn at an ever earlier age. But this activity is developmentally inappropriate for young children because they do not possess sufficient tactile dexterity to carry out complex actions with their fingers while looking at the computer screen. (Back when typewriters were in use, children did not learn to type until they were thirteen or fourteen years old. Most people take months to learn how to touch-type and don't remember how hard it was not to glance continually at the keyboard while memorizing the position of the keys.)

Learning to type is a difficult accomplishment involving a separation of the most natural eye and hand combination such as that which occurs in writing by hand. In the primary school years, children are still struggling with the basics of handwriting, copying words letter by letter or syllable by syllable. Expecting children to acquire sophisticated skills before they have become proficient at the basics might well cause them problems in the future because insufficient time and attention have been devoted to activities that would allow them to gradually build up their small-muscle coordination.

Of course, many of the computer programs designed for young children do not require fluent typing skills. But even when children have the motor skills needed to operate a program, they also need to be able to direct and hold their eyes on the details of what they are looking at on the screen. One behavioral optometrist reckons that "15 to 40 percent of primary children have not achieved a level in this skill needed for everyday classroom tasks."[34]

Activities such as learning to sew, modelling with clay, baking, catching a ball, knitting, marble games, or playing a recorder are much better ways to teach fine-motor skills, especially eye-hand coordination. They are far more appropriate from a developmental point of view, because they give a child more physical freedom and a sense of accomplishment. They are also much gentler on the eyes.

In *Mindstorms*, Papert describes how he used his body to think about gears. "I could feel how gears turn by imagining my body turning. This made it possible for me to draw on my 'body knowledge' to think about gear systems."[35] Given his age (he is now in his sixties), it is likely that he was encouraged to engage in much more physical activity than many children experience today. Without adequate experience of bodily movement, it is unlikely that he could have imagined the way gears move. Papert learned about abstract thinking by first using the concreteness of his body. It is ironic that in computerizing the classroom in the name of greater learning opportunities, a situation that Papert did much to bring about, this lesson has been ignored. In concentrating on the development of children's minds, we have all but forgotten their bodies.

Although the computer is touted by many as a complex multimedia machine, it relies mainly on only one sense: the visual. Bill Gates has said that computers can do a better job of supporting varied thinking than lectures and textbooks. He calls the computer "thought support" and suggests that students can more readily grasp complex processes while manipulating information in several media.[36] He would do well to acknowledge that, for children, the greatest aid to "thought support" is in fact the human body.

4

Online to Success?
Computer-Based Instruction
and Academic Achievement

We must guard against the belief that computerizing always represents progress. Convenience, speed, and accuracy are not necessarily tied to validity and importance.

D. LaMont Johnson and Cleborne D. Maddux[1]

P arents naturally want the best possible education for their children. Just as the parents of baby-boomers purchased home encyclopedias in record numbers, so today's parents are buying computers and software, hoping to give their children a head start. But while parents in the past might have waited until their children could read before purchasing a home encyclopedia, today's parents are buying computers and software for their preschoolers, including babies as young as eight months old. Hoping to give children a leg-up before formal schooling begins, parents are exposing them to computers at an ever earlier age.

Like the encyclopedia salesmen, software marketing companies are targeting families with young children as well as homing in on the lucrative educational market. According to *The Economist*, sales of educational software in the United States, much of it from the lucrative home-learning market, amount to between $750 million and $1 billion a year.[2] In fact, the home market for computers and learning software is growing even faster than the school market. Parents want their children to have this magical tool, whose use has become synonymous with academic success and marketable skills. They fear that without this vital piece of technology their children will be left behind and will end up intellectually undernourished and almost certainly unemployed.

Public perception of the computer as a passport to success has been heightened by the industry's relentless advertising campaign. Often the ads feature a child sitting beside a parent at the computer terminal, or depict the child with the computer as having gone to "the head of the class"—a favorite slogan in Apple's promotion of its technology. Another popular angle is to humanize the hardware, giving it a friendly personality and a desire to please in the face of the many different demands of its owners. "You won't believe the things I do for this family," says an AST computer, which then describes how it helps "Junior," "Ms. Social Success," Mom, and Dad.[3]

Apple and Microsoft also regularly advertise on television the virtues and advantages of home computing, although the scenarios presented are sometimes less than convincing. One recent Apple commercial shows a father and his young son apparently bonding while looking at the computer screen. At one point, the father smiles proudly and caresses the back of his son's head. But the child is oblivious to his father's touch; the screen totally absorbs his attention.

Behind the comforting assurance that computers are part of a close-knit family life there is another, more urgent theme: kids need computers because those who have them will outperform those who don't. That, at least, is the message insinuated in a number of computer hardware and software advertisements. Take, for example, a double-page ad for Microsoft's *Encarta 95* multimedia encyclopedia which appeared in the London *Daily Telegraph Magazine.* "Forget Goldilocks and the Three Bears, tell us about Sartre," the headline reads. The rest of the blurb begins: "'C'mon, dad, tell us about Sartre and existentialism and his belief in the inescapable responsibility of all individuals for their own decisions and his relationship with Simone de Beauvoir,' we pleaded as he tucked us in for the night." The ad shows the faces of two little girls, who can't be more than six years old.

Even less convincing (since no evidence of precocious development is produced) is a Sears Brand Central ad, which makes the following claim for the little girl who stands behind a computer with her arms stretched up above her head: "She may be only 5 but she's light years ahead. By the time she reaches first grade, she'll have *traveled* to Jupiter and back." The computer monitor shows two planets in misleading proximity to each other. What help "travelling" to Jupiter will be to a first-grader is left unexplained.

The overall message conveyed by this advertising onslaught is, then, quite clear: kids with computers will outperform those without computers. But do computers really enhance learning? Is there consistent and convincing evidence to support this view?

Research into the link between computers and improved academic performance has been going on for more than thirty years. In the past two decades there have been thousands of studies undertaken in North American classrooms in an attempt to examine the effectiveness of computer-based instruction.

The evidence that emerges is inconclusive at best. Taken together, reviews of research published between 1975 and 1995 show mixed and sometimes contradictory results.[4] For example, researchers at the Center for Research on Learning and Teaching at the University of Michigan, who analyzed the results of 254 controlled evaluation studies, concluded that computer-based instruction "usually produces positive effects on students." Specifically, their analysis showed that the average student in a class receiving computer-based instruction would outperform 62 percent of students in a class not using computers.[5] On the other hand, a research team from Florida A&M University and Florida State University found a number of reviews that showed no significant difference in performance between students who were using computers and those who were not.[6]

Results of a number of individual large-scale projects also do little to endorse computer-based instruction. For example, the Minnesota Technology Demonstration Project, undertaken in the mid-1980s, involved over 20 percent of the state's school districts. Researchers who studied the results of computer use with fourth- to sixth-graders over a two-year period discovered that, on average, these students did slightly less well in math, reading, and language arts than students taught by traditional methods.[7]

The efforts of one Midwest school district to integrate technology into the primary grades with a project known as "Computer Applications Now" (CAN) were similarly disappointing. Basing their study on classroom observations, student test scores, interviews, and questionnaires, a team of researchers evaluated the results of this project and concluded that there was "little reason to believe the CAN project has any significant effect on student performance."[8]

It is important to realize, too, that where the results were positive, not all students benefited equally. Generally speaking, boys appeared to perform better than girls, and low-achieving students showed more improvement than average students.

Studies looking at the effects of Integrated Learning Systems (ILS) show similarly unconvincing or, at best, problematic results.

In an ILS, a central management system links individual computers that are placed either in a computer lab or library or distributed in classrooms throughout the school. The system delivers courses as part of a school's standard curriculum, the subjects most commonly taught by this method being math, reading, and language arts. For a certain amount of time each week, students work on problems or practice drills presented on their computer screens, which act essentially as electronic workbooks. Newer applications have evolved into self-paced workbooks with graphics and sound.

A frequently cited advantage of the ILS is that it allows students to work at their own pace. The system determines the level each student has reached in each subject and presents the lesson accordingly. The computer provides immediate feedback to the user and records the student's work for later inspection by the teacher. By monitoring the results, teachers are ostensibly able to assess where their students are having difficulty and thus provide the necessary assistance.

It appears, however, that ILS programs have been, at best, only moderately successful in enhancing students' academic achievement, and that in some cases their effectiveness has been exaggerated. In an extensive review of ILS evaluation reports, Henry Jay Becker, of the University of California at Irvine, suggests that some studies (including the most widely cited) substantially over-report the effectiveness of Integrated Learning Systems.[9] Moreover, only low- and high-achieving students appeared to benefit from using this technology. Students in the middle range (the majority) did better when taught by their teachers.

Becker also cautions that evaluating the results of ILS programs is made difficult because of a number of factors that influence the quality of the research. In a majority of studies, for example, poor evaluation design (which includes failure to compare students' performance with that of a control group receiving traditional instruction) is compounded by inadequate data collection, poor data analysis, and/or inadequate description of how the program operated and the conditions in which it was used.

Even when every effort has been made to avoid these shortcomings, as was the case in a four-year project in New York City, the use of ILS programs remains problematic. The New York City Public Schools Integrated Learning Systems Project, which ran from 1989 to 1993 and involved thousands of students in grades three through five, failed to produce the expected improvements in math and reading. The researchers evaluating the project concluded that the results "were at best mixed and at worst negative."[10]

One reason why Integrated Learning Systems don't achieve more impressive results is that the learning environment they provide reflects a view of learning that, in Becker's words, "is individualistic and solitary at its core."[11] Integrated Learning Systems promote individualized problem-solving at the expense of interaction with peers. But much recent research argues that childhood learning is primarily a social activity. Young children especially learn a tremendous amount from talking with their teachers and with other students. They learn at least as much through dialogue with others as they do by solving problems on their own. Where an ILS is in place, children have less opportunity for discussion, not only with other children but also with their teachers. Given that self-paced instruction is possible with an

ILS, it is conceivable that each child could be working at a different rate on a different program. This means that there would be little context in which children could discuss their classroom work and so less opportunity to share problem-solving strategies. Such a system creates an enormous difficulty for the teacher in keeping a basic focus to class lessons and discussions.

Another reason given for the failure of ILS programs to boost academic performance is that their use has not been properly implemented. A two-year national study of ILS programs in the United States concluded that it was under-utilization of the systems that accounted for the poor results found by Becker and others. During the first year of the study, students in some schools "were spending as little as 10 minutes per week on the system!" But when schools improved their implementation, so that students spent "significantly more time" on the ILS and teachers were "much more involved" in integrating the system with other classroom activities, the results were "startling": students in ILS classes scored higher on standardized tests than those in conventional classes.[12]

These results, however, can be achieved only at considerable cost. The authors of the study believe that "it is essential that students spend a substantial portion of their day working on the computers. Our studies suggest that each student must spend *a minimum of 30 minutes per subject per day* on the computers to achieve significant learning gains."[13] Assume that the ILS is used in four subject areas, and you have students spending at least two hours per day on the system, about a third of the time devoted to instruction in a typical school day. If such a regime were to be established, time would have to be taken from other learning activities.

In many schools there would also have to be a substantial increase in the number of computers available for student use. If students did in fact spend a third of their time working on the ILS, each school using the system would need at least one computer for every three students. In U.S. schools the computer-student ratio is approximately one to nine, so in many cases "effective" use of an ILS would involve tripling the number of computers currently available.

By 1992, ILS programs were installed in about 25 percent of the school systems in the United States[14]; according to a 1994 estimate, 20 percent of all U.S. elementary schools had ILS programs installed and two-thirds of U.S. elementary schools with networked computers were using the systems. ILS programs account for a large share of spending on educational technology in the United States and are also used in a number of European and African countries as well as in Canada.[15]

Critic Douglas Noble views the growth in the use of ILS programs with foreboding. He believes that increased use of such systems "will almost certainly lead to more reliance on standardized testing to measure achievement," something for which an ILS is ideally suited. There will thus be a tendency "to reduce education to skills and facts pre-programmed into the computer, leaving little role for reflection, imagination, discovery, and creativity." This creates a kind of educational straitjacket in which "children are viewed as 'things' which are taught to perform specified tasks rather than as human beings to be cultivated."[16] The fact that ILS programs appear to be effective only if used intensively would seem to bear out his concerns.

In a climate of fiscal restraint, where there is a growing pressure for accountability and measurable outcomes, the computer seems, at first glance, to be an ideal means of objectively measuring student achievement. It looks like the perfect equalizer and does not appear to play favorites. Yet, not only does computer technology work better for some students than for others, it cannot come close to accommodating the wide variety of learning styles that are evident in any classroom.

Even where the use of computers appears to improve students' academic performance, there is reason for treating the results with caution. In the first place, most research studies take place over a relatively short period, often no more than three months. It's hard to tell whether gains made in such a short time indicate a long-term trend or whether they merely reflect students' increased interest and motivation as a result of the attention lavished on them by the researchers and the novelty of using computers. When the novelty wears off, students' interest and performance may well return to previous levels.[17]

In addition, the type of work that students do on computers—which, in spite of the existence of more innovative software, is still mainly drill and practice—is not likely to interest students much once the initial thrill of using a computer has gone. For example, Becker notes there is evidence that the enthusiasm with which students start ILS learning soon begins to wane. In spite of games and appealing graphics, once using a computer becomes routine, students find that they have no real control over what they are doing and that much of what they are required to do is dull and repetitive.

The fact that a "novelty effect" can significantly influence students' learning was confirmed in a Tennessee study that looked at the way students' perceptions about computers changed over the course of three years. In each year of the study, students in grades four through ten were asked to respond to a series of questions about "traditional literacy activities (reading and writing) and electronic media activities (using a computer and watching television)." They were asked "which one they would *prefer* in relation to the others, which one they would *learn more from*, and which one they would find more *difficult*," each activity being compared with all the others. The results showed that students' enjoyment in using computers "steadily declined" as they became more familiar with the technology, and that the longer they used computers, the less they considered they learned from them compared with other media. At the same time, greater experience and familiarity with computers did not appear to make using computers any easier. In addition, the older students were generally less keen about computers than younger students, and the girls' responses were consistently more negative than the boys'.[18]

The existence of a novelty effect puts into perspective one of the most persistent notions surrounding computer technology: the widespread belief that this technology plays a key role in motivating students in all areas of the curriculum. The degree to which a child is motivated to learn is among the more important factors in determining how well children do in school. Since children often appear to be completely absorbed when using a computer—one has only to observe children, even very young ones, playing video games to understand the machine's ability to capture their attention and compel them to remain at the screen, in some cases for hours—it is easy to believe that computers have a positive influence on all aspects of their learning. Not surprisingly, many teachers and parents are convinced that the computer can propel children into learning a wide variety of skills.

But even if computer use instills a positive attitude towards the technology, there is no proof that the enthusiasm spills over into other areas of learning. In a major one-year study, involving six schools and 803 children in grades one and two, researchers at the Tokyo Institute of Technology attempted to assess the effectiveness of using computers to enhance creativity and motivation in primary school children. Results indicated that the children who used computers appeared to have more positive attitudes towards computers—a finding that is consistent with a number of North American studies. Using a computer, however, did not encourage greater creativity, nor did it motivate these young children to study more. The research suggested that what *did* motivate children in their creative activities were experiences like reading books and saying rhymes.[19]

In addition to the novelty effect, there is another reason for having reservations about the results of research studies. This concerns the role of the teacher in implementing these studies. Students in experimental groups (those using computers) and those in control groups (not using computers) are often taught by different teachers, so that it is impossible to determine whether it was the teacher who made the difference or the technology itself.[20] If teachers enjoy working with computers and believe in their value as a learning tool, their enthusiasm is likely to rub off on their students, at least in the short term.

Some teachers do get excited about using new computer-based materials and approaches, but there are certainly other ways of giving them fresh challenges. Some schools, for instance, have discovered that when teachers use their professional development days to participate in workshops in the creative arts, their motivation and enthusiasm improve significantly. The use of computer technology is not the only way of invigorating a tired curriculum and listless students, and its success in doing so has not yet been proven in the long term.

So why hasn't there been more public debate about the limitations of computer-based instruction? The simple answer seems to be that there is a bias in what actually gets reported. Positive results get more attention and are more likely to be published than negative ones. Companies that produce and market educational computer programs conduct and publicize the results of their own studies, which tend to place their products in a favorable light. Discussion of research studies that are critical of computer-based instruction seldom makes its way into the mainstream media, which have happily played cheerleader to the technological revolution. The belief that computer technology will transform education is so widely held that few have questioned the extensive claims made for it. So rare is it to find critical writing in the media on the subject of technology in education that it is often difficult to separate journalism from advertising copy.

To take a sampling from the Canadian press: One column in *The Globe and Mail* about multimedia computers suggested that "early research indicated that the technology holds great promise—children appear to learn the three Rs more quickly and are more motivated to explore new subjects." An article in *The Toronto Star* proclaims, "Since word processing is a vital skill for the '90s, you can do your school-age kids a life-long favor by introducing them to word processing early." In another *Toronto Star* article about a math teacher who does not use computers in class, the writer asks incredulously, "So how come [he]— an educated professional—has no use for computers? How come he doesn't use them in his classroom even though his Grade 9 students— representing diverse learning levels—would benefit by working out math problems on computer?... How come he doesn't have one at home where his two young daughters could get a leg up on the technology that is changing the way we work, play and learn?"[21]

One notable exception to the uncritical media coverage comes from *The San Jose Mercury News*, a daily newspaper based in the heart of Silicon Valley. In 1995, the *Mercury News*, led by journalist Christopher Schmitt, undertook to examine the link between academic achievement and computer technology in the classroom. The purpose of the study was to discover whether or not schools with heavy investments in technology or with heavy technology use significantly outperformed schools with lesser investments or use. In other words, was computer technology a significant factor in improving students' academic achievement?[22]

The study used the 1994 results of a state-wide test, the California Learning Assessment Study (CLAS), to measure students' performance. Taking the average of each school's scores in the three major subject areas of the CLAS test—reading, writing, and mathematics—and correlating it with the density of technology in that school, the study attempted to find a link between schools with high technology use and those with high averages.

The *Mercury News* did not find in favor of the technology. "In general, the analysis showed no strong link between the presence of technology—or the use of technology in teaching—and superior achievement. The only exception was found in schools serving low-income students, where there was a stronger association between achievement and technology investment."[23]

The significance of the San Jose study, however, lies not just in its results but in the type of test that produced these results. Despite being politically controversial, the CLAS was regarded as an improvement over other standardized tests in that it attempted to measure the quality of students' thinking and their achievement across the curriculum, rather than their ability merely to memorize facts, fill in the blanks, or select the correct answers to multiple-choice questions. By using the CLAS, the *Mercury News* study provided a much broader assessment of students' abilities than is normally used in studies evaluating the effects of computer-based instruction.

One of the biggest problems with the premise that computers can improve academic achievement in students lies in the well-documented limitations of the standardized tests that are generally used to assess the effects of computer-based instruction. The rationale of standardized tests is that they measure students' ability to do well in school. But, to a large extent, how well students do in school is determined by the test scores they obtain. What a test does, therefore, is to measure how well students are likely to do in subsequent tests of a similar nature. High test scores are not related to the depth or scope of students' learning, but merely to their test-taking ability.

The origins of standardized testing go back to Sir Francis Galton, a cousin of Charles Darwin and creator of the infamous "bell curve." In 1869, Galton published a book called *Hereditary Genius,* in which he hypothesized that one could measure the degree to which people differed from one another in intelligence. He devised a way of representing the distribution of intelligence among a given population by constructing a curve, based on a purely imaginary scale, which showed that 50 percent of individuals would fall within the middle (normal) range, the remainder being divided equally among those of lesser or greater intelligence. The curve that resulted was in the shape of a bell.

Galton assumed, then, that intelligence could be measured on a linear scale and that such measurement would result in a bell-curve distribution. These assumptions were based on no scientific proof whatsoever.

Without going into the development of intelligence and achievement tests in any detail, it is important to understand that such tests are designed to produce scores that will conform to the bell curve. In other words, their level of difficulty is calibrated to ensure that half the students score above the norm and half below. Rather than assessing students fairly on skills and knowledge they might reasonably be expected to possess, the tests are constructed to create, as Herbert Kohl put it, "a hierarchy of success or failure."[24] And this is done in the name of an untested hypothesis that is supported by a completely arbitrary measurement of intelligence, a concept that in many respects still defies definition.

Certainly, the kind of intelligence required to do well in standardized tests is a very narrow measure of a person's capabilities. Harvard University psychologist Howard Gardner has suggested that everyone possesses a number of intelligences, which contribute in varying degrees to each person's potential. In his book *Frames of Mind: The Theory of Multiple Intelligences*, Gardner differentiates among seven different kinds of intelligence: logical-mathematical, linguistic, musical, spatial, bodily/kinesthetic, interpersonal, and intrapersonal.

Gardner contends that no one kind of intelligence is better than another. Each has its particular sphere of expertise. For example, writers are likely to be strong in linguistic intelligence, athletes in bodily/kinesthetic intelligence, visual artists and chess players in spatial intelligence. The traditional straight-A student demonstrates a high degree of logical-mathematical intelligence, this being the type of intelligence measured predominantly by standardized tests. By focusing on one type of intelligence, such tests ignore other forms of intelligence that can promote success later in life and, as a result, often fail to predict how well a child will do at the post-secondary school level or in the workplace. The fact that high test scores cannot necessarily be equated with later achievement lends support to the view that intelligence is multifaceted and cannot be measured by means of a simple test with "right" and "wrong" answers. Current modes of intelligence testing, while appearing to offer numerical precision, are more often than not conceptually flawed.

Just as disturbing is the fact that generations of researchers have discovered that standardized testing results in a narrowing of the curriculum. Where these tests are administered, teachers, and indeed whole school districts, begin to alter their curriculum in order to ensure that their students will achieve high scores on the tests. But the "teach to the test" approach has proven to be an unwise path to take in improving the quality of education. In order to do so, the teacher must break the curriculum down into highly structured units whose contents are the subject of tightly focused tests. In such a situation, students soon learn to be good test-takers, but it's questionable what else they learn.

So narrowing is the effect of test-taking that a Toronto Board of Education report found a negative correlation between scores on standardized reading, writing, and math tests and the number of times a student visits a public library or willingly reads a book. In the words of teacher and writer William Hynes, "What produces a good exam-taker is the opposite of what produces a citizen of literate habits."[25]

In addition, most tests do not teach students to analyze and solve problems and then to apply their skills and knowledge in other contexts.

Generations of research reveal that students who have been coached to do well on skill-testing are unable to apply the same skill when the question is phrased differently from the original one.[26] Indeed, without direct teacher involvement and evaluation, thinking skills are difficult both to teach and to measure in a meaningful way.

It is often claimed that computer use in classrooms gives teachers more opportunity to be involved with their students on an individual basis, thus contributing to better test scores, but direct teacher involvement can be better achieved by reducing class sizes than by putting children in front of computers. Smaller class sizes also have a positive impact on children's academic performance. This is especially true of young children in the early grades.

The 1984-90 Student/Teacher Achievement Ratio (STAR) Project study out of Tennessee provides striking evidence to support smaller classes. Involving more than seven thousand children, the study found that reducing elementary school class sizes gave students more contact with their teachers and resulted in strong academic and social gains. Students also achieved consistently higher scores in their state-wide tests. And in fact, these gains continued throughout high school. An added benefit was that teachers reported a greater awareness of their students' family lives, had fewer discipline problems with their students, and were able to give children more individual attention. Children who had learning disabilities or who were having trouble with reading or arithmetic were also identified earlier and given remedial instruction. With fewer students in the classroom, teachers suffered less from fatigue.

The cost to the state of Tennessee, a traditionally poor state, has been $1 billion. But the parents and teachers and school administration have said that the money is well spent. In 1988, elementary class sizes were cut virtually in half, and in 1989 the state legislated a fifteen-student cap on class sizes. Now seventeen other states have begun to follow Tennessee's lead. California, for example, has launched a program to trim class sizes in grades one through four, and in spite of difficulties in obtaining certified teachers and sufficient classroom space, teachers report high levels of satisfaction with the program. Perhaps if more school districts cut class sizes (and certainly this is a direction that early-childhood educators have urged for decades), there would be less reason to spend money on technology and more reason to focus on the relationship between students and their teachers. As it is, class sizes in many jurisdictions are likely to remain high, in part because of the costs of installing computer technology in schools.

At the same time, because of the emphasis on test scores, much of the computer work done by students caters to the limitations of standardized testing and consists mostly of drill and practice, which is seen as the most effective way to raise student achievement scores. Meanwhile, children with certain kinds of intellectual and creative gifts are overlooked and understimulated by being forced to gear their learning to test-taking. This means that students read less widely, have less time for hands-on learning activities, and spend more of their classroom time memorizing facts than exploring and learning from more open-ended kinds of experiences.

Another unfortunate effect of the test-score focus and of the educational software geared to it is that learning tends to be taken out of context. Most teachers believe that children need a meaningful context for learning so that they can make connections between abstract knowledge and concrete experience. In this way, information is acquired and facts are learned not in isolation but as part of a growing understanding of the topic being explored. This approach is quite different from what happens when children use educational software designed to enhance their factual knowledge: though they are presented with a vast amount of information, they are expected to answer questions and solve problems for which the only point of reference is the software program itself.

There is, in fact, scant evidence that using such software results in a better grasp of knowledge or makes children keener to acquire it. For example, a California study of fifth- and sixth-graders compared students who played *Where in the World Is Carmen Sandiego?* with students who drew maps and played non-computer games involving the same geography facts. It found no significant differences between the groups in their ability to recall facts or in their attitude towards the study of geography. The conclusion was that "non-computer games and activities can be just as beneficial as computer-based adventure games for reinforcing geography facts and student attitudes."[27]

The results of this study are significant because *Where in the World is Carmen Sandiego?* is by far the best selling piece of educational software in North America. The game first appeared in the mid 1980s and has been followed up by six sequels, three of which are also among the top five best-sellers. These programs use a detective-game format to teach geography and history. According to one review, teachers like the Carmen games because they send students scurrying to look up facts in the reference texts. (In the original versions of *Carmen Sandiego*, these consisted of *Fodor's USA Travel Guide* and *The World Almanac and Book of Facts*; later versions enable students to conduct searches on CD-ROM.) "The software," writes a *Home PC* reviewer, "gives children a context for the geographical and historical information they uncover, so they tend to understand and retain it.... The idea is to keep children from being passive learners."[28]

Thoughtful teachers, however, might have reservations about using a format that arbitrarily jumps all over the place, preferring an approach that allows children to explore a single topic from various angles and gives them time to absorb and fit together the details of what they are learning. While playing one of the *Carmen* sequels, *Where in Time is Carmen Sandiego?*, we discovered that the game propelled us round the world like a high-speed holiday package tour that never stopped long enough in any one place to show what was really going on. For example, during the game the following facts appeared on the screen, in this order:

- The founders of the unified Russian State were ruthless in the pursuit of their goals. Ivan the Terrible was notorious for the cruelty of his methods.
- Commercial dynasties such as the Medici family of Florence controlled much of the wealth and power in Renaissance Italy.
- Francisco Pizarro, a Spanish conquistador, sailed to Peru in the mid-1500s. There he ambushed the Incan ruler and forced him to pay a ransom of a room full of gold.

• Holland in the fifteenth and sixteenth centuries was first ruled by France and then by Spain. The 80 Years' War ended Spanish rule and ushered in Dutch independence.

Quite apart from the skimpy and sometimes misleading information these typical examples contain (as revealed by minimal research on the last two items: Pizarro in fact made two voyages to Peru, the first in 1526 and the second, his voyage of conquest, in 1531, and the unnamed Incan ruler was Atahualpa; and the Eighty Years' War in fact ended in 1648, in the middle of the seventeenth century), it is hard to see much educational value in this kind of whistle-stop info-tour, since the whole point of looking up information is to solve clues as to Carmen's whereabouts rather than to understand more about the times and places involved. Players cannot even do this at their leisure because they are given only a certain amount of time (which can be varied according to a player's ability) to solve the mystery. The only context, and the only real point of the exercise, is to find out where Carmen is—as quickly as possible.

The problem with games like *Carmen Sandiego* is that they provide no framework into which students can fit the facts they learn. Instead, people and places pop up as isolated phenomena which are discarded like unwanted playing cards as soon as they have served their purpose. To discover, for example, that "If that's the Eiffel Tower, Carmen must have gone to Paris" does little to teach children about the geography of France. Children are much more likely to develop an understanding of geography if they are first taught to find their way around their own neighborhood and then to create their own maps of what they have seen and experienced. And the facts they learn in this way are more likely to stick in their minds. While visiting an inner-city school in the United States, I noticed that it took the teacher several minutes to draw out of the students the name of the river that flowed through their city. This fact would have been known by every student in the grade four class if they had had the opportunity to take a single field trip to walk along the river's banks.

Writing a few years ago in the journal *Computers in the Schools*, the authors of a review of research on computer-based instruction pointed out that "society currently has some very specific measures for the effectiveness of its educational system: student achievement, attitudes, dropout rate, learning time. After nearly 25 years of use in instruction, the impact of computer applications on these measures remains largely an unknown quantity."[29]

This judgment seems to have been ignored. Vast sums of money are still being spent in our education system on integrating a technology whose effects are unproven and in many respects counter-productive. Computer drills might help in some cases to raise students' standardized test scores, but test scores are a narrowly based form of assessment and do not reflect the overall quality of students' academic performance. If computer use is to be assessed in terms of academic achievement, it needs to be considered in the context of a much broader range of skills and knowledge than is currently the case.

5

The Young Reader
and the Screen

The ability to read is of such singular importance to a child's life in school that his experience in learning it more often than not seals the fate, once and for all, of his academic career.

Bruno Bettelheim and Karen Zelan[1]

When people think about children learning to read, certain images spring to mind: a parent reading a child a bedtime story, a teacher pointing to the letters of the alphabet written up on the blackboard, or a child curled up in a favorite chair immersed in a storybook. These days, however, young readers are likely to be engaged in a very different kind of reading. When children visit their school library, the chances are they will spend some of their time in front of a computer screen rather than with a book. There is now a wide range of computer software designed to help children learn to read, and there is a growing list of storybook and reference CD-ROMs for children. These are widely used in homes as well as schools, parents being as much in the front line as teachers when it comes to children's literacy. But how much can computers help children become fluent and attentive readers? Will their effect necessarily be beneficial?

As spending on computer technology has increased, school districts and boards have often had to cut back the funds available to purchase books. To some, this reallocation of resources is justified: it signals the fact that one technology is giving way to another. According to this view, the way in which we acquire and communicate information depends less on the static technology of print and more on a dynamic interaction with image. That old cliché "a picture is worth a thousand words" has been given a new twist.

Yet learning to read unadorned text is as essential as it ever was. We are witnessing an exponential increase in the amount of data available, much of it in text form, even if it appears on-screen rather than on the printed page. Literacy remains of fundamental importance. Keeping up with the changes we are experiencing will largely be beyond the capabilities of those who are not literate. As one American educator has warned, "Children who cannot read fluently today will simply not have access to the responsible jobs of the future."[2]

With this much at stake, we should clearly be open to any approach that will yield improved results. But do such approaches include the use of computer technology? In the initial stages of learning to read, the answer seems to be no.

The basis of literacy is oral language—language spoken by real people in real situations experienced by the child—and the path to literacy begins long before children actually learn to read and write. The formal instruction children receive in school is in many ways a culmination of a process that has been unfolding practically from birth. Reading and writing are not isolated functions, they are inextricably linked with the acquisition of oral language. *Literacy for Life*, an Ontario Ministry of Education report on children's literacy, describes the relationship between speech and literacy as follows: "Without a mastery of speech, we would lack the internal voice that automatically accompanies us as we read and that we instinctively use to clarify meaning and interpret nuances of tone. Similarly, writing involves an internal dialogue that helps us to sort out our ideas as we set them down on the page."[3]

The first step towards literacy, then, is taken when a child starts to learn oral language. Since nearly all parents talk to their babies from day one, if not before, this learning begins long before the child is aware of what language is. Children learn to speak because speech is all around them; they instinctively realize that it is a useful and desirable thing to do.

Speech is not just a matter of communication; it also helps us to clarify our thinking. When children learn to speak, they do not just acquire a means of expressing their thoughts and feelings; they are also finding a way to sort out in their minds what it is they want to say. As their knowledge of oral language develops, this ability becomes more sophisticated and enables children to think about the situations and experiences they encounter in their daily lives. In doing so, children also develop the powers of reflection that are so necessary to their ability to read and write.

When young children are learning to speak, much of what their parents say to them is concerned with the nature of language itself. Many parents, for example, encourage their children to take an interest in language by reciting nursery rhymes and by playing word games with them. One of the virtues of word games and nursery rhymes is that they make children more aware of the existence of words as individual units of language.[4] Rhymes are especially effective in this respect because children have a natural affinity for them and delight in matching words that end with the same sound. In this way they learn that words are separate bits of speech that can be changed by replacing one sound with another. A number of studies have indicated that children generally find it easy to learn to read words by use of rhymes, and that their ability to do so is seldom affected by the nature of the vowels involved[5]—a significant finding in view of the fact that vowels often cause the most difficulty when children begin to read.

Even after the early years, when children are developing their reading and writing skills, oral language continues to play an immensely important role. By listening to and trying to absorb what they hear, children develop their memory and concentration. Without good auditory skills, children have a hard time learning to read and spell accurately. Their reading comprehension and writing ability also suffer, since they are often unable to remember something they read long enough to understand what it says or to keep the sound of a sentence in their heads when they want to write it down. The Waldorf schools place great emphasis on students' ability to reproduce orally in their own words what they listened to in a previous lesson before they put anything down on paper. In this way, the children assimilate what they have learned and make it their own. This process copies the way in which children learn to speak: by hearing others talk and by trying out words and phrases for themselves.

It is all the more important to remember the central role that oral language plays in children's learning now that so much information about the world comes to us in the form of images on a screen. Many teachers and parents introduce young children to computers in the belief that they will enrich and accelerate the children's learning, but if computer time becomes a substitute for talking and listening time, they are doing these children a disservice. Voices from the screen are no substitute for a parent's talk, because, unlike the latter, they are not connected with a close human presence that directs the children's attention to what is going on around them and responds to their reactions. Parents generally point to what they are talking about and tend not to refer to things that aren't there. By focusing on the child's experience of its immediate surroundings, they reinforce the child's understanding of language as a useful, meaningful accomplishment. Voices from the screen do not perform this critical function because what they talk about are only images of things, many of which the child has no experience of at all. What the child hears, as one researcher has put it, is "words without content."[6]

It's not just a question of how much parents talk to their children, however. What matters most is the *quality* of the oral language that children experience. By the quality of oral language, we mean quite simply that adults should talk with children in a caring and natural way, and that what they say should be authentic—that is, it should represent how they really feel. The Bristol Study of Language Development conducted in Britain in the 1970s followed the language development in a group of children from the age of fifteen months until they were over ten years old. A significant finding of the study was that the quality of the oral language with which children were surrounded had a considerable impact on their language development. It was also one of the most important predictors of their achievement in school.

When it comes to written language, children learn about print in much the same way as they learn about speech—as a part of their environment. But unlike speech, learning to read does not come naturally. As child psychologist Margaret Donaldson has written, "all normal children learn to use and understand speech in the first few years of their lives without specific instruction but...very few learn to read and write with equal success within the same period of time." There are children who *do* learn to read by themselves at an early age before they have received any formal instruction at all, but most do not, and even those who do start reading early "have learned to speak sooner."[7] Although most children in our society are surrounded by print in much the same way as they are surrounded by speech, they will not automatically make the connection between print and its meaning unless they are led to understand what print is and what it's for.

Frank Smith, an authority on reading, points out that "the first requirement for children who will become readers must be the recognition that written language exists, that there are aspects of the visual environment worth paying attention to in a particular way."[8] Children come across print in a wide variety of forms. Besides books and newspapers and magazines, there are labels and containers of one kind or another that have print on them, as well as flyers, signs, calendars, and posters. There are also letters and cards received and sent, shopping lists, recipes, address books, messages left on the fridge, utility and other bills, and so on. By involving their children in the activities that these various forms of print entail, parents can draw attention to the existence of print and demonstrate its uses.

If this happens, children can acquire a good deal of knowledge about written language by the time they actually start to read. In observing how a class of first-graders learned to read, one researcher discovered that "all were aware of the alphabetic nature of English print. They knew that the print in books and on other objects in the environment communicated written language messages. They knew how to handle books—which way was up, how and when to turn pages, and which aspects of print were significant for reading and which were not. They knew that print was read from left to right most of the time....They used pencils to write, observed the writing of others, and knew that what they had written could be read."[9]

Knowing what books are for and how they are used is particularly important, since this has been shown to have a strong positive effect on how well children do in their early years at school.[10] And it goes without saying that achievement at school is closely tied to the ability to read and write.

Some years ago, a friend of mine was relaxing in his study one day after lunch when his four-year-old granddaughter came in dragging a volume of the *Encyclopedia Britannica* that was almost as big as she was. She plumped herself down by his chair with the book in front of her. "Grampa," she said, "whaddya want to know?"

"Well," he replied after a moment's consideration, "what about elephants?"

"Elephants," she said. "Okay." She opened the book at the beginning and ran her finger down the page as if scanning the table of contents. "Elephants," she repeated as her finger stopped at what she judged an appropriate place. "Here we are." Then she opened the book somewhere near the middle and began to tell her grandfather what she knew about elephants. She couldn't, of course, read a word, but as a former educator, her grandfather realized that she would have no difficulty in becoming a reader. This episode demonstrated that she already knew what books were for, had a good idea of how one set about finding specific information in them, and was interested in doing so.

Children discover what books are for by seeing adults use them. My friend's granddaughter had no doubt recognized that books are things that contain useful information, having seen other members of the family referring to them for this purpose. These days, however, people increasingly consult CD-ROMs and electronic data bases rather than reference books. Computers, too, are increasingly becoming a means of introducing children to print.

For a young child, a computer screen merely presents another surface that displays print, and there is no harm in children discovering this fact and seeing the uses to which on-screen print is put. But far more problematic is the computer's potential impact on a child's concept of written language and on the practice of reading itself.

James Fallows, who has long provided intelligent commentary on computer technology, has remarked that reading on-screen "is so unpleasant—and the expectation is so strong that the computer will always be doing something more active than just displaying text—that computers will remain better suited to jumping from topic to topic than to the sustained intellectual, artistic, or emotional experience that print can provide."[11] The limitations of the screen as a medium for reading might lead a child to form a limited idea of what reading entails. Watching an adult access computer-based texts, the child will tend to gain the impression that print is something to be searched with maximum speed and efficiency for specific information. This is a perfectly valid use of print—a newspaper reader scans a story in much the same way—but it presents reading as having a purely functional value; it does nothing to convey the intellectual, emotional, and imaginative dimensions of writing that is read for pleasure and enlightenment.

There is also the possibility that, by being conditioned to expect "something more active" on the computer, children will tend to devalue text itself, focusing instead on the pictorial or animated aspects of the screen. There is already some evidence that this happens when children look at electronic books. Far from being an encouragement to read, the visual excitement of much "edutainment" software could actually impede reading development. "Reading," writes Jane Healy, "demands sustained voluntary attention from a mind that can hold a train of thought long enough to reflect on it, not one accustomed to having its attention jerked around every few seconds."[12]

Even if children do read what they see on the screen, they might not be able to absorb its content because of the way the text is presented. This is because electronic print lacks the structure and permanence of print on paper. If we pick up a book, we know at a glance how long it is, and by turning to the table of contents we can see how the author approaches the subject and, often, by noting the emphasis given to certain topics, what is his or her point of view. Flipping through the pages, and stopping when our eye catches something of interest, can give us an idea of whether the book lives up to our initial expectations. In other words, we get a sense of the work as a whole. Moreover, the contents of each page and its relationship to the pages that precede and follow it remain the same no matter how often we turn to it, so that each time we refer to a book we reinforce our understanding of its structure.

On-screen, however, things are very different. A CD-ROM cannot be physically handled and explored like a book. True, we can move easily from one part of its contents to another, but the linearity of consecutive numbered pages often gives way to a more flexible and dynamic—but potentially far more confusing—form of presentation. Instead of turning pages, which have a fixed position within the work as a whole, the on-screen reader is confronted with a series of screen-sized packages of print, whose order of appearance can be changed at will. And unlike the content of a book, which remains physically present in its entirety no matter which page you are reading, print on the screen comes and goes at a click of the mouse, as if it were constantly on the move. Even when scrolling up or down, the text seems to flow past, rushing quickly into and out of sight. It is not fixed but fluid.

Because of these fundamental differences, readers respond to electronic and printed texts in different ways. Derrick de Kerckhove, director of the McLuhan Centre for Media Studies at the University of Toronto, thinks it essential that children start with fixed text before they experience "movable text." The reason for this is that fixed text lets the mind move at its own pace, it allows time for reflection and stimulates the imagination. With electronic movable text, on the other hand, the mind stands still while the text flashes past, screen by screen. Unless the user already understands the concept of "fixed text technology" (that is, the structures and uses of printed materials), the result can be a confusing blur. As de Kerckhove puts it, "Mobile data will turn your mind to static."

These qualities of electronic print are easily overlooked in the rush to provide children with the latest offerings in reading and storybook software. After all, the argument goes, the computer environment, with its sights and sounds and interactive possibilities, is so much richer than that of a book. But as with any kind of learning, it is the quality not the quantity of stimulation that counts. And the current tendency to believe that more technology means better results must not be allowed to obscure the value of a simple and low-tech activity that plays a vital role in the development of children's literacy: reading stories to children.

It is widely agreed that reading to children is particularly important in preparing them to be readers themselves. For example, *Becoming a Nation of Readers*, the report of the U.S. Commission on Reading, noted that "the single most important activity for building the knowledge required for eventual success in reading is reading aloud to children"; and Marilyn Jager Adams, whose book *Beginning to Read* contains an exhaustive survey of research on how children learn to read, writes that "the most important activity for building the knowledge and skills eventually required for reading is that of reading aloud to children."[13]

More than probably any other activity, reading stories to children makes them aware of the range of possibilities of written language. They not only discover that written language is different from speech, they also learn that it can be organized in particular ways—for example, stories have a formal structure: a beginning, a middle, and an end. Reading stories to children helps them develop their listening comprehension, their ability to follow and remember a sequence of events and details of description. And it continues to be valuable beyond the stage at which children are able to read for themselves, since their comprehension of oral language will be in advance of their reading ability for some time to come. By listening to stories that they would find too difficult to read on their own, children have opportunities to enrich their vocabulary and develop an understanding of more complex narrative structures.

Perhaps most important of all, reading to children opens up new worlds to their imagination, worlds that lie beyond their own personal observation and experience. The images that children create in their minds are among their most powerful and emotionally satisfying responses to story reading. These images, unique to each child, are the means by which children make a story their own, absorbing it as part of their experience of life. This imaginative capability develops even more strongly when children become readers themselves.

The introduction, through computer technology, of new forms of storybook reading may well undermine these crucial benefits. Intended as a supplement to, or even a substitute for, the human reader, electronic books on CD-ROM enable children to look at and listen to text that appears on-screen accompanied by colorful illustrations, which are often enlivened by animation. One of the best-known examples of these electronic books, which are appearing in increasing numbers, are the titles in the Living Books series from Random House/Brøderbund, found in many school libraries in Canada and the United States.

Electronic books offer a new experience to young readers by combining the traditions of storytelling with the interactive attractions of multimedia technology. Children have always been active participants when stories are read to them. They ask questions about the story, pass comments on characters or events, and sometimes direct the reader to repeat a passage they especially enjoy. Electronic books try to take this involvement with the story a stage further by enabling children to access features of the program that provide information about the story's content, help with unfamiliar words, or activate additional elements of the animation and sound track. It is the last of these features—the animation and sound track—that constitute the main attraction, and it is here that drawbacks to the high-tech approach become apparent. "More technology" may be equated with "more fun," but the danger is that the multimedia dimension of electronic books will lead to less attention being paid to the story itself, and hence will do less to develop listening and reading skills than the traditional activity of reading aloud. Children whose parents don't have time to read to them would be better off listening to stories on cassette. Apart from the fact that the sound quality on a cassette player would generally be superior to that of most home computers, the children would also have to listen carefully to the story to understand what it was about.

The trouble with the multimedia features of electronic books is that the story itself takes second place to a variety of visual and aural diversions. The small amount of text that appears at the top of the screen is visually overwhelmed by the colorful scene that comes with it, and animation and sound effects provide additional distractions as the reading proceeds. Moreover, by selecting the "play" option, which most children prefer to do, the reader can activate a number of "hot spots" on each page with a click of the mouse. When this is done, the person(s) or object(s) in question perform some kind of action, accompanied by dialogue and/or sound effects. The reading of the text thus becomes a formality to be gotten out of the way as quickly as possible so that the real fun can begin. With a finger on the mouse, readers are free to pursue whatever interactive opportunities they can find.

In some cases, the extra dialogue adds to the storyline. For example, in Aesop's "The Tortoise and the Hare" in the Living Books series, the words of the hare reveal his vanity and self-satisfaction, while those of the tortoise demonstrate his earnest desire to do his best. Often, however, what happens has nothing to do with the story at all and appears to be chosen purely for its entertainment value. One page of "The Tortoise and the Hare" is devoted to musical effects, in which a group of birds, introduced by a suave snake emcee coiled round a nearby branch, bursts out in a nifty little 1960s Motown number, and one of the cabbages in the allotment where the hare stops for a snack levitates and turns into a flying saucer.

While one must admire the ingenuity, and often the whimsical sense of humor, that has gone into these special effects (one of our favorites is in "Arthur's Teacher Trouble," also in the Living Books series, in which some of the cookies on a baking tray grow legs and walk around munching happily on the others), they can have a negative effect on the child's appreciation of the story itself. Since the hot spots provide what one might call the "real entertainment," the reader (or viewer) invariably spends a good deal of time crisscrossing the screen to make sure that none of them has been overlooked. As a result, children are distracted from the story and quite likely lose track of it altogether. Not surprisingly, some teachers have found electronic books to be "too busy" for their students. Many children, we were told, react in a very passive way, just staring at the pictures and paying little attention to the accompanying text.

A serious drawback to electronic books is that the story is only part, and by no means the dominant part, of the presentation. It is the pictorial aspect of each page that commands attention. There is evidence, as Bruno Bettelheim and Karen Zelan have pointed out, that pictures can "retard or interfere with learning to read." Bettelheim and Zelan make this point in connection with reading primers whose text has little or no intrinsic interest for children. "The trouble with pictures is that the printed text becomes even less appealing in comparison. Worse, being able to guess from the pictures what the text is about, a child who is reluctant to read has no incentive to learn." This tendency is reinforced when, as is often suggested in teachers' guides, children are asked questions about the pictures before reading the story.[14]

The visual impact of electronic books causes a similar form of interference with reading. The animated sequences perform in ways that make the accompanying text largely irrelevant. Good illustrations should work with the text rather than against it. Pictures are a means of extending the reader's imagination. Their function is not just to let the reader see what things look like but also to tell the story in another way. They do this by giving a heightened sense of certain aspects of the story, which adds to the impression made on the reader.

Celia Lottridge is a Toronto-based storyteller and children's book author. Her award-winning book *The Name of the Tree*, a retelling of an African folk tale, starts with a full-page illustration of the sun shining over the parched land while a line of animals files by in search of food. One small boy who saw this picture said it hurt his eyes to look at it "because the sun is so hot." Although the book was produced primarily for children, the illustrations are not meant to distract readers but, rather, to enhance their appreciation of the story, a fact that this child had no difficulty in recognizing. As Lottridge says, "We underestimate children's ability to relate to subtle and imaginative art." There is nothing subtle, however, about the visual appeal of electronic books. Software designers seem unable to resist the temptation to upstage the text, invariably emphasizing flashy multimedia effects over educational goals.

Interactive fiction (sometimes referred to as hypertext stories) takes the hands-on approach of electronic books a stage further by allowing the reader to manipulate the text itself. By selecting from a number of options at various stages in the story, the reader can exercise some control over what happens next. The reader thus becomes an "active" partner with the author in determining how the story will unfold. In fact, in the words of one researcher, "one of the most striking ways that computers distinguish themselves as storytellers is by blurring the boundary between teller and audience."[15]

Is this a good thing, especially for young readers? Hypertext stories sacrifice a good deal for direct reader participation. It is our ability to identify with fictional worlds that makes fiction so satisfying to read. But we must believe in the characters and what they do. Writers of children's books need to create a world that is authentic and consistent on its own terms, a place the reader can inhabit without being constantly reminded of its artificiality. When we ourselves can choose the way a story develops, our involvement as readers undergoes a fundamental change. We begin to indulge in a game of "Let's see what happens if ..." and thus we become more interested in what we can do to the story than in what the story is all about.

If a story is to have meaning, the reader needs to find out and understand what it is all about. As they become familiar with a story, children gain a sense of the *shape* of things. Once they know how the actions and events unfold and fit together, they come to realize that life doesn't happen in unconnected bits—they learn, for example, that problems develop, reach a climax, and are finally resolved. Realizing that there are certain patterns in human experience is an extremely important step for young children who are still trying to make sense of the world around them. Good stories help children to make that step; it is a part of their enduring popularity.

This appeal is as much emotional as intellectual. The fact that a conventional (as opposed to a hypertext) story is always the same no matter how many times it is revisited provides reassurance, and this emotional connection with the story can be a spur to further learning. When a child of two or three, on a visit to a children's bookstore, asked for a copy of a story he already knew, his mother suggested they get something different, a book he had not been read before. The child protested: "But sometimes I need it," he said, "and sometimes I don't have it."[16] Because it was familiar to him, the story was a resource, something he could count on when the rest of the world didn't make sense.

For children, stories are not just a form of entertainment; they are alternative *realities*. "Stories," writes Smith, "do not *represent* experiences for children; they *are* experiences as immediate and compelling as actual events."[17] Children therefore need stories that make sense to them, and to help them unravel the meaning of what they listen to or see on the page they need an understanding guide. Another *person* must be involved. The guidance might come from a parent or from an older child acting as a reading buddy, a practice widespread in North American schools. Computer technology does not offer any real alternative. Sending children off to "read" an electronic book on their own is a grossly inadequate substitute, since the kind of assistance provided by the voice of an electronic book is extremely crude compared to what an older reader would offer. Reading stories to and with children opens up a dimension of childhood that cannot be explored in any other way.

Reading stories is only one side of the learning-to-read equation—the side that stresses what is referred to as a whole-language approach, in which children learn to read by searching for the meaning contained in print. On the other side is the viewpoint that emphasizes the need for basic skills to "decode" the signs of written language into the sounds of speech, a process that is taught by phonics.

Phonics is enjoying something of a comeback these days. There is a good deal of evidence that children who have had difficulty learning to read have made good progress after phonics instruction. With phonics, children learn the sounds associated with letters and then learn to combine these sounds to read (that is, sound out) complete words. Perhaps more importantly, phonics instruction also teaches children that they need to pay attention to each letter in a word in order to identify it correctly, and that there are certain spelling patterns that make word recognition easier. According to Adams, "Laboratory research indicates that the most critical factor beneath fluent word reading is the ability to recognize letters, spelling patterns, and whole words effortlessly, automatically, and visually. The central goal of all reading instruction—comprehension—depends critically on this ability."[18]

It is a fact that a child who cannot recognize individual letters or words is not going to be a fluent reader. It is also a fact that many children start school with little or no ability to identify written words, let alone read continuous text. Some may have very little idea of what reading is all about. Many educators see the use of phonics as necessary in helping these children get started.

Phonics involves drills. But children do not necessarily find drills boring or meaningless, especially if they are told the point of the exercise and what it is all about. They like the sense of achievement they derive from mastering new skills. Jeanne Chall, author of *Learning to Read: The Great Debate*, visited more than three hundred schools in the course of her research, and with regard to the view that "it is the story—the content of what is read—that makes for interest and enjoyment," she had this to say: "I did not find this assertion valid. The little children I watched were as excited and keenly interested in words, sounds, spellings, and rules as they were in stories. They did not seem to find studying letters and sounds and rules dull or abstract."[19] Much depends, however, on the means used to teach phonics. Adams cites studies of phonics teaching in first-grade and special-education classes which showed that much of the time devoted to phonics occurs as seatwork rather than supervised instruction. In other words, children have to plough through workbooks on their own. In such circumstances, they are likely to lose interest in their work.[20]

In many ways, computers are tailor-made for phonics instruction. They combine sound and visuals, so that children don't just see the words but also hear them. They provide instant feedback as to whether an answer is right or wrong. And exercises can be played over and over again. Software programs for teaching phonics have been and continue to be widely used both in homes and at school. Perhaps the most widely used is *Reader Rabbit*, which is still one of the most popular pieces of educational software on the market. It first came out in 1984, and since then it has sold more than two million copies.

Some children will be more receptive to on-screen phonics games than to workbook exercises, but it is far from certain that such games provide an effective means of learning basic reading skills. For one thing, they offer a limited range of activities (*Reader Rabbit* has only four at each level) and lack the variety and flexibility of teacher-directed exercises. Another factor to be considered is that a drill program cannot distinguish among different types of errors. All it knows is that a wrong answer has been given, and it responds in the same way, regardless of why the answer is wrong. But children need to know why an answer is wrong if they are to learn from their mistakes.

Research in fact indicates that learning-to-read software programs are no more effective than other materials in helping children acquire basic reading skills. A number of studies have found that using computers has little effect on young children's ability to learn basic skills such as matching letters, recognizing letters and words, and spelling simple words.[21] Nor are computer games necessarily favored over other forms of learning. In one of the studies just referred to, the children who had been using computers showed a clear preference for toys and books over the machines. This was in contrast to the children in the control group who had had no access to computers and who initially indicated they would rather play with computers than with toys and books. Once they were allowed to use the machines, however, they soon changed their minds and, like the children in the treatment group, ranked the computer last in order of preference.[22]

Commercially successful though they may be, computer drills such as those in *Reader Rabbit* can have only a supporting role in helping children to read and write, since they each deal with a relatively limited set of skills and provide little or no opportunity for extended reading and writing. As such, they do not seriously attempt to change the environment in which children learn. But much computer-based learning is more ambitious in scope. In the realm of language arts instruction, one program that has received a good deal of attention is IBM's *Writing to Read* (*WTR*). *WTR* is designed to help kindergarten and first-grade students develop reading and writing skills. The children work in rotation at five "stations," each providing a different activity, most (but not all) of which involve computer use.[23] As the name of the program indicates, emphasis is placed on encouraging children to begin writing before they can read and spell. The program was developed in the early 1980s and was published in 1983. It was eventually mandated by several U.S. governors for all the elementary schools in their states, despite, as one commentator puts it, "devastating research results" concerning its lack of effectiveness.[24]

WTR certainly appears to have yielded unspectacular results. Studies involving kindergarten students in California, first-grade students in Georgia, and second-grade students in Iowa indicate among other findings that the program had little or no effect on the children's reading and writing. And a study of the use of *WTR* in British Columbia found that, at the end of the first full year of implementation, there was no significant difference in children's reading readiness compared with previous years.[25]

Moreover, *WTR* is typically used to supplement existing language arts programs. Therefore, children in *WTR* groups tend to receive more language arts instruction than other children, and this, rather than the effectiveness of the program, could account for any positive results. According to a research review, where children spent more time on "structured story writing followed by reading, discussing and expanding on the stories," the results of reading comprehension and general reading skills were much the same as those obtained with *WTR*. "This finding suggests that many of the benefits attributed to *WTR* can, in fact, be explained by increased instructional time devoted to writing activities in the classroom rather than the technological innovation of the program."[26]

It's worth bearing in mind that these results were obtained at considerable cost, in terms of both personnel and resources. Using *WTR* in a lab usually requires the presence of at least three adults while the children are working on the program.[27] When *WTR* was first installed in two British Columbia school districts in 1985, teachers found that a teacher's aide was essential in each classroom where it was in use. Since there was no funding for teacher's aides, schools enlisted parents as volunteers. These volunteers, however, needed training and orientation; and because they were volunteers, many of them did not last long, so that new recruits were continually sought.[28] On top of these staffing considerations, there is the cost of the equipment, which, for a lab designed for twenty-four to thirty students, might run to nine computers and at least one printer, as well as tape-recorders, cassettes, and the program software.[29]

There were a number of other unwelcome surprises in store for the teachers in B.C. when *WTR* was installed. They found, for example, that many of the books to accompany the taped readings at the listening station were not available in local libraries, so that teachers had to make cassettes of books of their own choosing. Some of the accents on the tapes (e.g., Southern U.S.) were also inappropriate for Canadian children. But perhaps the most serious stumbling block was the nature of the program itself. Some teachers resisted the rigid routines on which *WTR* is based. They did not like being told "that they had to follow a preset routine, where some kind of sound goes off every fifteen minutes to signal to the children to move from one station to the next."[30]

WTR is designed to operate in a controlled environment. Far from providing the flexibility that would allow children to learn in the way that suits them best, the program possesses the shortcomings of so much computer-based instruction. Interactive it may be, but what this amounts to is that children do what the computer tells them, when it tells them to do it. One U.S. researcher observed that "whether they were listening to tapes, using the software, or working in the workbooks, students had few choices about what, where, or how they could learn." They couldn't choose the stories on the tapes and were not encouraged to bring in others of their own. They also spent a good deal of time waiting, either because their classmates were not ready to begin or because they had finished at a work station ahead of time. The greatest frustration occurred when children were at the writing station. If they had difficulty in getting started, they would sometimes end up with "only three or four minutes of actual writing time." On the other hand, time was still a problem when the children got down to their writing straightaway, since in this case, their frustration "resulted from being interrupted when they were deeply involved with their stories."[31]

No doubt the developers of *WTR*, like those of other computer-based learning programs, assumed that once their program had been devised, it would be implemented on its own terms and left to run in the way intended, which leaves little room for teachers to exercise their own judgment and creativity. The notion that computer-based learning programs can be perfected, to the point that teachers just get in the way, has unfortunately been around for some time. Donald Parker, who sold his reading program to SRA in the early 1960s, explained his approach as follows: "Leave the teacher out of this....That's the magic of this. To hell with the teacher.... She wouldn't know what to do."[32] But Chall concluded that children's interest in reading is not determined by the method of instruction or the materials they use. Instead, "it was *what the teacher did* with the method, the materials, and the children rather than the method itself that seemed to make the difference."[33]

Bruno Bettelheim and Karen Zelan remind us in their book *On Learning to Read: The Child's Fascination with Reading* that "for most children, learning to read is not an entertainment but hard work, a difficult task requiring serious application."[34] Children are unlikely to apply themselves seriously to this task unless there is a commensurate reward, and the reward of learning to read is being able to read. How the prospect of this reward is presented is of crucial importance.

Drills have their place, and software programs can make such drills more palatable for some children, but they must be seen as just a means of helping children towards the only goal that counts: that of being able to read on their own. It is in this latter context that computer technology could end up having unfortunate effects. The multimedia attractions of electronic books and CD-ROM encyclopedias might well lead children to equate reading with visual entertainment, so that, in Healy's words, they "keep looking around for meaning instead of creating it inside their own heads."[35] At the same time, as they begin to discover the vast amount of print that can be accessed by computer, children might develop a purely functional approach to reading, one that is limited to finding facts and processing information.

Reading is much more than this. Children need to have stories presented in a way that appeals to their imagination and opens the door to new worlds they can create inside their own minds. The most effective way of doing this is to read books to and with them. One might call this a low-tech approach, but there is nothing unsophisticated about the imaginative, intellectual, and emotional development it fosters.

6

The Young Writer and the Screen

Using word processing, in and of itself, generally does not improve the overall quality of students' writing.
Marilyn Cochran-Smith[1]

Some years ago, a computer researcher and consultant asked professors in the Artificial Intelligence (AI) lab at the Massachusetts Institute of Technology "what kinds of programs would be most useful to students and writers." The answers from eminent computer scientist Joseph Weizenbaum and author and mathematician, Douglas Hofstadter, a visiting professor, were the same: "Better word processors."[2]

Their emphasis on word processors was well placed. Word-processing programs bring immense benefits, as any writer knows. Whether or not you compose on one, the labor saved in revising and retyping is beyond question. Avoiding this kind of repetition is a boon to any writer.

But there is more to using a word-processing program than the fact that it's easier and quicker than typing or writing by hand. Many professional writers who became enthusiastic about computers also found that the process changed the way they wrote and the nature of the relationship between themselves and their writing. The ease with which text could be entered and changed on the computer screen made it altogether a more fluid medium of expression than typing words or writing them down by hand. And because the process of text creation was more fluid, writers believed they could explore ideas more freely than they could before.

There is, however, an immediate problem with transferring this view to the writing that goes on in schools. Professional writers bring a formidable array of writing skills and strategies, and often a depth of subject knowledge, to their work; children generally do not. If children are still learning the basics of writing, it may be difficult, if not impossible, for them to take advantage of the greater flexibility offered by on-screen composition. Writing is at the heart of so much of children's learning in school. Well-developed writing skills are critical for academic success. The question that must be asked, therefore, is: Does the use of word processing help young students in the development of their writing skills and strategies, as many educators seem to believe?

What made word processing so attractive to the educational community was that it promised to make writing easier for students and to encourage more creative thought in the process of writing. It would thus address a problem that teachers commonly encountered in their students—a reluctance to engage in writing because of the physical tedium of correcting mistakes and recopying—while at the same time helping students express themselves more effectively through their writing. A kind of virtuous circle would be created in which the more students wrote, the better they would write, which in turn would lead them to write even more. If this happened, a major stumbling block would be removed.

Writing is difficult, even for experienced writers. It is full of false starts and dead ends. It is often hard to get started; it is easy to get stuck. A computer screen can appear to be a more forgiving medium than a blank sheet of paper because a writer does not, to the same extent, have to "live with" his or her mistakes. Text on the screen can be changed almost instantly if necessary; what has been written on the page can only be crossed out or erased. Children, it is claimed, are more likely to take risks and try out their ideas on the screen, and will revise more often and more thoroughly, than they would normally do when writing by hand.

At the same time, it is argued that the computer screen is a much more visible medium than a sheet of paper. The text it displays can be easily read by more than one person as the writing takes place, making students' writing more accessible to comment and criticism. This encourages teachers to engage students in discussions about what they are writing, and students are able to work together and critique one another's work as they are producing or revising their texts.[3]

The overall effect of the computer screen is thus to make writing a process that can be talked about *and observed* at the same time. As one researcher puts it, "What was once the hidden process of mentally re-arranging information becomes visible in our word processors."[4] As a result, it is argued, children become more aware of what goes on in their minds when they are writing, more conscious of what it takes to produce a written text, and this realization plays a vital part in the development of their writing skills.

The combination of these factors, many educators believe, makes writing with a computer a very different experience from writing with pencil and paper, one that does not inhibit children's natural desire for self-expression. They have more freedom in determining the order in which the various parts of their text are written—there is no need to start at the beginning and work straight through to the end—and in choosing the way in which they are finally arranged. A thought or an observation can be put on the screen as it occurs and then fitted in with the rest of the text when its appropriate place becomes apparent. Because writing on-screen encourages discussion and collaboration with other children, young writers come to see that in many ways writing is not so different from speech, and this realization can help them come to grips with an activity that is still relatively new to them. And finally, use of a computer creates a different view of the nature of writing. Instead of approaching their writing as something that is fixed and immutable once written, students see that it can be continually subject to revision and change. This knowledge gives them more confidence and a greater sense of control.

This view of writing coincides with what is normally referred to as the "process approach," which sees writing as consisting of a number of stages, some preceding and others following the actual writing itself. Pre-writing activities involve thinking about what one wants to write about, researching facts and developing ideas about the topic, and deciding how these facts and ideas should be organized. The writing that is then produced is seen as only a first or working draft, one that students are expected to revise several times as a result of their own rereading of what they have written and in response to comments and suggestions received from other students and their teacher.

With so many advantages claimed for word processing, one might expect that the use of computers has led to dramatic improvements in students' writing. The results, however, are decidedly mixed and far from convincing.

A sample of research studies published between the mid-1980s and the mid-1990s show results fairly evenly balanced among positive, negative, and insignificant effects.[5] In some cases, the writing appeared to improve as a result of computer use, being generally of a higher standard and containing fewer grammatical and spelling errors. (It's worth noting that the greatest improvement appears to have been among students receiving remedial writing instruction.) In other cases, the writing produced by hand was better. One particularly telling comment concerned some grade three students whose handwritten work "appeared better organized, was longer, and seemed to better express what the child was thinking." In contrast, the writing they did on computers "appeared stilted, was brief to the point of insignificance, and had only one point of superiority—neatness."[6]

Why such inconsistent results? An obvious answer is surely that individual students respond to computers in different ways, depending, among other things, on their temperament and their style of thinking and learning.

Many students clearly do enjoy working with computers, and there is some evidence that computer use can create a more positive attitude toward writing, although not all research has come to the same conclusion.[7] It may be, in fact, that positive attitudes have less to do with writing than with computer use.[8] Nevertheless, a willingness to write could be a potent factor in improving students' performance, at least in the short term.

A major attraction of writing with a computer is that when students see their work printed out, it appears to be more "finished" than if they had written it by hand. This doesn't necessarily have any bearing on the quality of the work produced, but it could explain why students writing with computers obtain greater satisfaction from their work, as well as higher marks. The professional appearance of a computer printout can make it easier to overlook shortcomings that would not be ignored in handwritten work. One ten-year-old boy said he liked the computer because it "makes my writing look better than it is."[9] It seems that teachers often fall into the same trap. Many admit that they have a tendency to give higher marks to papers that are computer-typed than to those that are handwritten, even if the quality of the writing is similar.

On the other hand, some students find that using a computer inhibits their ability to write because they lack the necessary keyboarding skills and knowledge of software commands. Writing with a computer is obviously harder than writing by hand if you cannot type and are unfamiliar with the word-processing program you are using. And it appears that many students do not find it easy to reach this basic level of computer competence. Until they do, students focus primarily on how to get the technology to work. The computer, far from making writing easier, presents a barrier that must be overcome.

For example, preliminary findings of a two-year study of students five to ten years old indicated that the students needed time to learn word processing before they could use a computer productively for writing. "Regardless of the tasks that teachers assigned during the learning period, children focused their attention on mastering the word processing system and on developing keyboard familiarity, rather than on the content of their writing."[10]

This problem is not confined to young children. One study of students in grades seven and nine found that, although they had had considerable typing and word-processing practice, they still had difficulties in using the computer and, as a result, wrote less on the computer than they did with pencil and paper. According to another study, students in grade eight managed a typing speed of only about eight words per minute. And grade ten students with little computer experience tended to write a good deal more when writing by hand than when they used word processing.[11]

There are also some students who prefer the more intimate relationship between thought and word that occurs with handwriting. One such student was George, a fifth-grader at a public school in the northeastern United States, who said, "I don't like the computer. I like writing in pencil. When I first started writing I got a bump. [He held up his middle finger.] Then I started writing, writing, writing. Now I'm used to it and it doesn't hurt any more. I like writing a lot. I can't do that much by hand because [the teacher] tells us to do it on computer. But I can do some of it by hand. The only thing I like about it [the computer] is that it's got games. Other than that I don't like anything about it." George's handwriting was very small but quite legible, and, from my observation, it was clear that he was a fluent writer who was perfectly comfortable with his chosen medium. He had not been put off by the initial discomfort caused by the bump on his finger. He knew that using a pencil was right for him, and he persevered.

Not all children, therefore, will immediately want to compose text on-screen, and it seems reasonable to allow them to write by hand if they want to. Some young writers do better on the computer, and some do worse, and it is reasonable to conclude that students' personal preferences play a large part in determining the outcome.

The way in which students are introduced to word processing will also have an effect. Approaches to computer use for writing vary widely. For example, the report from a three-year study in southern Ontario describes a situation in which the computer was seen largely as a motivating tool that would encourage students to write (and write better), even if they had been previously reluctant to do so. In contrast, a long-term project in Winnipeg, Manitoba, emphasized the computer's role as a writing resource, part of the learning environment needed to support young writers.

The Ontario study was carried out from 1992 through 1994 by researchers from the Centre for the Study of Computers in Education at York University. It involved students in two elementary schools in the same school board. In one of these schools, students made extensive use of computers for their writing assignments; in the other school, word processing was infrequently used. The purpose of the study was to assess the effects of computer use on the development of students' writing skills as they progressed from grade three to grade five.[12]

By the third year (grade five) the students who had regularly been using computers for writing achieved higher scores than the students at the other school, although their scores had been lower in the two previous years. The students using computers were not only judged to have produced better writing, they also wrote more. Since the two groups of students were similar in terms of their socioeconomic background and academic achievement, it appeared that it was the regular, everyday use of computers that accounted for the difference.

One category of writing, however, appears to have had a disproportionate influence on the results. The computer-using students appear to have excelled in fictional narrative rather than in other forms of writing, such as research reports and essays. By grade five, computer-using students with average writing ability were writing stories of more than two thousand words, and in some cases the stories were considerably longer. These fictional narratives in fact represented a very large proportion of all the writing these students did, and although the study compared students' writing in a number of categories, the impression gained from a close reading of the report is that these fictional narratives were what put the computer-using students ahead.[13]

In encouraging their students to write stories on the computer, teachers at the computer-intensive school were prepared to let students choose what they wanted to write about and then let them go at it. They made limited use of pre-writing activities such as brainstorming to develop ideas, and students often started writing as soon as they had selected a topic for their stories. There was also less emphasis on correct spelling and grammar, at least in the drafting stage. Two of the teachers, in particular, stressed the importance of getting ideas down "on paper" (that is, onto the computer screen) before worrying about editing their work. And the students seem to have had little help from their teachers in making revisions.

As a result of the freedom they were allowed, it seems that the computer-using students became less inhibited about writing and pursued it with genuine interest as they developed their stories. Moreover, their teachers encouraged their growing involvement with their compositions by extending their deadlines, often by as much as two months. Hence the unusual length of their stories.[14]

Length is not everything, however, and if the work of three computer-using students featured in the study is representative, the quality of much of the writing produced may have suffered from too much emphasis on quantity. In two of the stories, written by students who were rated low and average respectively, there was much youthful energy and spontaneity but an uncertain control of the conventions of written language. The story written by the low-rated student is essentially a series of action sequences with a strong comic-book flavor. Much of the writing sounds rather like a mono-logue a child would maintain while playing with action dolls. The average-rated student tends to write in a kind of headlong rush, in the manner of a breathless child whose words come tumbling out so quickly that one has difficulty keeping up with what he or she is saying. Only in the story written by the high-rated student do we encounter writing that has a sense of command and self-assurance (the writer is skillful in evoking the protagonist's feelings of uncertainty and fear, and there are some nice touches of descriptive detail), but even here the story would have been better if it had been quite a bit shorter.[15]

Important as it is to encourage imagination and self-expression, it's not clear whether an emphasis on creative writing, such as occurred at the computer-using school, will help students develop the skills needed to produce other forms of written communication that will be increasingly required in the higher grades. How well prepared will students be when it comes to producing clear, coherent essays and reports? How will they compare in the long run with students whose teachers have given them more practice and guidance in these forms of writing? In many ways, the real test of this approach to writing with computers is still to come.

Writing is essentially driven by thinking, and one of the greatest challenges students face is quite simply to develop the ability to think clearly about what they are writing and how they are going about writing it.

The River East School Division Literacy Initiative represents an ambitious attempt to use computer technology to create the conditions in which students can improve their writing. This project, carried out between 1988 and 1996 with fourth- to ninth-grade students in the River East School Division in Winnipeg, Manitoba, adopted a broad definition of literacy that included "the ability to think critically, reason logically, and be technologically aware and capable."[16] Its underlying premise was that because writing, especially non-narrative writing, is difficult to learn and difficult to teach, but so important for students to know how to accomplish, a number of factors needed to be combined to create an environment strong enough to provide students with effective support.

The Literacy Initiative addressed three basic needs. Students needed to learn strategies that would help them overcome problems and refine their ideas; they needed software that enabled them to move easily between the various aspects of the writing process; and they needed to be able to share and exchange their writing with other students.

Otto Toews, Deputy Assistant Superintendent, Curriculum, at the River East School Division, and Joan McCreath, principal of Sun Valley Elementary School in the same division, developed the strategies in a document suggestively called *Think More ... Write More*, which identifies and describes fifty-eight thinking and writing strategies commonly used by good writers. The idea is that if students are to improve as writers, they need to be able to think about their writing, approach problems, and seek solutions in the way that experienced writers do. For example, students are frequently asked to elaborate on a certain aspect of their report or essay. But they don't always know what this means: it's not just a matter of writing more. "Elaborating," one of the thinking strategies, includes a list of nine approaches to this task: writing a description; clarifying a position; thinking through a process; organizing through classification; drawing comparisons; making an analysis; drawing an analogy; identifying assumptions; and generating hypothetical instances. By selecting, say, "drawing comparisons," students can discover two ways of making a comparison and can read an explanation of why comparisons are used and how they are made. They can then use this information to help them draw comparisons of their own. The other strategies provide help in a similar way.

Writers' KnowledgeBuilder™, a software program that enables students to access any of the *Think More ... Write More* strategies at any stage of their writing, was developed with the financial support of a grant from the Apple Canada Education Foundation and piloted in the River East School Division. *KnowledgeBuilder* brings together a wide range of writing functions: researching, preparing notes, organizing material, drafting and revising text, producing graphics, and publishing.[17] And because their computers were networked, students could exchange information and provide feedback to one another as they progressed with their work.

To judge from the results, the Literacy Initiative proved a success. A number of studies conducted during the course of the project found that there was significant improvement in the thinking and writing skills of the students involved. The Literacy Initiative, however, was considerably more than an exercise in computer use in which students got to play with fancy new software while their teachers looked on admiringly. Teacher training in the instructional uses of the writing strategies was an essential part of the project, since without teacher guidance, many students would probably not have known how to benefit from the sophisticated software they were using.

Equally significant is the fact that Sun Valley Elementary School, where 49 percent of students were writing above their grade level, has an overall emphasis on literacy. The school has a summer reading program, a home writing program in which parents work with their children, and a remedial reading program. In addition, all professional development days focus on aspects of reading and writing. As principal

McCreath emphasizes, many factors, not just the technology available, contribute to the school's high standards of literacy.

The results of the River East Literacy Initiative support the view that it is unrealistic to expect that students will become competent writers simply by using a computer. No amount of technology can substitute for a teacher's guidance: students need teachers to show them how to develop and revise their written work. As one word-processing software writer has pointed out, "It is teachers who have to help students learn how to start an assignment, frame an argument, and select which revision processes are most productive, and then teach students how to use the new technology to make the most of it as a creative medium. THE WORD PROCESSOR WON'T DO ANY OF THAT."[18]

So what does the word processor do? Unlike a sheet of paper, which just lies there waiting to be written on, a computer screen offers all sorts of possibilities for action depending on the software being used. The danger is that young writers will be seduced into exploring these possibilities rather than concentrating on the real task at hand: learning to develop and express their thoughts in a clear, coherent way and to give authentic expression to their feelings.

One of the hardest things about writing, especially for young writers, is getting started. Children often don't know what they want to write about or how to approach their chosen topic. No problem: a number of writing software programs provide help by suggesting ideas; some will even compose sentences from randomly selected words or phrases. For example, as one enthusiastic newspaper article explained, "The top level of the *Creative Writer* 'house' is the 'ideas' attic. If you get stumped for a getting-started idea, you can pull the lever of a slot machine that will put three random parts of a sentence together. It delivers nonsense sentences such as 'the likeable ornithologist blasted into reverse close to the magic garden.' Sometimes these contain the germ of a good story."[19]

Similarly, the writing component of Logo enables children to make random groupings of different categories of words that might eventually result in "meaningful" or "poetic" statements. Students are directed to make up vocabulary lists for each part of speech—article, noun, verb, adjective, adverb, pronoun, etc. Each list is then subjected to a randomizing process as part of a program for stringing words together in some specified order.

This is all very well, and no doubt affords a certain amount of fun, but it surely encourages a scattershot approach to writing in which words and phrases are played around with at random. Such an approach is incompatible with the idea that good writing requires disciplined thought in order to achieve clarity and coherence. It also overlooks the value of using children's own observations and sensory experiences as a basis for their writing—for example, having them listen to the wind or the rain and then describe the sound it makes. Simple activities like this are good at stimulating children's imagination and encourage them to look within themselves (rather than at a computer screen) for insights and ideas.

Even if the promptings of the software do spark ideas, there is nothing to show that this kind of gearing up is more effective than other kinds of preparation for writing. For example, the narrative compositions of primary school children have been found to benefit from the students' prior participation in drawing and drama sessions. The children who took part in these sessions produced writing of a quality that was "consistently and significantly different" from that of children who had only had a discussion of what they were going to write. It seems that since drawing and drama are both creative activities, they are particularly effective in helping children to test and sort out their ideas before the actual writing begins.[20]

Moreover, drawing and drama are meaningful activities. The random-selection approach ignores the fact that creative writing has meaning and associated feelings that are rooted in the experiences and imagination of the writer. Commenting on Logo's poetic programming, Theodore Roszak questions whether the result has any validity as an expression of human thought and feeling. "Aren't poems *about* something? Don't they have a *meaning* that comes out of somebody's life? When the children make up poems, their own minds would not seem to be doing anything at all like the poem-program. They mean to *say* something, and that something preexists the words as a whole thought. They are not shuffling parts of speech through arbitrary patterns."[21]

Besides prompting children to play around with random words as a preliminary to writing, word processing also encourages them to play around with how the words will look on the screen before they actually begin. Type size, typeface (font), line spacing, all can easily be changed, and even the color of the text on-screen can be varied. For mature writers, these are options that are selected according to need. For children, on the other hand, they seem to exert a strong fascination.

This is certainly the impression given by the three-year Ontario study of students in a computer-intensive school. According to the authors of this study, "after lengthy observations with a number of students it became apparent that student creative activity was often being subverted by the students' obsession with formatting their texts. By allowing students greater freedom to produce a stylish product, the computer seemed to be diverting them away from sustained creative effort." In what is described as a "typical sequence" in one grade four class:

> First [the student] changed the fonts, then he changed format size,
> after which he changed the text style to bold, introduced lines,
> changed font again, re-changed the font, changed text size, changed
> the font again, changed text color to red and then to black, then
> green, and then changed the font and font size.

The teacher was apparently unaware that this kind of compulsive re-formatting occurred so frequently, perhaps because from a distance the students appeared to be busily working away. Nor was this behavior confined to a single class. In another grade four class taking part in the same study, students seldom produced "an extended piece of writing" without making changes to the format of their text.[22]

Other researchers bear witness to the truth of these observations. A group of grade eight students was monitored by electronic videos using screen-recording software, which provided a running account of everything they did while writing on the computer. An analysis of their actions found that the menu-bar option most frequently used during the drafting session was the "format" label, which made layout features available.[23]

Some teachers who have observed this kind of compulsive formatting believe that it undermines the usefulness of computers as writing machines. At the Louis Riel elementary/middle school in Calgary, Alberta, language arts teacher John Portway now insists that his grade seven and nine students use pencil and paper to draft their stories instead of attempting the first draft on the computer. He thinks the students become lost in playing with the headlines, fonts, and other formatting features, and are distracted from the actual act of writing. Portway concedes that computers are good for teaching formatting and for getting students to write to a specific length, but overall, he says, "I would swear that [the computer] is more detrimental than beneficial for creative writing. It's not that the technology is inherently bad, it's just that it is very distracting."

Portway, a published writer as well as a teacher, believes that the computer has had a bad effect on the way students approach their writing. "The process of writing is lost," he says. "It becomes a visual medium. The kids go in without a working draft, it goes down, and it doesn't change. It looks good, so the students think it *is* good." Portway found that his students made only superficial revisions on a computer. When he switched them from composing on-screen to writing a draft by hand, they were more prepared to edit and change their work and they produced more text as well.

The ease with which text can be entered, erased, and entered again is another aspect of on-screen writing that can, paradoxically, be a disadvantage for inexperienced writers. It means that they do not feel so committed to their initial choice of words, since it requires no effort to change them. As a result, text may be drafted less carefully than when written by hand. A number of high school students in a British study pointed out that, "because of the tedium involved in rewriting handwritten text, they had to be clear about what they wanted to say before handwriting, whereas on the word processor they 'wouldn't really bother."[24] In fact, they generally felt that they planned *less* when using the computer, a response that seemed to indicate a diminishing respect for the discipline that writing requires.

Nor does it seem likely that word processing facilitates more effective revision than writing by hand. The underlying assumption is that the more students review and revise what they have written, the better their writing will be. And since it's easier to revise on-screen, the argument goes, using computers will enable students to revise more, and thus their work will improve more than if they were writing by hand. But the quality of the writing that results from revision depends on the nature of the changes that are made. And there appears to be little evidence that revising on-screen helps students to improve their writing in terms of the logic of its structure or its clarity of expression.[25] The grade eight students in the study that monitored keyboard actions had ample time to revise their texts once the first draft was completed. Yet no in-depth revision was attempted. Of the three students whose work was featured in the report, the first two neither elaborated on their ideas nor added any descriptive detail to what they had written. The third student, described as a "graphics experimenter," managed to produce only five sentences in his first draft, and his final version was not so much a revision as an extension of what he had previously written.[26]

Using revision time simply to add on more to the end of the existing text is in fact another common tactic among computer-using students. One researcher, who observed this approach among seventh- and ninth-graders, linked it with the fact that when students revised on the computer, they no longer had to recopy what they had written. Recopying has often been cited by students as one of the things they like least about writing,[27] and has been condemned by many educators as being a waste of time; but this researcher concluded that recopying "is not the meaningless process it appears to be" since it "slows the writer down" when reviewing the text and "leads the writer to focus on each word." The students in this study appeared not to have done this and evidently did not focus on the overall content and organization of their writing, either, since many of the additions they made "related to ideas that could have been developed more fully in the body of the text."[28]

If, as much research shows, many students do not write better or revise more thoroughly with word processing than they do when writing by hand, it would appear that pencil and paper still have their uses. Writing by hand might present physical challenges for young children, but it allows them to concentrate more on the writing and less on the technology they are using. When children write with computers, some of their attention is bound to be directed at the capabilities of the software. Writing with a pencil, a familiar and much simpler tool, leaves them freer to concentrate on what they want to say.

Pencil and paper have another advantage over computers in that the writer can review several pages at the same time; with a computer, unless the composition is short enough to be viewed in its entirety on a single screen, it is not possible to see the complete text all at once. As one grade eleven writing-class student complained, "You don't have your full story in front of you."[29] Yet at both the drafting and the editing stage, the writer (or editor) needs to be able to view the text as a whole in order to see how its parts fit together and whether they do so in a way that makes sense. Here, too, word processing makes additional demands on students' attention, since, because of the physical limitations of the screen, they must either hold more of their composition in their minds or else continually scroll up and down to remind themselves of what they have written. The answer to this problem is for students to print out what they have written and revise the "hard copy" after a careful reading. Unfortunately this stage is often skipped because revising on-screen appears to be more efficient.

Writing requires focused attention, and anything that diverts attention away from the process of writing (in particular, thinking about what to write) is going to affect the quality of the work produced. It is true that some aspects of writing can, with mastery of the keyboard and of program commands, be performed more quickly and easily on a computer than by hand. Correcting spelling errors with a spell-checker is an obvious example. But without a teacher's careful intervention, the use of computer technology tends to undermine the development of many of the skills that are needed to produce good writing: in particular, the ability to think clearly, to choose words carefully, and to organize one's writing into a coherent whole. Teacher guidance is even more essential when students use sophisticated programs like *Think More ... Write More* and *Writers'KnowledgeBuilder*™, which are designed to support these skills. Unless they are appropriately used, such programs can be a powerful drain on students' attention, placing an additional burden on what is already a demanding task.

The technology of paper and pencil cannot simply be dispensed with, because there are skills associated with learning to write by hand that are not adequately developed in other ways. What we must focus on is learning to take advantage of both kinds of technology. "The benefits that flow from writing letters using small muscles are different than those that flow from the ease of revision on a computer," says Judah Schwartz, co-director of Harvard's Educational Technology Center. "With any luck we'll learn to reap the benefits of both."

7

The Information Maze

Infomania retards rather than accelerates wisdom.
Michael Heim[1]

One of the greatest advantages of the computer is its ability to access, store, and retrieve information quickly and efficiently. In many situations, computers and electronic data bases have replaced the older technology of print because they provide a less cumbersome means of search and retrieval and they require less space for storage. Some techno-enthusiasts go so far as to suggest that print collections held in libraries should, and eventually will, be abandoned altogether.

The move to electronic sources of information is beginning to change the way children learn in our schools just as it has already changed the way many people work at their jobs. Some schools with a heavy reliance on computer technology have almost dispensed with textbooks entirely. At the Saturn elementary school in Ohio, for instance, children do most of their reading and writing on computer and use data bases instead of a newspaper to get their daily dose of current affairs. And at the River Oaks school in Oakville, Ontario, mathematics is the only subject still taught using a textbook.

Even at more conservative schools, libraries are buying fewer books and magazines, replacing them with subscriptions to electronic data bases on the Internet or, at the very least, with CD-ROMs. Unlimited information on any subject, teachers and students are told, is now just a touch away.

Electronic data bases promise a new and better way of acquiring information. No more slow browsing through library stacks or card catalogs. No more dusty volumes on crowded, poorly lit shelves. No more bottlenecks where access is restricted by the number of copies of a particular book. A few deft strokes on the keyboard will pull up precisely the right piece of information, or point the way to the best authority on the topic at hand.

Along with this seductive promise of instant, universal access comes the notion that it is mere child's play to gain access to this vast body of information. There is a widespread belief that computer technology makes it easy for children to learn on their own, and that it will lead to a new era of child-centered education, with the computer as an omniscient tutor free of the shortcomings of any human teacher. No longer will a child's question go unanswered by a busy teacher, or her curiosity be thwarted by the limitations of her local library. With the whole world of knowledge accessible from her desk, she will be able to find her own answers to any question she could possibly pose.

Proponents of computer use in elementary schools believe it will create a learning environment that will nourish independent, motivated learners. As one elementary school principal explained, "Knowledge is doubling every fifteen months, and we want our students to be exposed to the most up-to-date information. Classrooms are information-poor; the computer makes them information-rich."

That, at least, is the theory. However, if we look at what goes on in schools when students use electronic data bases, and consider the quality of materials involved, a rather different picture emerges.

Contrary to the assurances of cyberspace advertising, surfing the Internet is fraught with diversions and difficulties for the learner. For one thing, there is just too much to see. Picking one's way through the

Internet is like walking through a giant shopping mall—there's a lot of interesting stuff to dazzle the eyes and pique the interest, but how do you find what you're looking for? And the possibilities for distraction are endless. Children who have access to a vast and ever-growing body of information are likely to be briefly dazzled, and then confused, by all the choices that confront them.

The Internet also offers many activities that have little or nothing to do with learning in any formal sense, and these tend to have a strong attraction for student users. Many websites provide entertaining animation and games for children, and these are soon preferred to more tedious research tasks. In other words, without teacher guidance and supervision, the computer winds up, more often than not, being used in trivial ways. The technology, by itself, will not inspire children to learn. To say this is not to blame the students. It's simply unrealistic to expect children, on their own initiative, to start using the computer as an academic research tool, especially when there are other, easier uses that have an instant appeal.

Nor is it rational to expect children to find their way unaided around the surfeit of information a computer can provide. Using computerized data bases is, in fact, anything but child's play. While any child can easily go to the library and browse through a section of books on, say, wildlife, browsing on the Internet is a far more complicated undertaking. A child whose reading skills are minimal can still take a book from a library shelf. If she can't judge the book by its cover, she need only open it to see what's inside: flipping through its pages will give her a sense of what the book is about. But little can be gleaned about a website without extensive reading on-screen. Children can assess the relevance of a reference book far more quickly and easily.

Using a card catalog or a computerized catalog system is a relatively easy way of finding out what books a library has on specific topics and where they are to be found. Readers are also able to locate books on similar or related subjects because they are grouped together on the shelf. If a student is looking for information on, say, black bears for a science project, she'll likely come across information about other mammals, like wolves or raccoons, that share the same habitat. But if she's searching for black bears on the Internet, her chances of success are nowhere near as good. She might stumble across all kinds of irrelevant information—chat rooms, advertisements, or games.

A certain amount of technical knowledge is required simply to get into the system. Different data bases have different access routes and information protocols. They also have different focuses and functions: some are good for current affairs; others are much better for finding out about business, science, or technology; others focus on music; and a few are valuable for historical or literary research. The success of a search thus depends largely on knowing which data base will be most likely to contain the information you are looking for.

Data bases work by highlighting individual words in a document or text, in a procedure known as Boolean logic. Learning how to focus the search so as to find what you want can be difficult and time-consuming for an adult, let alone a child. For example, while doing a trial search across the Internet for information on the Long March of the Chinese communists in 1934-35, neither I nor the librarian I worked with was able to find relevant material. Instead, we came to a great many dead ends, including a game entitled "Mao Tse-tung." In an hour of searching, we found nothing of value.

Our experience was by no means unique. Steve James, a British journalist who tested the effectiveness of the Internet as a research tool and wrote about his experiences in a July 1996 article in *The Guardian Weekly*, found himself at first in some very strange places quite unrelated to the subjects of his search. One of the topics he selected concerned the British Tory party and its split over the repeal of the Corn Laws in 1846. When he searched under "Corn Laws," top of the list of finds was "Breast implant firm halts compensation claim," an article on the lawsuits involving Dow Corning, an American manufacturer of silicone breast implants. Using "British political history" as a new parameter with a number of different search engines produced equally unpredictable results, including abstracts on the history of British Columbia. The next day, however, a new engine did lead him straight to a description of the Corn Laws. As James commented ruefully, "If only this had happened earlier."[2]

This example illustrates two major difficulties that can be encountered in Internet research. First, the search must be clearly focused. Because of the vast scope of material on the Internet, a too-general inquiry will result in a listing of hundreds of websites, with no indication as to which really has the information you are looking for. Second, you cannot assume that search engines categorize information in the same way that you do. Some are better than others (although all probably have their eccentricities), and experience will tell which are to be trusted.

Searching online, therefore, involves fairly sophisticated decision-making, and children will need a good deal of training and careful, ongoing assistance when using the Internet. Most elementary schools have discovered that students, especially young ones, cannot be left to navigate the Internet on their own. Guidance is necessary, and it's the teachers who have to provide it. As well as helping students find their way around, teachers must continually spend time tracking down pools of information that will be useful for students. Examples might be websites for environmental groups or human rights organizations. This process is called "bookmarking." It is essential that teachers do this (often in conjunction with librarians), since so much of what a child can find on the Internet is overly complex or simply irrelevant. And given that websites are constantly being constructed and abandoned, keeping up with all the changes is an ongoing job.

In fact, far from allowing students to be independent learners, working on the Internet takes a great deal of one-on-one tutoring. When a classroom gains access to the Internet, it falls to the teacher to spend much of her time supervising her students in their forays into cyberspace. Not to do so will likely lead to misguided or ineffective use. Children who are given unlimited access to information—whatever its form—without ongoing guidance will often be unable to distinguish among the important, the trivial, the inadequate, and the simply erroneous. They can be sent wandering off in a kind of cyberchaos, buffeted by bits and pieces of unrelated and often unreliable material. Without guidance, a child who has spent several hours surfing the Internet might have learned little or nothing of any value by the end of the day.

Even with careful supervision, there can be unwelcome surprises in store. A teacher from Toronto described how two random Internet links on the classroom computer landed her and her grade five class in the middle of a Nazi bulletin board. On another occasion, one of her children, who was searching the Internet for information on chickadees, wound up connecting to a sex chat-room. Many parents have also expressed concern about the possibility of their children encountering online pedophiles.

The fact that information is available on the Internet is no guarantee that it is accurate or unbiased. Information that appears in print may not be accurate or unbiased either, but at least with print there are certain well-established procedures to inform readers of the author's identity and point of view and to ensure that the material has been vetted—by publishers' readers, by editors, and sometimes by fact-checkers. Websites generally dispense with these formalities. The information they contain could have come from anywhere and been put together by anyone. And since there are few recognized forums for discussing their contents, such as book reviews, Internet users are generally left to determine the value of a particular site for themselves. This is a lot to expect of young children.

There are similar problems with CD-ROMs. Teachers rarely have time to screen and evaluate such material (previewing a CD-ROM is a much more difficult and time-consuming undertaking than skimming a book, both because of the way information is presented and because of the amount of material a CD-ROM contains), and published reviews are generally uncritical. Consequently, material is purchased on the basis of packaging and advertising. Yet proper review is even more necessary than with books because the haste with which new CD-ROMs are being placed on the market has led to very uneven quality. For example, a topic much in vogue at the moment is dinosaurs. When dinosaur specialist John W. Merck, Jr., undertook a thorough review of four CD-ROMs designed for the school market on the subject of dinosaurs, in the magazine *The Sciences*, he found the quality ranged from "terrible to pretty good." The content of one CD-ROM even failed to give an adequate definition of the term "dinosaur" and made fundamental errors, sinking into "a welter of shallow, inaccurate and misleading information."[3]

One writer of CD-ROM text confirms the poor quality of much CD-ROM material. In a provocative essay published in *Harper's* magazine, "Virtual Grub Street, Sorrows of a Multimedia Hack," Paul Roberts writes with despair about the quality of writing for CD-ROMs. Noting that the writers of this material are not experts, he describes them as merely "filters, whose task is to absorb and compress great gobs of information into small, easily digestible, on-screen chunks. Brevity and blandness; these are the elements of the next literary style. Of roughly one thousand 'essays' I've 'written' for CD-ROM companies here in Seattle over the last year and a half, fewer than forty ran longer than two hundred words—about the length of the paragraph you're reading now—and most were much, much shorter.... Nowadays, whole months go by when I do nothing but crank out info-nuggets on whatever topics the multimedia companies believe will sell: dead composers, large African mammals, sports stars of yore. It is, without question, hack writing."[4] Roberts points out that, typically, the budget for writing is much smaller than the budget for the video or audio components, a fact that reflects the low status of the text itself.

The trouble is that the multimedia attractions of CD-ROMs can distract users from the quality of the factual information presented. This certainly seems to be the case with CD-ROM encyclopedias. Until recently, the *Encyclopedia Britannica* and *The Book of Knowledge* were considered the best encyclopedias for use in schools. But the advent of encyclopedias on CD-ROM has created a situation in which slick marketing and glitzy graphics—which eat up space and memory and are produced at the expense of the text—can make inferior encyclopedias look good. Few schools, for example, wanted to own the Funk and Wagnall's encyclopedia before it got animated.

Another very popular CD-ROM encyclopedia is Microsoft's *Encarta*, and this, too, has its limitations. When the 1994 Encarta was reviewed by *The Economist*, a number of irritating quirks were found, as well as some serious shortcomings. Acknowledging that, as an

American encyclopedia, *Encarta* would naturally pay more attention to American subjects than to others, the reviewer still found it "hard to believe that Deng Xiaoping merits only an entry equal in length to that of Donna Shalala [U.S. Health and Human Services Secretary in the Clinton administration]; and the French reader, seeking an account of his own country, will be puzzled by a presumption that it is not yet a member of the European Union." Although Microsoft updates *Encarta* annually, many entries in fact had "hopelessly antique statistics."[5]

Encarta also shows a fascination with the computer industry, for an obvious reason, and devotes particular attention to Microsoft itself. There are separate entries for Microsoft Corporation, Microsoft Windows, and Microsoft DOS, as well as for William Gates III, whose biographical note is longer than those of Deng Xiaoping and Donna Shalala put together. This might be nothing more than a forgivable piece of ego-boosting, but it does suggest that Microsoft is perhaps using what should be an impartial source of information as a marketing tool.

The CD-ROM version of the *Encyclopedia Britannica* currently sells for $400, though some electronic encyclopedias cost as little as $80. This might seem inexpensive, but the relentless pressure to upgrade software brings other costs, not least the need to upgrade hardware every few years since older machines often cannot handle the latest software. Buying new machines in turn carries additional costs such as installation and training. As well, if a library has only one computer on which to run the electronic reference material, only one child can use the encyclopedia at a time, resulting in long line-ups at the computer. With a printed edition of an encyclopedia, most of the class can use it at the same time since there are many volumes to go around. Few schools can afford to purchase all the computers and CD-ROM licensing fees necessary for an entire class.

With so much new information on the market and so many new data bases being set up, the filtering task of school librarians has never been more necessary. Librarians, like teachers, have a bigger job to do than ever before, sifting through an ever-increasing volume of material to ensure that what gets into the library or classroom is appropriate and has educational value.

As the budget for technology increases, however, the amount available for librarians' salaries decreases, and with it the number of librarians. This is true in both public and school libraries.

The time-tested way of building library collections was to read the review journals and then the recommended books themselves. With fewer qualified school librarians, there is less opportunity for this kind of personal selection. As a result, school libraries increasingly rely on material collected for them by others, usually large, market-savvy book distributors who send out pre-packaged selections of printed material, with return freight paid. When schools are forced to rely on wholesalers to do their ordering and buying for them, the material that arrives is increasingly homogenous and of dubious quality. According to Anne Letain, a library consultant in Alberta, one series of books shipped from Florida contained a number of errors in both geographical and historical facts about Canada.

After undertaking a tour of some eighty schools in the province to look at the state of their library collections, Letain described the situation as "very discouraging." Many schools were using volunteers or library clerks to staff their libraries. "Where there might have been a teacher-librarian in the past, they'd usually put in another person. This might even have been a mother who'd spent a lot of time in the school, and was now functioning as a volunteer librarian." These replacements lacked the background and experience of a qualified librarian and had little detailed knowledge of curriculum requirements. "So what you'd see—even though these people were very well-meaning—was that they'd been buying books at the local grocery store. You'd see a library full of Disney books. It was enough to make you cry."[6]

Joanne Schott is a former children's resource collection specialist at the world-renowned Lillian H. Smith Library for Boys and Girls in Toronto. Like many of her colleagues, she is deeply concerned about the deterioration in the quality of collections that serve children and the adults who teach them. While the number of staff in her library has grown smaller, the volume of inquiries has increased. Since less time is available to examine materials before buying them, the tendency is to purchase popular, if mediocre, series publications over more demanding, higher-quality books. These series are at least a known quantity, and there is no time to look further.[7]

The biggest dilemma now facing children's librarians, says Schott, is the fact that staff have less time for the kind of brief but meaningful interviews that were once a significant part of the job. Whereas a librarian would once question a child about her interests and reading level and then steer her towards a good book, now there is rarely the time available to do so. Thus, even when good books do enter the library, they don't get read because no one has brought them to the attention of children or their parents. There is also the danger that, when it comes time to weed through the collections, the tendency is to dispose of any books that have not been circulating.

These are not isolated problems. Pressures on library services are widespread. When the California State Library commissioned a study to evaluate public library reference material, it found that, while the demand for library service was very high, the human resources needed to meet this demand were inadequate. Between 1978 and 1993, when the California study was commissioned, the number of queries for information went way up,[8] but cuts to staff resulted in shorter library hours, with more requests handled by each staff member. This meant that librarians spent less time on each reference question. In some libraries, staff cuts meant that *fewer* requests for information were handled. This led to a decline in service that staff described as "reduced goodness (completeness, authoritativeness, soundness) of answers."[9]

The California study also cites the loss of school librarians as a factor in placing a heavier burden on library resources. Also, students find it harder to find their way around the public library, not only because it is more complex but also because they are receiving less library instruction in school than they did in the past.

The irony of all this is that the new information technologies were supposed to make everything easier, while at the same time providing library users with access to a vastly expanded range of information. By allowing the librarian's role to be largely superseded by online services, many library systems have left their users confused and baffled by all the choices open to them. Where, they wonder, should they begin? The obvious answer is that they should consult a librarian—if they can find one available.

In the view of Thomas Childers, director of the Library and Information Science program at Drexel University in Philadelphia, "the 'new' public library is so complex that effective self-help is virtually impossible, without more bibliographic instruction or better tools, such as good electronic gateways." Childers, a consultant to the California State Library and author of the California library study, says that most people simply have no idea how to build the right search strategy or how to evaluate what they find. While electronic information systems sometimes make finding information (and more of it) faster, library users generally cannot be relied upon to find the best sources for themselves. Librarians are critical to the quality of a search.

Particularly worrisome for children are the brutal cuts to library services and the steadily diminishing number of school librarians or teacher-librarians—a profession that has existed for about thirty years. In Alberta alone, the number of school librarians has declined since 1983 from about seven hundred to less than two hundred. And in Nova Scotia, the government has been removing teachers from the school library and putting them back in the classroom, often replacing them with less qualified, but cheaper, library clerks or computer technicians. Similar instances are reported in the United States.[10] One Calgary teacher-librarian I spoke with described how he had to leave the elementary school where he worked because it had decided to redefine his position as that of a computer "technologist." Although offered the new position, he preferred to stay in his chosen field and so had to move on.

This is an unfortunate and misguided trend. It stems from a view of libraries that values the technical knowledge required to keep the system going above an understanding of the sources of information the system makes accessible. Replacing librarians with technical staff might mean that students learn to change the paper on a printer or to initialize a disk, but will they acquire the skills they need to navigate their way through the sea of information that awaits them?

Even if students receive the kind of guidance and assistance they need, the use of electronic information technology encourages certain tendencies that conflict with educational goals. In the first place, the ease with which the computer can copy and print material has created more tempting opportunities for plagiarism than ever before. Librarians and teachers frequently report incidents of students copying out entire articles or sections of material and turning it in as their own. (In one example, a student copied a thirty-five-page biography of Shakespeare from an electronic data base. The librarian was alerted because of the amount of time the printer was on and because of the amount of paper used.)

Plagiarism has always existed, but in the past students were at least required to write out or type the text they were using, ensuring they read what they had purloined (though their use of the material remained plagiarism nonetheless). With a computer, they can easily skip this step. As one librarian said, "Sometimes people think that because they are working on a computer they don't have to read. Often students hand things in without reading the material they have copied." Teachers predict that this will become a much bigger problem than it is right now. District meetings and school seminars are now being devoted to ways in which this problem might be addressed.

If students haven't read the material they use, they won't have made notes, either. Yet note-taking is a vitally important skill. Only by writing things down in our own words do we make them part of our working knowledge. If we do not take notes, we reduce the likelihood that what we have read will be fixed in our minds. Note-taking forces us to read carefully and reflect on the text we are referring to, for only in this way can we determine what our notes should contain. This is a critical step in writing good essays.

Another problem is that information obtained from a data-base search is often devoid of context. For young children especially, context is essential if they are to arrange what they learn in any meaningful way.

Books, with their clearly defined scope and linear organization, are good at helping children fit new information into a broader framework; computer data bases are not.

In presenting information, the computer screen tends to break it up into separate little chunks, or "mind bites." Often what we see on the screen are boxes of text and/or illustration, each under a particular heading, which are not necessarily related to each other in any formal way. Some may be useful for the task at hand, others not. In the latter case we quickly move on. Thus, like birds feeding on a lawn, pecking whenever a tasty morsel comes in sight, we hop around our research topic from one box to another, keeping a sharp eye out for tidbits that appeal to us.

Hypertext links, which are programmed into many electronic data bases and CD-ROMs, give an exponential boost to this kind of learning. Using hypertext, we can branch off into related topics and pursue associations beyond the context in which our research originated. For example, a piece on fashion that mentioned cotton could lead to the topics of how and where cotton is grown, suitable climate conditions, the need for pest control, the economics of production, etc; and each of these topics could lead to others in turn. In enabling us to do this, however, hypertext tends to undermine our sense of context even further, since we soon leave behind the particular concern that started us off in the first place.

Students need discipline to keep on target when researching hypermedia, but the trouble is that it's often hard to know what the target really is. There are so many tempting side roads along the way that might lead to new and unexpected discoveries. As one researcher has pointed out, "Placing an inquisitive, undisciplined young learner in a rich hypermedia environment may be similar to giving a remote control unit to a student in front of a television with 80 channels of action programming."[11]

For those who are enamored of the new information technologies, the goal of contemporary education is not to master any particular body of knowledge; nor is it to inhabit the classics of literature or study the details of the world around us. What lies behind current beliefs about education in the information age is the notion that children should be exposed to, and become used to handling, an increasingly varied range of information from a vast body of growing data.Yet, given the exposure children already have to different media—from the total environments of shopping malls, to television, to computers—it could equally well be argued that they are already drowning in a confusing sea of information.

As it is, with the resources currently devoted to computerizing education, and the increasing role played by private business in shaping curriculum, it is hard to escape the conclusion that navigation of the information highway has become *the* primary goal of contemporary education. Children, just like their adult counterparts in the workplace, are cast alternately in the role of data processors and information consumers.

8

Caught in the Web: Children's Advertising on the Internet

The online services emerging today are in some ways like television networks. They suck in an audience, and distribute entertainment and information. They are a destination rather than a jumping-off point into cyberspace.
The Economist[1]

Oh. Uh … sorry, you surprised us. Well, you're welcome to look around of course. But there's really nothing to see around here. Yup, pretty quiet at the old library.… Just a couple of books, nothing more. But feel free to sit for awhile and read quietly.
M & M's website[2]

As the number of Internet users (some 60 million people in 1997) continues to increase, the World Wide Web is drawing more and more young people into this new electronic environment. Children as young as two can be found sitting at a terminal using an online service. According to Jupiter Communications, approximately 5 million children between the ages of two and seventeen used online services in 1996.[3] Conservative estimates suggest that by the turn of the century between 12 and 15 million children will be connected to the Internet either at home or in school. By the year 2002, as many as 20 million children will have access to the Internet in their homes and more than 90 percent of these children will have access in school.

While many parents and teachers view the Internet as a resource for the education of the young, a very different role has caught the attention of corporate advertisers. A growing number of companies are devoting significant resources to turn the Internet into a potent marketing tool that will allow advertisers unprecedented access to children in the classroom and at home. When students in Peoria, Kansas City, or Toronto turn on their computers each morning, the first image they see might well be an advertisement for Pepsi, the figure of Ronald McDonald, or a Burger King logo.

The use of the Internet to mount a massive advertising campaign aimed at children has brought a new dimension to the infiltration of corporate values and objectives into the classroom. Computer companies have long known the advantage of supporting computer use in schools by donating equipment and software: it helps to build a customer base of loyal users. Now they are being joined by a raft of other companies who have realized the potential of the Internet as a means of pitching their consumer goods to students. Increasingly, the price for, say, visiting an environmental website or using *World Book* in its electronic version is first to run a marketing gauntlet. In an even more disturbing twist, some schools are receiving corporate funding in exchange for downloading advertising via the Internet onto the screen-savers of students' computers. In seeking this kind of corporate sponsorship, made necessary by the high cost of computer technology and the decline in funds for education in general, schools are in effect leasing out the time and minds of their students in order to finance their education.

At a marketing conference held in New York in 1995, a representative of one of the world's largest advertisers said of the Internet: "There is nothing else that exists like it for advertisers to build relationships with kids." This remark, from Erica Gruen, former director of Saatchi & Saatchi Interactive, was made during a discussion about how best to tap into one of the most lucrative markets for advertisers—the children's market. Catching kids early, advertisers know, is the best way to instill brand loyalty in everything from high-tech consumer goods—computers and computer games—to soft drinks, candy bars, fast food, and clothes. Children are no longer just the consumers of tomorrow but a prize market from babyhood on. In 1996, American children age fourteen and under spent $20 billion, money they got as gifts, allowances, and pay from part-time jobs. Teenagers spent an additional $67 billion. Together, the two groups exerted an influence on their parents' annual spending to the tune of an additional $200 billion.[4]

In advertising parlance, the market for children online is known as the "lucrative cybertot category." By 1995, Saatchi & Saatchi had already set up special teams to gather information about the habits of children online in order to develop sophisticated techniques for marketing to kids in cyberspace. This multibillion-dollar company has hired cultural anthropologists and psychologists to study "kids' culture" and to determine how children process and respond to information online. Speaking at the conference in New York, Gruen said that the online world corresponds to "four themes of childhood … attachment/separation, attainment of power, social interaction, and mastery/learning."[5] Each area corresponds with an important stage in child development. Children need to feel secure, but at the same time they want independence and need to explore the world on their own. They also want to bond with people or characters who are familiar to them. Children like to demonstrate that they have control over their lives, and playing on the computer gives them a sense of power. Social interaction on the Internet frees them from adult supervision and allows them to form independent relationships. Finally, children who have mastered basic computer skills will apply their understanding to an exploration of websites.

Here, child psychology is, in effect, harnessed to sell products. Perhaps more tellingly, advertisers at the conference spoke of how much pleasure children got from using the computer and how this "flow state," a state characterized by sensations of pleasure and absorption, could be used as a perfect vehicle for advertising.

The advertiser's first objective, getting children in front of computer screens, has been achieved without much difficulty. In fact it was largely handed to them. In most cases, children can be sure that a request to spend time on the Internet will meet with adult approval.

With their target audience within reach, advertisers are hard at work looking for the best ways of presenting their products to young and highly impressionable minds. At the present time, their options are virtually limitless because no regulations restrict the content or format of Internet advertising. And since much of children's time on the Internet is unsupervised, in school as well as at home, there is little input from adults to mediate or criticize the forceful commercial messages that are presented in increasingly subtle and seductive ways.

Young children are especially susceptible to the lures of advertising. Bonding with role models, among whom well-known advertising characters must certainly be included, is a natural part of their social and emotional development. Such emotional ties lend particular force to the advertising messages children see on-screen because of their belief in the "friendship" and "goodwill" of the messenger. If Ronald McDonald and the Power Rangers tell them how good it is to eat hamburgers and play with plastic toys, these are what they will urge their parents to buy.

Children under the age of seven do not possess the ability to distinguish between what is real and what is imaginary. Many young children regard the characters from storybooks, comic books, and television programs and commercials as no less real a part of their social and emotional landscape than family members and friends. The deep emotional bonds children form with these imaginary characters create the contours of their emotional landscape, which accompanies them into adulthood.

Once upon a time the characters of childhood came to life in stories told or read by parents or grandparents. These stories generally had some moral purpose beyond the desire to entertain. They showed what happens to people who are good and kind or selfish and uncaring, brave or cowardly, clever or stupid, persevering or lazy. They dealt with the most basic of human motivations, the most powerful of human emotions. But with the coming of television, and now even more so with the Web, children's fantasy lives have been invaded by a host of one-dimensional, disposable creatures whose sole business it is to capitalize on the naturally suspended disbelief of children for the purpose of turning them into lifelong consumers. Some of the traditional fantasy figures of childhood have also been co-opted. Thus, the fantasy life of children on the Web is permeated not only by the iconography of advertising, but also by icons that the advertising industry has begun to appropriate for itself.

The Internet provides a particularly favorable environment for children's advertising. Unlike watching television, playing with a computer gives a child a sense of having control over his or her environment. Sitting by oneself close to the screen—tapping out commands on the keyboard, seeing one's name appear in a "personal" message—creates an intimate atmosphere and gives the child an impression of close contact. In such circumstances, it is easy for children to think that they can make friends with Sailor Moon, Ronald McDonald, the Power Rangers, or the Tooth Fairy, creatures they believe to be real. These are the "people" who will make their wishes come true. In fact, they are also the ones who are trying to influence what these wishes will be.

But the interactive nature of the medium and the sense of trust and security that is established have consequences that extend beyond the creation of a desire for certain products. By playing on children's need for attention and understanding, website advertising can easily persuade children to give out very personal information about themselves and their families, information that will enable advertisers to target individuals in just the way that will appeal to them. After all, what child can resist having a personalized e-mail birthday card arrive from the Blue Power Ranger or an e-mail message from the Tooth Fairy?

Colgate's Tooth Fairy site has been discontinued, but it provides a good illustration of how a recognized character can be used to elicit personal information from children and deliver an advertising message to them under the guise of advice from an understanding and supportive friend. When children surf into Colgate Kids World, they are asked to type in their name (though if they leave the name blank, they can still advance to the next page). Upon entering the "Tooth Fairy" site they were asked: "Lost a tooth? Visit this location to get a special message from the Tooth Fairy!" Children were then told to "Fill in the blanks below, get a good night's sleep, then check your E-mail tomorrow for a message from you-know-who." In order to get this message, of course, children had to enter their names, e-mail address, and age. The submit button for this form read "Put Your Tooth Under Your Pillow." The next day, children received an e-mail message. One such message read:

Dear Jane Smith,

Hi! I got your E-mail. I'm the Tooth Fairy ... and I watch over your baby teeth.

So, you've lost a baby tooth. That means you're growing up! It also means that now it's up to you to watch over your grown-up teeth.

You need to take care of those new teeth coming in. They are yours for the rest of your life! Here are some of the tips I've learned, hopefully they'll help you too! Don't forget to brush your teeth at least twice a day with fluoride toothpaste. And visit my friend the dentist every year ... that's really important! And my last advice is to limit your snacks. Healthy snacking is good ... but don't snack all the time!

Now it's up to you. Good luck! If you follow my advice, you'll help to keep your teeth healthy and your smile shining bright!

Keep smiling!

Your friend the Tooth Fairy

While it is certainly laudable to encourage children to take care of their teeth by brushing regularly, the underlying message is that the Tooth Fairy wants them to brush with Colgate. In children's minds, this brand of toothpaste soon becomes inextricably linked with their feelings about the Tooth Fairy—feelings that this toothpaste manufacturer hopes to capitalize on.

If getting a message from the Tooth Fairy is compelling, equally enticing are the products given away just for parting with personal information. Jelly Belly, for instance, gives away five hundred free samples per day to people who send in their names. (The day we visited the site all of the samples were gone and we were asked to try again.) The Pepsi site promotes "Pepsi Stuff"—merchandise given in return for points collected from buying Pepsi products. Walt Disney offers online sweepstakes. On the Nickelodeon cable television channel website, children are offered the opportunity to win "tons of prizes" by submitting their name, street address, and sex. They must also answer questions about their pets, the sports they play, and other online games and activities they engage in. Glossy, a website for "Glossy Girls," asks girls to tell about their favorite magazines, their favorite music, why they surf the Web, when they will graduate from high school, etc. In return for this information, Glossy promises to send along a free compact mirror.

Another hook is the offer of certain privileges in exchange for information. If children wish to play at Nintendo's "Loud House" site, they have to become members, and while membership is free, registration means a child must divulge the following information to Nintendo: name, password, birthdate, e-mail address, and game preferences, including whether or not they like action, street-fighting, role-playing adventure, puzzles, etc. Sega allows visitors to send Sega online postcards to friends called "Segagrams." In return, visitors must give the name and e-mail address of both the sender and the recipient, as well as the message to be delivered. The Nabisco Kids site offers a downloadable Chips Ahoy! screen-saver for visitors who send in information about their favorite TV show, favorite hobby, favorite meal of the day, favorite time to snack, etc. This offer is accompanied by a request for their sex and age.

Openly offering incentives in exchange for information might appear to be harmless, but the implications are disturbing. Children become, in effect, unwitting participants in what amounts to an online focus group; their personal preferences are being noted and tabulated and in some instances sold to other agencies for marketing purposes. This allows marketers to create one-on-one relationships with children, effectively micro-targeting them.

Such relationships are dangerously unequal. In the view of Michael Brody, a child psychiatrist, advertising on the Internet exploits children's lack of judgment. While representing the American Academy of Child and Adolescent Psychiatry at a Federal Trade Commission workshop on privacy protection, Dr. Brody was shocked at how little discussion there was about child development theory. We must remember, he says, that children are not little adults, that their cognitive development takes place in stages.[6] It is particularly exploitative for Internet advertisers to use well-known characters such as Batman and the Power Rangers as spokespersons to sell consumer products to children (something that is not allowed on television) because these characters are among children's most trusted role models. Brody emphasizes that role models are exceedingly important to children. "They help with impulse control, the ability to learn, and how to socialize." But what lesson will children learn when their role models tell them to buy, buy, buy? This question seems to be largely ignored when considering children's use of the Internet, perhaps because they appear to be so adept at handling this medium. Brody finds this shortsightedness especially troubling. "It takes a whole village to raise a child," he insists. "It takes only one corporation to exploit one."

Equally indefensible is the practice of collecting information without the user's knowledge. The electronic gathering of information online is carried out by what are known as "cookies" or "magic cookies." This is technical jargon for a way of secretly keeping track of the visitor's movements through an Internet site. Surreptitiously tracking the amount of time each visiting child spends at a site, a program logs the activities and interests of that child in order to develop a marketing profile. Jeremy Hoey, a Vancouver writer for *Adbusters*, kept a running tally of how many "cookies" were blocked after he installed a "cookie blocker" on his computer. In the first week it had blocked 212 banner ads (ad space, often animated, at the top of a Web page) and 325 cookies. Since he only surfed the Web for about five hours, his program blocked approximately 42 ads and 65 cookies an hour. "It serves," Hoey wrote, "as a sobering reminder of the extent to which we are inundated with marketing messages each day without fully realizing it."[7]

Without software that blocks the gathering of this kind of information, children, teachers, and parents will not know when such information is being collected, let alone who is collecting it or how it is being used.

The Center for Media Education, a Washington-based children's advocacy group, has been documenting the numerous sophisticated techniques that advertisers are using to target children online. In a report entitled *The Web of Deception*, the Center concludes that the boundaries between website content and advertising are often so blurred that in many cases they are being eliminated altogether.[8] In cyberspace, for example, there is nothing to prevent the alcohol and tobacco industries from targeting children as future consumers, and doing so in a way that masks their real intentions. Cuervo Tequila has a cartoon character called J. C. Roadhog, a "cyber-rodent" who inhabits the virtual community of the "Republic for Cuervo Gold." As part of an online game, this character races through a desert littered with empty tequila bottles displaying the company logo. Visitors are urged to "defect" and join the Republic, a land of "untamed spirits." To advertise its product online, Budweiser beer has a radio network, "KBUD," hosted by a DJ, which brings children a stream of interviews with rock stars, music, and reviews of albums, along with promotions for beer. Its online promoter is a character called Budbrew J. Budfrog, whose online biography announces that he "drives a German luxury car, has memorized the entire Oxford English Dictionary, and likes to hang out on the beach with a hot babe, a cold Bud, and a folio edition of the Kama Sutra in its original Sanskrit." Another brewer, Amstel, has a "virtual bar" and a friendly barkeep named Hank, who dispenses advice on relationships and beer.

Chat rooms for smokers, which are numerous and easy to find, offer similar enticements. These range from Smokey's Cafe on the Smoker's Home Page, where visitors can view photographs of glamorous celebrities smoking, chat with other smokers, and read pro-smoking articles, to advertisements for specific brands.

Innocent searches for information on the Web can easily lead children into websites for tobacco and alcohol. A study that searched key words children might commonly look for turned up several alcohol and tobacco links for topics like "games," "entertainment," "music," "contests," and "Halloween." The Budweiser Budfrog character even popped up during a search for "frogs."[9] It is also possible for those underage to buy alcohol and tobacco from the Internet. Few or no questions are asked, and products are delivered directly to the home. If sellers do ask if a buyer is old enough, there is no mechanism for verifying the answer.

In another study, published in 1997, the Center for Media Education examined the information collection practices of thirty-eight websites specifically targeted at children, and noted that 90 percent of all websites actively collected personally identifiable information from them. "Cookies" were used by 40 percent of the sites. Only one site in five asked children to "check with your parents before releasing information," and not one site asked for verifiable parental consent before collecting this information. One quarter of the sites sent an e-mail message to children after their initial visit. In addition to this, several sites used product spokes–characters (like the Tooth Fairy) to solicit information. Forty percent of sites gave away free merchandise, ranging from screensavers to sweepstakes prizes, in order to encourage children to give out personal information.[10]

Once this information is obtained, there is no knowing where it will end up. There is nothing to stop a company that collects information on the Internet from selling it to other users. This should be a matter of considerable concern, since such users could have other than legitimate motives. For instance, *Money* magazine described how a TV reporter, who posed as the wife of a man on trial for the abduction and murder of a twelve-year-old, was able to obtain a list of the names, sex, addresses, and phone numbers of 5,500 California children from a company called Metromail, simply by using an alias, a mailing address, and a disconnected cellular-phone number. This information cost the reporter only $277. Metromail says that it no longer sells mailing lists of children, but as the reporter, Anne Reilly Dowd, discovered, other companies do. A firm in Tucson, Arizona, will sell children's names for 8.5 cents each and a copy of the material you plan to use to advertise to them. The company will give out as many as 8 million children's names designated by sex, age, and city.[11]

Only a very few companies warn those online that the information they are collecting may be used elsewhere. On the Colgate website there is a link called "Legal Statement," part of which reads, "The communications and material you send to www.colgate.com or to Colgate by Internet electronic mail are on a non-confidential basis with no promise by Colgate not to use." And in a fine-print disclaimer the Jelly Belly site says, "... anything you disclose to us is ours. That's right—ours. So we can do anything we want with the stuff you post. We can reproduce it, disclose it, transmit it, publish it, broadcast it and post it someplace else." A spokesperson for candy-maker Herman Goelitz told *The Wall Street Journal* that it has no intention of selling or renting this information but rather was issuing a warning for all Internet users.[12]

Given the political capital that the Clinton administration has invested in computer technology, it is unlikely that the U.S. government will attempt to regulate the current free-for-all. In 1997 the Federal Trade Commission (FTC) ruled that certain practices were deceptive and unfair, specifically citing KidsCom (an entertainment corporation) for soliciting personal information in a deceptive manner and for failing to "fully and accurately disclose the purpose for which it collected the information and the uses made of information" (KidsCom was releasing the information to other companies for marketing purposes). However, KidsCom modified its conduct and the FTC did not take any action. KidsCom now sends parents an e-mail when kids register at its site and will not release personally identifiable information to other parties without parental approval, either by return facsimile or by mail.[13]

As for blocking commercial advertising, politicians are opting for a technological solution, hoping that a V-chip will be developed in order to block commercials as well as pornography. However, the blocking technology is simply one more thing teachers and parents have to worry about. They must buy it, install it, and monitor the children who are using it. While a number of software packages exist that promise to block "cookies" and advertising banners, and to keep children from straying into websites parents and teachers don't want them to see, these are far from foolproof. While playing on the Internet at a friend's house one day, my twelve-year-old daughter and her friend were quite easily able to remove the Net-minder that my neighbor—a knowledgeable and technically proficient librarian—had painstakingly installed.

Commercial interests of course are eager to reach young consumers directly and would like nothing better than to do an end run around the teachers and parents who try to control their children's exposure to online advertising.[14] Such tactics can be more easily pursued if corporations are involved in partnerships with schools, a fairly common practice in the United States.

Unlike their American counterparts, Canadian schools have yet to embrace wholesale commercialization within their curriculum. While there are ten thousand or so American schools that subscribe to Chris Whittle's Channel One commercialized newscasts, there are few instances of widespread corporate sponsorship of schools in Canada.[15] The wolf, however, is at the door, and some school boards have made the decision to generate revenue by granting computer-based advertisers access to students.

The Peel Board of Education, just outside Metropolitan Toronto, has signed a contract with ScreenAd Digital Billboards Inc. that allows the company to transfer advertising images to the board's website, from which they are downloaded as screen-savers to classroom computers. Starting in the fall of 1997, students in elementary, middle, and high schools began viewing a variety of commercial messages on screen for such products as Trident Gum, Burger King, Pepsi, and Minute Maid. These electronic ads, known as "digital billboards," are displayed only when a screen has been inactive for more than ten minutes. So, in theory, as long as students don't pause for too long, they can expect to do their school work uninterrupted by advertising. Just what effect such interruptions will have when they do occur remains to be seen. There are also bound to be periods when the computers are turned on but not in use, so that the digital billboards will be displayed for a considerable length of time.

The Peel Board now receives approximately 32 cents per screen per month. It hopes to be able to attract more sponsors as time goes on, the goal being to generate about $500,000 in the first year of the program. The school board and individual parent councils have drawn up guidelines that govern the content of the advertising, and local dentists, community colleges, the milk marketing board, and a fruit-growers' association are being brought in to "balance" advertising for fast food. As well, messages to use the library, stay in shape, apply sunscreen, stay in school, and be "environmental" are being added to the mix. When the program is up and running, Peel hopes the venture will bring in about a million dollars per year.

Other Ontario school boards, equally short of funds, have decided not to pursue this option. In the spring of 1997, the Lakehead Board of Education in the Thunder Bay area voted not to approve a ScreenAd pilot project in some of its schools. Like the Peel Board schools, the schools in this northern Ontario city found themselves in a cash-crunch in the wake of continual government cuts to education.[16] But Lakehead's thirteen school trustees held a spirited debate and decided that they would not lease out the minds of their children to corporate sponsors. "The school, classroom, and teacher lend credibility to anything," said Arlene Gervis, president of the Thunder Bay area Ontario Secondary School Teachers' Federation. "Children are apt to think that a product is good because the teacher says it is. My teacher said drink Pepsi and my teacher said Nike is best. As well, children are apt to re-member what they learn in school and we didn't want corporate sym-bols following them for the rest of their lives." Many older teachers remembered the old Neilson's maps that were used in classrooms in the 1960s. Gervis took one of these maps to the trustees' meeting, and after thinking about the effect of corporate sponsorship on themselves, the trustees voted against it. "We just don't want to promote corporate symbols," said Gervis. (There is considerable irony in the fact that some years ago the Ontario government ordered the removal of all corpo-rate symbols from the classroom, including Neilson's maps and Royal Bank book covers. Today, the province is actively encouraging schools to seek the sponsorship of corporate advertisers.)

Teachers in Thunder Bay were also offended by the continual flashing of corporate logos, which went on and off every fifteen sec-onds. The speed at which the images changed caused teachers to be concerned that the screen-saver ads would simply be a distraction, making it more difficult for students to pay attention and focus on their work. Even if students are not actually watching the screen, the constant repetition of advertising images can have a subliminal effect. In Gervis's view, what results is really a kind of "subtle brainwashing."

Children already spend more time learning about life through the media than they do in any other way. It is estimated that by the time most North American children graduate from high school they will have watched some 22,000 hours of television, of which up to one fifth could consist of commercials.[17] The commercialization of the Internet provides one more arena in which children's assimilation of consumerism can occur. By bringing computers into the classroom, the potential exists for children to receive a bigger dose of advertising than they are already getting at home watching television.

While television remains a strong influence in the lives of children, the Internet, with its sense of intimacy and interactive attractions, could become an even more potent force both at school and in the home. Yet if it has any potential for good in children's education, this has been seriously undermined by its slide into commercialism. As commercial opportunities are opened up, the Internet is becoming more like television, more a mass-merchandising tool than anything else.

But the greatest danger to children from advertising lies not so much in the seductive promotion of corporate agendas as in the more subtle effects on children's imaginative lives. As Stephen Kline writes in *Out of the Garden: Toys and Children's Culture in the Age of TV Marketing*, "Although there has been constant criticism of the tediously violent stories that television feeds to children, one factor has tended to be overlooked: that the rise in character marketing has all but eliminated images of real children playing in the normal course of their lives—in dramas or narratives about and for the young."[18] A lack of such images is leading to a gradual deterioration in the imaginative life of children.[19]

Television has already staked out a colonizing claim on children's imagination, and now the Internet has also moved in on the territory.

These invaders, with the odds currently stacked heavily in their favor, can do much to undermine children's sense of self. Young egos are in the early stages of development and are highly susceptible to outside influences. As children spend less and less time with their busy parents, they are far more at the mercy of role models that come from television or, increasingly, the Internet. If children cannot imagine futures for themselves other than those that are provided for them by the entertainment and advertising industries, what resources do they have to solve the personal problems of their lives, let alone the vast difficulties facing the planet?

It is a sad reflection on the current state of education that such a dangerously influential force as advertising should be allowed to intrude on young children's learning in school. Advertising is not just a distraction, it is altering forever the mental terrain of children with an infusion of fast food and plastic toys and other consumer goodies. Kalle Lasn, editor of *Adbusters*, sees it as a pollution of the mental environment. And it is coming with the tacit approval of a great many teachers, parents, and policy-makers. We would do well to begin considering the mental environment in which their children learn as seriously as we consider the state of the physical environment in which their children live.

9

The Physical Effects
of Computer Use

What could possibly be harmful about striking a key at the computer?
Nothing—unless you do it several thousand times a day.
Deborah Quilter and Emil Pascarelli[1]

We tend to think of the computer primarily as an extension of our intellectual capabilities, allowing us to access vast amounts of information and to perform almost instantaneous calculations at the touch of a finger. As a result, most of the discussion and research about educational computer use focuses on the cognitive effects on students and largely ignores what is happening to them physically as they sit and gaze at the screen in front of them.

Computers do have physical effects on those who use them, and these effects can be serious and long-lasting, even permanent. Moreover, they contribute to a wide range of disorders—to muscle, joint, and tendon damage, to headaches and eyestrain, to seizures and skin problems. Toxic emissions and electromagnetic fields produced by computers and video display terminals are also serious potential health hazards.

To start with the more obvious concerns, it does not take much imagination to see that working at a computer is hardly a healthy form of physical exercise. However flexible it may be as a means of accessing and manipulating information, for the user the computer is a kind of straitjacket into the which the body must adapt itself. The eyes stare at an unvarying focal length, drifting back and forth across the screen. Fingers move rapidly across the keyboard or are poised, waiting to strike. The head sits atop the spine balanced, in the words of one physician, like a bowling ball. Built for motion, the human body does not respond well to sitting nearly immobile for hours at a time.

The most prevalent injuries suffered by computer users are musculoskeletal ailments that fall within the broad category of repetitive strain injury (RSI). The tendons, tendon sheaths, muscles, ligaments, joints, and nerves of the hand, arm, neck, and shoulder can all be strained by repetitive movements such as those involved in keyboarding or clicking a mouse. Caused by a combination of bad posture, improper technique, badly designed or set up work stations, and simply working for too long without a break, these types of injuries have reached epidemic proportions in today's computerized workplace. Most at risk are those who spend a good portion of their day keyboarding in front of a video display terminal (VDT). Journalists and data-entry clerks, for example, are particularly prone to these disorders.

Since RSI arises from cumulative trauma to the body, it can take years before its symptoms become apparent. Studies by the U.S. National Institute for Occupational Safety and Health (NIOSH) show that it often begins with "occasional" discomfort in the back, neck, and shoulders. According to the NIOSH reports, more than 75 percent of VDT users experience these symptoms from time to time, and more recent studies indicate that 20 percent of users experience daily discomfort. British researchers have recently suggested that mouse use and keyboarding contribute to sensory nerve damage in the hands and wrists. Jane Greening of University College London and neurophysiologist Dr. Bruce Lynn say that people with RSI have reduced vibration sensitivity in the hand area, especially in the median nerve, the major nerve in the hand.[2] Overuse of the hand and arm can cause the joints in the hands to swell and ache so badly that sufferers wake up at night.

As children spend more time using computers, both at home and at school, it becomes increasingly likely that they too will experience these ailments. In fact, there is evidence that this is already happening. "Anecdotally, physicians and rehabilitation therapists say that the average RSI patient is [getting] younger and younger," says Deborah Quilter, author of *The Repetitive Strain Injury Recovery Book*.[3] Canadian chiropractor Richard Pilkington agrees. He says that he is beginning to see younger and younger patients with injuries consistent with computer-related RSI.[4] Most are boys, some as young as seven. The most common complaints are headaches and neck aches. An Occupational Health and Safety consultant in Canada, with a practice in Oshawa, Ontario, Pilkington believes these injuries are caused by poor posture at the computer. Children who use computers often display worse posture than adults—lounging, lying on the floor, hunching themselves across the keyboard, or leaning on their elbows. These postures all place added strain on the arms, neck, wrists, and spine.

Dr. Mark Gilbert, a noted specialist in chronic work-related injuries, who prefers to use the term work-related musculoskeletal disorder (WMSD), has found a similar trend in certain sectors of the population. Musicians are a case in point. "Ten to twenty years ago," he says, "the musicians would get WMSD later in their thirties, forties, and fifties. Now it's showing up in their teens." Gilbert speculates that by spending time on a computer as well as playing a musical instrument like an electronic keyboard or piano, young musicians are overtaxing muscles in their hands, neck, shoulders, and arms. Having treated hundreds of patients at his Toronto clinic, some of them very difficult cases, Gilbert strongly believes that children should be educated about the importance of taking safety precautions when using computers—including rest breaks, stretching, and aerobic activity.

While we have much to learn about these injuries, they are unquestionably painful and disabling. When Paul Taylor, a science reporter for *The Globe and Mail*, undertook to write an investigative piece on RSI in 1993, the damage to the nerves and muscles in his hands was already so severe that he was unable to type the article himself. Journalist Tony Wong was only thirty-one years old when a computer injury sidelined him as a political reporter for *The Toronto Star*. At their worst, his injuries prevented him from driving, cooking, and even opening doors. Wong, who was working long hours covering an election, blames his injuries on poor posture and hours of using a laptop computer. Although their respective employers have equipped both men with voice-activated computers, both Taylor and Wong are now suffering from repetitive strain injury to their vocal cords.

Repetitive strain injuries are also alarmingly widespread in the workforce. The U.S. Bureau of Labor Statistics reported 302,000 new cases in 1993, up from 281,000 in the previous year. In 1994 there were 332,000 new cases. Approximately 2.5 million workers are affected annually in the United States alone. (In 1993, according to the American Occupational Health and Safety Association, RSI cost American business $20 billion.) According to the Workers' Compensation Monitor, the average claim for RSI cost $11,479 in 1997.

Deborah Quilter and Emil Pascarelli, a doctor who runs an RSI treatment clinic out of Columbia Presbyterian Hospital in New York City, are co-authors of a book entitled *Repetitive Strain Injury: A Computer User's Guide.* They say that two to four hours a day at a computer is enough time to put someone at risk. There is a wide range of opinion in the medical profession about how best to treat such injuries—everything from hand splints, which must be worn to bed, to surgery. But health care professionals who deal with RSI agree that the best treatment is prevention.

Only in the past few years has there been a growing understanding of the importance of creating ergonomically correct workplaces. A well-designed computerized workplace should have adjustable tables and chairs to minimize strain on the body, as well as good lighting. Some computer companies are making keyboards that split in the middle, which allegedly allow the operator to maintain a more natural position. To date, however, no one has designed a computer keyboard, video screen, chair, or table with the health and safety of children in mind.

Given that millions of North American children now have access to computers at home or in schools, there is reason to be concerned. Women in the workplace have been frequent victims of RSI, not only because of the high preponderance of female secretaries and data-entry clerks, but because office furniture has been designed mostly for men.

Children fare even worse. Computer work stations are simply not made to fit the size and shape of a child's body. An elementary school classroom outfitted with computers, or even a library where children go to do research, will typically have the computers placed on ordinary desks with unadjustable chairs. Given the greater variation in size among children, especially in multi-age classrooms, this equipment is patently unsuitable. A desk that is too high, for example, forces the shoulders to be elevated and causes muscle fatigue and attendant pain across the shoulders and base of the neck, often leading to headaches. Many children are introduced to the computer at such an early age that they have no hope of achieving correct posture at the computer screen.

While visiting a computer lab with my daughter and her grade two class, I watched while the children got a crash course in the use of various software programs. Although the chairs swiveled and were adjustable, they had clearly been made for adult bodies. My daughter, who is tall for her age, was using a chair at the same height as a boy who was about four or five inches shorter. Neither the instructors nor the teacher took the time to discuss basic safety precautions. Missing from the lesson was any guidance on correct hand and body posture at the keyboard. No one mentioned that the chairs were adjustable and could be made more comfortable for children of different sizes. There was no talk about eyestrain or muscle strain, or the need for the children to take regular breaks to refocus their eyes and to stretch their muscles. The equipment was completely out of proportion for virtually the entire group of seven-year-olds. Consequently, all of these children spent the morning with their heads tilted upwards at the screen in a posture designed to put strain on the spine and give them sore necks. Even at the River Oaks Public School in Oakville, Ontario, a school specifically designed to house the latest computer technology, there is no allowance for adapting the dimensions of the work stations to the growing bodies of young children. A school I visited in New York City had work stations so out of proportion to the children using them that many kids were kneeling on their chairs in order to look up at the screen.

While this issue has been ignored in North America, the Swedish Institute of Working Life has begun to examine working conditions for children who use computers in schools and to make children aware of their own working environment. A survey designed in Sweden is now being distributed in Japan by the National Institute for Health, in Italy by the Institute of Occupational Health, and in the United States by Nova Solutions, Inc. Japanese researchers at Waseda University in Saitama have already reported that there is a huge mismatch between the size of a child's body and the dimensions of the computers. Researchers Kageyu Noro, Tatsuo Okamoto, and Minako Kojima have suggested that no matter how much an adult work station is adjusted it remains a makeshift measure for most children. They conclude that it is essential to design work stations of various sizes to suit children.

Like adults, children need to limit their computer time and take frequent breaks when using computer equipment, but the strong attraction exerted by the software favored by children (video games in particular) makes it unlikely that they will do so unless their time is monitored by a parent or teacher, which is not always the case. Many children in fact are spending far longer at video display terminals than either their parents or teachers realize, and the overuse is resulting in physical distress.

Few parents are aware that children can sustain injuries at the computer so they tend not to worry about how much time their children are spending with it. Even when confronted with an injury that has been caused by computer use, parents or children themselves often attribute the pain to other sources, such as a sports injury. "Children can be suffering from wrist, elbow, or shoulder strain and the parent won't know," says Pilkington.

High on the list is an injury referred to by kids themselves as "Sega thumb," which comes from playing high-speed video games. Because the thumb is a weak joint to begin with, heavy action with a joy stick, which drives the thumb continuously and rapidly forward, overtaxes the joint. The result is a painful condition much like skier's thumb—the kind of injury skiers get from jabbing their ski poles into the snow and jarring their thumbs. Pilkington says this is quite a routine injury in his practice. Computer games tend to utilize only one hand, placing tremendous strain on the index finger or thumb and the wrist.

The mouse poses another problem for children. Many adults suffer from RSI as a result of continuous use of this piece of equipment, because of the continual pressure placed on the index finger. Since the mouse is designed for adult hands, children are at an even greater disadvantage. The mouse is dangerous to use, says Deborah Quilter, because it can lead to the overtaxing of the index finger and also cause arm and neck strain.

Pilkington and others who have begun to consider the long-term effects of computers on a child's developing body are concerned that these effects are not fully understood. Moreover, since repetitive strain injuries are cumulative and can take years to show up in adults, there is reason to believe that the full extent of the damage to children will not be evident for many years to come, so that in the meantime the gravity of the problem will be overlooked. It is very possible that children suffering from RSI will not get appropriate treatment and will be vulnerable to long-term injuries.

Another major concern about children's use of computers is the extent to which the eyes are affected by staring for long periods at a video screen. Good vision is essential for academic success. Children who cannot see properly, either to focus on the blackboard or to do close work like reading or writing, will naturally make more mistakes and so find learning a frustrating experience. In the workplace, adult eyestrain results in loss of productivity. Children react differently, often by simply avoiding the task at hand. A child experiencing eyestrain related to VDT use might simply begin to avoid all academic work linked to that activity. Parents might become aware of a problem with vision only when their child's school work begins to decline, by which point the attendant damage to self-confidence might also need repairing. The child's teacher might also fail to realize that the problem is related to the tools, not the child.

The American Optometric Association recommends that, to be effective, eye exams for school children should test how well their eyes actually perform in classroom conditions. This means checking near and far vision, how quickly the eyes can switch focus from near to far, and how well both eyes work together as a team. If children are using a computer, then an eye exam should take this into account.

The effects VDT use has on the eyes is an area that has been studied in some depth, but the research to date has been conducted on adult eyes. We simply do not know what the long-term effects of heavy computer use will be on children's eyesight, but it is logical to assume they will be no less serious than they are for adults. Until the full effects of VDT use on a child's developing visual system are understood, it makes sense to limit the amount of time spent on computers during those early years and to make safety an automatic concern.

As far as the effects on adults are concerned, in 1991 alone, American optometrists treated more than 7 million patients with VDT-related vision complaints, according to Dr. James Sheedy, chief of the VDT eye clinic at the University of California at Berkeley. At Dr. Sheedy's clinic, 80 percent of the patients reported eyestrain and 50 percent reported blurred vision and headaches.

Spending too much time in front of a video screen is known to cause intermittent blurring and general eye fatigue, because looking at the screen forces the eyes to work continuously at one focal length. Toronto optometrist Barbara Caffery has seen an increase in the number of adults and children who need eyeglasses as a result of computer use. "What we used to ignore, we now end up giving a prescription for glasses for, because [the client focuses] on one focal distance for such long periods of time." Any close work like reading or sewing can also cause eyestrain, but unlike a book, the computer screen emits light and reflects glare, putting the eyes under additional strain.[5]

Staring for hours at a computer screen can also produce a "charley horse" of the eyes. Sheedy says that because the computer tires the eyes' ocular focusing mechanism (their ability to shift focus between varying distances), the eyes don't readjust to distance viewing after being in this position for a long time. This happens, according to Sheedy, even when a person is wearing eyeglasses or contact lenses. The result, as a number of studies have shown, can be a rapid onset of transient myopization (temporary nearsightedness).[6]

There is no way of knowing which children are predisposed to-ward myopia, but adults whose vision is less than 20/20 are more likely to develop both myopization and other eyestrain symptoms after working with a VDT. "The significance of these individual differences is very important for children," writes researcher Shirley Palmer of Ohio State University. "Some children could rapidly develop my-opization as a result of VDT work, while others might not be much affected."[7]

Since transient myopia is temporary, we might be tempted to think that it isn't serious. However, a Japanese study has reported that, after a ninety-minute stint at a VDT, the eye can take up to an hour or more to recover its full ability to see at other focal lengths. This finding indi-cates that students who spend significant amounts of time at computer terminals might have difficulty readjusting their eyes to other visual tasks, and thus be unable to concentrate on other learning experiences, immediately afterwards.

Another common complaint reported by VDT users is dry, itchy eyes. This occurs for two reasons. First, there is a consistent tendency to reduce one's normal blink rate by as much as 80 percent when reading from a VDT. Second, compared with printed material, VDTs are posi-tioned relatively high out in front of us, causing us to open our eyes wider and expose a larger portion of the eye's surface. Together, these factors substantially reduce the eye's tear film or surface moisture, which causes irritation. Contact lens wearers are particularly suscepti-ble. Although children have a better tear film than adults, they too can suffer discomfort.

It is reasonable to conclude that if students spend more time learning via computers the incidence of eyestrain will increase. The fact that many children can read text on-screen without significant loss of comprehension is seen by some as a vindication of the merits of computer-based learning, and in the general enthusiasm, the pos-sible physical effects of such learning are overlooked. A study testing the assumption that it is harder to read text on-screen than on the printed page found that there were no clear disadvantages to reading text on-screen, except that 20 to 30 percent of children who were using computers "said it hurt their eyes." This startling observation is all the more provocative in that it drew no comment from the research team.[8]

Even under the best workplace conditions, VDT operators still suffer from eyestrain. In classrooms, where computers are frequently inadequately lit and poorly positioned, the chances of eyestrain would seem to be a good deal greater. Eyestrain often occurs in tandem with muscle pains because, as Sheedy says, "the eyes lead the body." When, as is often the case, eye defects in children go undetected, the risk of VDT-related eyestrain and other injuries increases. Children who need corrective lenses but don't wear them, and who thus have difficulty seeing the screen, will compensate by squinting or by craning their necks to get a better view. Such postural contortions can result in neck strain and headaches and contribute to generalized poor posture that is hard to fix later on.

VDT operators who are aware of the risks of eyestrain know to assume a correct posture, take frequent breaks, do eye exercises, and use proper lights. Such essential health and safety precautions are rarely taken in school. Poor lighting conditions still plague many school children today and may even be getting worse. Schools routinely put computers into brightly lit classrooms, creating problems of glare from computer screens and working surfaces and subjecting children to too much light or the wrong kind of light, two causes of blurred vision and eyestrain.

The quality of lighting appears to have wide implications for human health. John Ott, a pioneer in the area of light research and founder of the Environmental Health and Light Research Institute in Florida, suggests that the mix of spectral light we ingest affects our physical well-being. He says we are in many cases "starved" for natural light spectra and that we receive too much light from the spectra that come from artificial lighting: incandescent, fluorescent, mercury vapor, sodium, and video screens. He describes the effect of inadequate lighting on the body as "malillumination."

While little research has been conducted in this area, a study undertaken for the Alberta Department of Education indicates that children's health and cognitive development can be correlated with the kinds of light their bodies ingest. The study found that full-spectrum lighting—illumination approaching daylight in its color quality—appeared to enable children to improve their scholastic achievement and their health. Children who experienced full-spectrum lighting grew faster, had better attendance, and even had fewer cavities than children who were exposed to the pinky-orange glow of high-energy sodium-vapor lights. The latter were absent a lot more, got lower marks, and showed signs of slower physical development. Dr. Warren E. Hathaway, author of the study, said that its conclusions show that lighting systems are not neutral with respect to their effects on people.[9]

If school boards and teachers are going to set up classrooms with computers in mind, they should be aware that the correct lighting for computer work (which entails, for instance, blocking out natural sunlight to avoid glare) does not necessarily promote the health, or the academic achievement, of the children.

. Another health concern is the association of epileptic seizures in children with the playing of video games. According to a study carried out in Seattle, epileptic reactions in children occur more often than previously thought, although the frequency is still unknown. The study reported on video-game-related seizures in thirty-five patients between the ages of one and thirty-six. Most of this group was composed of teenaged boys. While epilepsy has been known to be triggered by strobe lights or even sunlight shining through leaves, many of the patients in this study were not light-sensitive. The researchers concluded that the video games set off the seizures. Of the thirty-five patients studied, twenty-seven had never suffered a seizure before being exposed to computers. The youngest patient who suffered a seizure, a one-year-old girl, was standing next to her brother while he was playing a game. While scientists do not think the video games actually cause epilepsy, they do believe the games can trigger a response.[10] In Holland, warning about possible injury from seizures is now required when marketing such games.

Skin problems also appear to be associated with VDT use. Studies have generally shown consistent correlations between VDT use and increased reports of problems such as rashes, dryness, itching, and burning. In some cases, the reported incidence of facial skin conditions and/or rashes was twice that among non-VDT users, and these conditions appeared more frequently as the time spent in front of VDTs increased.

Just why VDT use should have this effect remains unclear, but it is likely that increased stress is a factor. The computerization of work is often accompanied by higher stress levels, and stress is known to produce skin reactions and conditions in many people. Another possibility is that the static electric charges of the VDT screen might cause ambient, potentially toxic airborne particles to be deposited on the face of the user. A further possible source is the toxic chemicals given off by new computers.

Toxic emissions introduce a new dimension to the health hazards of a computerized environment because they affect not only those who are actually using computers but also anyone who happens to be regularly in the same room with them. The U.S. Environmental Protection Agency (EPA) has identified a series of chemicals that are found in the off-gassing from hardware construction materials and internal components.[11] Such emissions are highest when equipment is new, and the EPA estimates that it can take from 144 to 360 hours for them to dissipate completely. "The implications of these emissions can be particularly significant in an indoor environment containing several new pieces of electronic equipment, e.g., a computer room in a school."[12]

Exposure to such chemicals has been shown to cause ear, nose, and throat irritation, as well as skin problems for office workers,[13] and the effects on children are not likely to be less harmful. Edward Lowan, an environmental consultant to school boards across Ontario, believes children, especially those with allergies, may be affected by the gases given off by new computers. He cites figures showing that traces of three hundred different chemicals have been found in the vapors given off by new computers. The result is that some children generally don't feel well and so don't enjoy school or work to their full potential, while others get sick a lot and miss days at school. Since most people are unaware that off-gassing of potentially harmful chemicals is taking place, children's symptoms and sicknesses, whether skin rashes or ear, nose, or throat irritations, are often put down to unknown causes and not properly diagnosed by parents or family physicians.

Toxic emissions are, however, a temporary hazard. The effect of electromagnetic radiation (or electromagnetic fields or EMFs), on the other hand, is a permanent concern. This is a particularly significant issue for school-age children, because of the association that has been established between childhood leukemia and exposure to EMFs from power lines.[14]

EMFs of differing strengths are present with all everyday electrical sources—televisions, computers, radios, dishwashers, electric hair-dryers, house wiring, power lines, etc. Video display terminals are likely to be the most constant source of exposure for children. For many, this exposure begins in kindergarten and will continue throughout their working lives. Many children already spend large amounts of time sitting in front of computer screens, playing video games or doing schoolwork. And while children are often told by their parents to sit well back from the television, they are frequently found sitting closer to their computer screens than the twelve-inch (30 cm) recommended minimum. Field strength from the back or side of a VDT is typically two or three times higher than in front. Yet in schools, terminals are often placed close together, so children are also exposed to the fields emanating from the back or sides of the computers around them.

Cathode-ray tubes, which are found in television sets and inside VDTs and the display screens of virtually all desktop computers and computer network terminals, emit radiation across the frequency band, from X-rays to extremely low frequency (ELF) electromagnetic fields. But the cathode-ray tube is not the only source of EMF radiation. All components, including the tube, the main processor, and the drives, operate on an alternating current that generates fields and charges of various frequencies and intensities.

Citizens' groups in both the United States and Canada have lobbied for a standard for individual EMF exposure. The current Swedish standard, known as MPRII, sets an allowable EMF emission level at 2.5 milligauss at 30 cm (1 foot) from the source. The TCO standard (a standard developed by Sweden's white-collar union) is even more stringent—2.0 milligauss at 30 cm (1 foot). Computer manufacturers are almost always unwilling to give out information on their computers' EMF emission levels, although many will say they meet the Swedish standard. However, because computer parts can be manufactured at different sites, different units of the same make and model can register different emission levels. When several schools in Toronto requested that Ontario Hydro measure the EMFs from computer terminals (as well as power lines), they discovered great variance among machines of the same make and model.

Many scientists consider the 2 milligauss level to be safe, but there is in fact no hard scientific data upon which to base this estimate, partly because it is impossible to find a control population that has never been exposed to artificial EMFs. So any standard, for the time being, remains an arbitrary one. It is also important to note that this is a standard driven by technology, not health—that is, it represents the standard to which the computer industry manufactures the equipment.

While many studies have sought to correlate biological effects with EMF field strength, recent research suggests that more significant factors might be the shape of the pulsed wave form, the frequency, and whether or not the field is continuous or intermittent. Researchers Indira Nair of Carnegie Mellon University and Jun Zhang of the Oak Ridges National Laboratory have noted that, while the EMF strength from a VDT is similar to or lower than that from sources like hair-dryers or toasters, it has different attributes.[15] Most notably, it tends to fluctuate suddenly. They argue that this fluctuation could have significant health effects. Consequently, lowering field strengths might not be as protective as has been believed.

There is growing suspicion that EMFs can disrupt the production of melatonin. Produced by the pineal gland, this hormone is linked to the visual system. Melatonin appears to include among its functions the inhibition of tumors by "mopping up" free radicals and thereby preventing damage to DNA.[16] The work of Russel Reiter, a neuro-endocrinologist at the University of Texas Health Sciences Center at San Antonio, appears to indicate that melatonin production is suppressed by static and by extremely low frequency EMFs.[17]

Other researchers believe that electric and magnetic fields disrupt the circadian systems (or biological clocks) of humans and primates as well as other animals.[18] Whether such effects are harmful or long-lasting is not clear. Disruption of the circadian system has also been associated with physiological and psychological disorders, including altered sensitivity to drugs and toxins, interrupted sleep, and psychiatric disorders such as chronic depression.

These studies and the questions they raise underline the complexity of the factors that affect the functioning of the human body. Given that children today likely spend more time at computer screens than any before them, it seems only prudent to teach them to keep at a safe distance from VDTs, and to recommend that parents and schools purchase computers that meet the lowest possible emission standards.

The precautions described above might help to mitigate some of the adverse health effects of a computerized environment. But they do not address a more basic problem: the long-term effects of the sedentary habits encouraged by television watching and computer use.

There has already been a marked decline in the physical fitness of North Americans, children included. For example, Canadian children now expend 40 percent less energy than children did forty years ago, and 60 percent of them do not meet average fitness standards.[19] This trend has been accompanied by a steady increase in childhood obesity. Long-term studies show that in the past thirty years the proportion of overweight American children between the ages of six and eleven has roughly doubled, from 5.2 percent to 10.8 percent. The greatest increase, however, has occurred since 1980, a development attributed to the prevalence of sedentary pursuits, such as watching television and playing video games, and the eating of high-calorie food—the latter no doubt often taking place in front of the TV screen.[20] (Just how sedentary one can become was discovered by researchers from the University of Memphis. When they focused on the resting metabolism of children between eight and twelve years of age, they found that the amount of energy being expended was higher when the children were doing nothing than when they were watching television.[21])

Another danger of prolonged periods of physical inactivity is that blood cholesterol levels can rise, with potentially serious long-term consequences. Clinical research by Dr. Kurt Gold and his colleagues at the University of California has shown that the longer children spend in front of a television set or video game, the higher their cholesterol levels will be. Gold discovered that children who had the TV on at least two hours a day were twice as likely to have cholesterol levels over 200 milligrams than those who watched less. Children watching for four hours or more a day were even worse off, being four times more likely to end up with cholesterol levels above 200. Gold cautions that children who are physically inactive so much of the time face an increased risk of cardiovascular disease later in life.[22]

The increase in computer use means that children are spending a much greater part of their day in a way that exposes them to a number of serious health hazards and deprives them of healthy physical exercise. In North America, the average child already spends twenty-six hours a week watching television and another twenty to thirty hours sitting in class. The current generation of children is the least physically active one there has ever been. The situation will hardly improve if we increase the amount of time young children spend in front of a computer screen. Yet this is what many computer advocates are suggesting we do.

Schools have routinely ignored health and safety issues around the use of computers. One ergonomically conscious educator, Janetta Wilson, has come up with a proposal to build work stations appropriate for elementary school children, but so far no company has stepped up to manufacture it.[23] Similarly, one primary school in Toronto tried to work with a furniture company to produce a work station of suitable dimensions for a child, but all the companies approached were reluctant to become involved. For some problems, however, there are practical solutions that could be implemented without too much difficulty. Toxic emissions through off-gassing, for example, could be avoided. Edward Lowan recommends that parents and school boards purchase secondhand computers so that off-gassing will be reduced, though with state-of-the-art technology increasingly seen as a necessity, this recommendation is unlikely to be heeded. As an alternative, Lowan suggests that computers be purchased at the end of the school year and left turned on in unused classrooms (with the windows open) for the summer, so noxious chemicals can dissipate while children are out of school.

Often, however, one must go beyond the technology itself and consider the state of the environment in which the computers are placed. The problem of air contamination, for example, is compounded by the fact that the ventilation systems in many older schools simply fail to meet current building standards. A bank of computers running constantly can heat up any classroom, but particularly one that is inadequately ventilated. Air-conditioning, which is the obvious solution, is yet another expense to be added to the school budget. Similarly, a combination of carpets and computers can spark a build-up of static electricity, aggravating dust problems for children with respiratory difficulties. The solution here would be to replace carpeting with another form of floor covering—again, a considerable expense.

New applications of computer technology, such as virtual reality simulations that have particular side-effects of their own, are already on the horizon.[24] Our children will be the first generation to use computers from "the cradle to the grave." Neglecting the safety issues that confront them, especially at an early age, could mean serious problems for them later in life. While computer-related injuries in the workplace have cost society dearly, few resources have been devoted to studying the physical effects of computer use on children. "It hasn't been studied yet," says Pilkington "because it hasn't cost society any money yet."

10

The Art of Intelligence

The new technology is not just an assemblage of machines and their accompanying software. It embodies a *form of thinking* that orients a person to approach the world in a particular way. Computers involve ways of thinking that under current educational conditions are primarily technical.
Michael W. Apple[1]

What happens a lot of times in education is that your imagination and vision is the last thing that you're exposed to.
Nan Elsasser[2]

I f our children are to escape from the confines of an education that values technical reasoning above all else, we need to recognize that there are more attractive alternatives. And if we are to place our children in schools that will educate them in a broad sense, as opposed to merely training them in technical skills, we need as a starting point the broadest possible understanding of the nature of intelligence.

One of the most promising approaches to developing all aspects of children's intelligence is to place greater emphasis on the arts and to integrate arts education into the core curriculum. Arts education, however, has been under severe pressure. With more money being spent on computer technology at a time when educational budgets are being squeezed, many schools are faced with a hard choice. If their students are to have computers, what will they have to do without? In many cases, it's an arts program that has to go.

As we have noted, a number of school boards and districts in Canada and the United States have already axed arts programs to accommodate spending on computers and Internet connections. Others are finding it impossible to maintain their level of arts programming within current budget restraints. For example, the Toronto Board of Education, one of the largest and richest in Canada, is faced with a budget cut of 25 percent, which poses a serious threat to its music programming. School choirs, itinerant music teachers, and "movement and music" classes might all be terminated. A Coalition for Music Education has been formed in Toronto to try to prevent these cutbacks. But many educators and parents seem willing to sacrifice arts programs, because they consider that learning to use computers is more important.

It is easy to pay lip service to the importance of the arts in education—almost everyone within the educational establishment does so. Yet when it comes to taking action, the arts too often get relegated to the sidelines. The 1994 Ontario Royal Commission on Learning, for example, sternly proclaims that "any school system that fails to open up the spirit of the arts to its students is unworthy of public support."[3] Yet after this resounding pronouncement, the commissioners say virtually nothing more about the arts, and do not make a single recommendation as to the role the arts could play in revitalizing the curriculum.

At the same time, there is no lack of certainty when it comes to the pursuit of academic achievement as measured by test scores, and the acquisition of the skills and knowledge required to succeed in this form of assessment. Schools typically reward and encourage the child with good logical-mathematical and linguistic abilities, since this sort of child will usually produce high grades and good test results. But high scores on math tests, an ability to memorize facts for science quizzes, or being able to write grammatically correct sentences indicate a limited range of abilities and do not even begin to hint at the potential in each child.

Unfortunately, computer use often results in an even more intense focus on this narrow view of intellectual achievement. Drill-and-practice programs, with their emphasis on "right" answers, are used because they are seen as a means of acquiring basic skills and knowledge that will help children to get good test marks.

There is a persistent view that spending time on the computer will yield significant advances in higher-order thinking skills, or what we can more generally call intelligence. But not enough attention has been given to the range of contexts and activities in which intelligence can be applied, or the various forms it can take. Indeed, intelligence is often defined in extremely limited terms (for example, IQ test scores, or technical reasoning) that ignore certain types of intelligence altogether. As Douglas Sloan, professor of history and education at Teachers College, Columbia University, points out, "cognition involves a rationality much deeper and more capacious than technical reason."[4] We have failed to develop a critical perspective on the role of computers in education because of a misconception of what it means to nurture the potential in each child.

Howard Gardner's theory of multiple intelligences suggests that the full potential of a child's abilities needs to be nurtured and developed by a wide range of activities that correspond to the range of aptitudes children possess. Most parents are well aware of what those aptitudes are. They are often heard making such comments as "Robin is an avid reader and makes up wonderful stories" or "Max draws from dawn till dusk and has an amazing visual memory" or "Jimmy has a real ear for music and Alicia is so athletic." Some children are continually tinkering with mechanical objects, taking things apart and putting them back together; others dance expressively or like to put on performances. Yet others demonstrate a creative imagination through their use of language: An eight-year-old I know suggests that a squeaky washing machine sounds "just like a cricket," and another child wondering about the origin of the word "*helmet*" asked, "Are they like hell to wear because they're so hot?"

Many of these aptitudes involve artistic interests and abilities, which are downplayed in standardized assessments of academic achievement. Yet the arts should not be seen as a fringe activity to be fitted into time left over from the "essential" elements of the school curriculum. In fact, there is a growing body of research indicating that arts programs actually improve students' performance in core academic subjects. For example, two recent studies have demonstrated that students who received early training in music and the visual arts did better in reading, mathematics, and foreign languages than students who were taught a conventional curriculum.

At the Music School in Providence, Rhode Island, Martin Gardiner and a group of his colleagues looked at the effects of music and visual arts teaching on primary school children aged five to seven years. One group of four classes was enrolled in a special program designed to develop musical and artistic skills in a systematic way. Another two classes were taught according to the standard syllabus. After seven months, all of the students were tested in reading and mathematics.

What Gardiner and his colleagues had not known until this point was that the group in the special arts program had been underachievers according to their kindergarten records. So the children who did *not* receive the special arts training were already ahead academically when the study began. In spite of this, however, the tests indicated that the underachievers had caught up with the other children in reading and were outperforming them in math, and they continued to do better in math until the end of the study the following year.

The Music School researchers believe that children who discover the pleasure inherent in the arts become motivated to acquire these challenging skills. This is echoed in the teachers' evaluations, which concluded that attitudes toward school and behavior in the classroom improved when children received an arts-enriched program. Gardiner himself thinks that musical and visual arts training stretches the mental capabilities of children, making them readier to absorb learning in other areas of the curriculum, including mathematics.

The second study, undertaken in Switzerland and Austria, came to similar conclusions. Conducted by Maria Spychiger, then at the University of Fribourg in Switzerland, and Jean-Luc Patry, from Salzburg University in Austria, this study involved a much larger number of students—about 1,200 elementary and high school pupils participated. Seventy classes of children took part in an enriched music program, receiving five music classes a week instead of the usual one or two. This increase was made at the expense of lessons in mathematics and languages. Thirty-five classes continued with the standard curriculum. After three years, the students who had taken more music classes and received less teaching in math and languages were as good in math as the control group and showed better results in languages. The "musicians" were also more cooperative with each other.

Too few experiments of this nature have been carried out, but there is a good deal of anecdotal evidence to suggest that arts education has many positive spinoffs for students. Perhaps if a fraction of the time and money that has gone into analyzing student responses to computer technology had been channeled into examining the link between the arts and academic achievement, more resources would now be devoted to arts education. (In France, for example, the arts are considered such an important part of education that schools all across the country close every Wednesday afternoon—time that is made up on Saturday morning—to coincide with free admission to virtually every art gallery and museum in the country.)

An active involvement in the arts helps to develop aspects of children's intelligence that are seldom called into play in traditional academic programs (and even less in much computer-based instruction). Howard Gardner's theory of multiple intelligences indicates what these aspects are: for example, ability in music and the visual arts is linked with musical and spatial intelligence, while dance not only involves both of these but relies on bodily-kinesthetic intelligence as well. The work of Robert Sternberg on successful intelligence and that of Daniel Goleman in the field of emotional intelligence reinforce Gardner's theory and bring further dimensions to this complex field of investigation.[5]

Sternberg, a psychologist at Yale University, distinguishes between three different kinds of thinking: analytic, creative, and practical. He believes that one must be able to think well in one or more of these different ways if one is to be "successfully intelligent." Having successful intelligence does not necessarily mean one does well in school. As Sternberg points out, "Many people with modest test scores are nevertheless highly intelligent." Our system of education tends to value only one way of thinking: analytic, or "critical-analytic" intelligence, which has much in common with Gardner's logical-mathematical intelligence. There is, of course, nothing wrong with this kind of thinking, but Sternberg emphasizes that "no one way is any better than either of the others, and, ironically, the style of intelligence that schools most readily recognize as smart may well be less useful than the others to many students in their adult lives."[6]

Overvaluing critical-analytic intelligence can have unfortunate consequences. In the first place, many children, rather than having their abilities acknowledged, are labeled below average and, seeing themselves fall behind their peers, lose their enthusiasm for learning in school. Children capable of writing an original essay or designing an imaginative science project might be passed over because they do not perform well on standardized IQ tests. These children do not test well, not because they aren't bright, but because the tests are unable to evaluate their abilities.

Second, children who are good at analytic thinking and who do well in tests are often encouraged to believe that this type of achievement on its own will lead to success later in life. In many cases, they will be disappointed. Students with extremely high IQs often go on to lead rather ordinary lives. The kind of textbook problems that "bright" students are good at solving (problems that have a "right" answer) do very little to prepare them for real-life situations that require original ideas and creative solutions.

Creative intelligence is well suited to just such situations, but its contribution to a child's overall performance is seldom recognized or formally assessed in schools. Creativity doesn't show up on report cards. In fact, Sternberg claims, if anything, teachers tend to discourage it because creative children are liable to disrupt well-established classroom routines or produce work that does not meet conventional expectations. Yet creative intelligence should not be associated only with the waywardness that is often assumed to accompany artistic inclinations. While a creative imagination is essential in any artistic endeavor, it also functions in other spheres of activity. Sternberg cites the instance of a child who, as well as being artistically gifted (some of her art work was selected to represent her school at a regional art show), considered science her favorite subject in school. She devised her own science projects at home, growing bacteria, collecting insect specimens, and, on one occasion, making a model of the human digestive tract out of a balloon. "Thus, she was really good at generating interesting ideas and at carrying them out independently."[7]

One program that has shown that arts education can have a positive effect on creative thinking and academic performance is SPECTRA+, which began in January 1992 in two elementary schools in Ohio. The program aimed to provide one hour of instruction per day in music, drama, dance, art, or media arts. It featured artists-in-residence and intensive arts experiences for teachers as part of their regular professional development activities. Results of the first two years of the program (as measured by a variety of tests) showed that the SPECTRA+ students did at least as well as, if not better than, students at two other schools in the same communities who were in either a "traditional" curriculum or in an innovative whole-language program. The SPECTRA+ students made greater gains in creative thinking, generally did better in math, and at one of the schools showed greater improvement in reading. They also had higher self-esteem and, not surprisingly, they demonstrated a greater appreciation for the arts.[8]

The other style of thinking Sternberg refers to is practical intelligence. Children who exhibit intelligence of this kind are often socially adept; we might call some of them "street smart." Such children are skilled at adapting to new situations because they see what needs to be done and know how to go about doing it. They have an instinct for what will and will not work and are good at fitting in.

Sternberg tells the story of one ten-year-old girl who had a low IQ and needed help in basic academic subjects. In fact, she was having a harder time than other children in her group. When they were transferred full-time to a regular class, however, she was the one who did the best. This was because she knew how to ask the teacher for help, how to function independently in the class, and how to get along with the other children. Her practical intelligence enabled her to make "the best possible use of the abilities she had, whereas the other children in her group, despite their higher IQs, often failed to mobilize their abilities effectively without the constant adult direction and supervision available in a special-education setting."[9]

This type of thinking shares certain characteristics with Goleman's concept of emotional intelligence, which includes "self-control, zeal and persistence, and the ability to motivate oneself."[10] Goleman, who has taught at Harvard and covers behavioral and brain sciences for *The New York Times*, believes that emotional intelligence is as necessary as other kinds of intelligence to leading a successful and satisfying life. Many people with high IQs flounder because they cannot motivate themselves, or control their impulses, or get along well enough with other people to get into positions where their latent talents can be productively employed. They are unable to manage their own feelings and deal effectively with the feelings of others. On the other hand, people with well-developed emotional skills are at an advantage, even if they have moderate IQs. Their emotional intelligence helps them to think clearly and make good decisions, while preventing emotional outbursts from clouding their judgment.

Our emotions, in other words, can help us move forward or can hold us back, depending on how well we are able to harness them—and this applies to all aspects of our lives. As Goleman writes: "To the degree that our emotions get in the way of or enhance our ability to think and plan, to pursue training for a distant goal, to solve problems and the like, they define the limits of our capacity to use our innate mental abilities, and so determine how we do in life. And to the degree to which we are motivated by feelings of enthusiasm and pleasure in what we do—or even by an optimal degree of anxiety—they propel us to accomplishment. It is in this sense that emotional intelligence is a master aptitude, a capacity that profoundly affects all other abilities, either facilitating or interfering with them."[11]

The ability to delay gratification is an important aspect of emotional intelligence. Many people regard it as an essential part of growing up. But it appears that learning this ability at an early age is more than a matter of modifying behavior by controlling emotional impulses; it also has long-term consequences for children's social and intellectual development.

Goleman refers to research carried out by Walter Mischel at Stanford University in the 1960s which tested four-year-olds by presenting them with a choice: they could each have a marshmallow immediately if they wanted to, but if they waited awhile they would each get two. Years later, these children were revisited when they were graduating from high school. The differences between those adolescents who, as children, had been prepared to wait for two marshmallows and those who had wanted a single marshmallow "now" were "dramatic." The former were self-assertive, were able to cope with stress and frustrations, and were persevering in the face of difficulties. The latter tended to be more easily upset, had a more negative image of themselves, and were often unable to control their tempers. Those who had waited at the age of four were also doing better academically. In particular, they had "dramatically higher scores" on their SATs.[12]

Delaying gratification, developing the self-discipline to persevere in order to attain one's goal, is a vital part of any engagement with the arts. In learning to draw or dance or play a musical instrument, children must achieve a measure of control over what they do, and they generally will not succeed in doing so if they go about this in a haphazard way. It takes concentration and practice to develop the appropriate techniques and an understanding of the materials they are working with. (By contrast, the vast majority of software available for children caters to what is perceived as a child's need for some kind of satisfying result regardless of the effort expended. It doesn't take much to get something of interest up on the screen, or to change it when interest wanes.)

Arts activities also provide valuable experience in working with others, since many kinds of performance depend on a cooperative effort. Although each individual's contribution is important, it's the performance of the group as a whole that determines the overall result. Children who learn this through their experience in the arts not only have the satisfaction of pleasurable achievement but also develop abilities that will serve them well throughout their lives.

For example, being able to work well together is becoming an increasingly valued quality in the workplace, as skills become more specialized and productivity depends on coordinated teamwork. Goleman points out that when people come together as a team, "there is a very real sense in which they have a group IQ, the sum total of the talents and skills of all those involved." The most important element in group IQ, it turns out, is not so much intellectual brilliance as emotional intelligence. Studies at Bell Labs found that emotional IQ, especially a talent for building good relationships and establishing informal networks, was what made the difference between outstanding researchers and those who were merely average.[13]

Clearly, helping children develop the kind of intelligence that will promote social harmony is a worthwhile goal, and it appears that education in the arts is an effective means of achieving it. (It's worth noting that music has long been recognized as a means of improving harmony within the community. The Greek historian Polybius, writing in the second century BCE, ascribed the cruelties that the citizens of Cynaetha inflicted on one another to a general neglect of the teaching of music to the young.)

A two-year study of the effects of a creative drama program at a middle school in North York, Ontario, found that the creative drama classes had a noticeable and extremely positive effect on students' behavior.[14] Compared with a control group, the students who took part in the classes "developed greater self-control and a better understanding of themselves and others. They engaged in more cooperative group work, took initiative in solving problems, and showed a greater willingness to take risks. Students learned to listen to each other more carefully and improved their ability to concentrate on what they were doing. The most spectacular change in behaviour occurred in shy, insecure, or emotionally withdrawn students ... who in some cases exhibited abilities and/or personal qualities that had not been revealed before."[15]

The students themselves were aware of the changes that had occurred as a result of the program. "Most of the students felt that they had become more confident, open, mature, involved; that they were less shy and understood themselves better; that they had greater respect for what others were feeling; and that they were no longer afraid to speak in front of an audience, or to say what they really think."[16]

Similarly positive signs were evident when I visited the Gateway Boulevard elementary school in Toronto. This school places a strong emphasis on the arts, using a kind of back-to-basics approach, in which the basics include drama, dance, visual arts, and music. Its success is all the more striking in view of the fact that 70 percent of the more than eight hundred students who attend the school speak English as a second language and that there is not one single-family dwelling in the school's entire catchment area.

At the invitation of the principal, David McGee, I took my two children to see the school play, *The Wizard of Oz.* The talent was well rehearsed and there was no shortage of it—kindergarten students made endearing Munchkins and the eleven-year-old who played Dorothy was riveting. Additional dance numbers had been added to showcase the abilities of 120 student performers. I learned that one of the leads was played by a child with a serious learning disability, but I wouldn't have known from watching the show. The child's mother said the experience of performing had "transformed" her formerly withdrawn daughter. McGee described how another member of the cast, a boy with behavioral problems (previously known for punching teachers as well as other children), had turned into a "great kid" since getting involved in the drama program. "The real magic of the arts," said McGee, "is that they give kids the internal discipline they need to manage their lives."

Creative programs for children that have been shown to motivate students and deal with problem behavior are not necessarily confined to traditional arts programs. Etobicoke, Ontario, for instance, has a Classy Clowns program that introduces students suspended from school to the art of clowning. Students who have been disruptive enough to be suspended from anywhere from six to twenty days learn the art of clowning, along with techniques of anger management and conflict resolution. The program has proved to be a resounding success, amazing teachers, principals, and the parents of the students involved.

Self-discipline and social harmony provide a potent antidote to the increasing violence that is occurring among children both in and out of school, violence that many link to the effects of the electronic media. Goleman notes that although boys on the way to becoming delinquent tend to have lower IQs than others of their age, it is their inability to control impulsive behavior that is a more direct cause: "impulsivity in ten-year-old boys is almost three times as powerful a predictor of their later delinquency as is their IQ."[17]

There is a persistent view that presumes that logical-mathematical, or critical-analytic, intelligence is the dominant part of the intellect, the glue that holds all the other areas together, and the sole ingredient of technical expertise.[18] The greatest problem with this view, according to Gardner, is that, like most previous approaches to intelligence, the information-processing model "is studiously non- (if not anti-) biological, making little contact with what is known about the nervous system."[19] Paying scant attention to the interplay of senses, through which the body feeds, and thereby shapes, the contours of the mind, we see the intellect as a self-sufficient entity in a sharply divided hierarchy. Rarely do we reflect upon the varied roles that the body plays or the feats of physical dexterity necessary to accomplish a wide variety of "mental" tasks. But the movements of the body are a language unto themselves, which we ignore at our peril. Many kinds of work require great precision and subtlety of physical movements—think of a surgeon or a painter, for example—and much theoretical knowledge is meaningless unless accompanied by a corresponding bodily or kinesthetic understanding.

Paul Demsey, an artist and art instructor at the Ontario College of Art in Toronto, notes that tactility is extremely important in the artistic process. "When drawing, there is a relationship between the kind of movement on the page and the physical movement of the body." Drawing an arc on a computer screen using only the forearm and a finger clicking on the mouse limits the intuitive process and the possibilities that can arise when using the whole arm or moving the entire body. A sculptor and print-maker, Demsey has studied modern dance, mime, martial arts, and music in order to keep growing in his work as a visual artist.

The effects of music, too, demonstrate the complexity of the interrelationship of the brain and the sensory system. The fine-motor coordination necessary to learn to play a musical instrument seems to stimulate intellectual development, and, as we have seen, there is a link between the ability to keep a steady beat and the ease with which children learn to read. It also appears that listening to certain kinds of music (especially classical and jazz, though not atonal music) awakens or invigorates areas of the brain that are connected to memory and to visual or spatial reasoning, a form of intelligence used by mathematicians, physicists, and engineers, as well as by sculptors, dancers, and chess players. Experiments by psychologist Frances Rauscher at the University of California at Irvine showed that after listening to ten minutes of Mozart's Piano Sonata K 448, college students had increased their spatial IQs.[20] An amalgam of abilities, spatial intelligence is characterized by the ability to form mental images of physical objects and to recognize and remember variations in their shapes and positions. Sound, in effect, enhances vision.

In another study, Rauscher found that preschoolers also benefited from exposure to music through keyboard instruction and group singing lessons. After eight months, the children who had been taking music lessons did far better on spatial reasoning tests, which included putting together cardboard puzzle pieces and describing what was "wrong" or "silly" about a picture, than the children who had not had any musical training.[21]

The education we provide for our children must move beyond an emphasis on test scores towards a broader, more integrated curriculum that acknowledges the full range of human intelligences and the connections among them. The arts surely have a major role to play in such a movement since they encompass so many different yet complementary abilities, physical as well as mental. Dance, for example, is as much about concentration in listening, watching, and memorizing as it is about coordinated movement and spatial awareness. Even a simple warm-up routine demands discipline and self-control.

In fact, the arts provide far greater opportunities for interactive learning than anything a child is able to do on a computer, currently regarded as the interactive tool par excellence. Drawing and drama, for example, have been found to be excellent means of preparing young children to engage in narrative writing. A study of second- and third-graders in a rural Rocky Mountain region found that children who took part in drama or drawing activities produced writing that was "consistently and significantly different" in quality from the writing of children who had been part of a discussion group. The authors of the study explained the difference in terms of creative interaction. "As they involve creative products in themselves, drama and drawing allow the writer to test out, evaluate, revise, and integrate ideas before writing begins. Thus, drama and drawing are more complete forms of rehearsal for writing than discussion."[22]

This study provides a small-scale example of how arts activities can be successfully integrated into learning in core subject areas. On a much larger scale, there is the Different Ways of Knowing program launched by the Galef Institute of Los Angeles. The purpose of the program was "to develop an instructional approach based upon the premise that integrating visual and performing arts with social studies and other core curriculum subjects would improve learning outcomes for high-risk elementary school children." A three-year study of the program as implemented in four schools, two in the Los Angeles area and two in Boston and Cambridge, Massachusetts, found that it produced impressive results. After one year, children in the program recorded gains on a standardized language arts test over children not in the program, and these gains were even higher after two years. Children with three years in the program had "significantly higher report card grades" in language arts, math, reading, and social studies.[23]

It has long been a tenet of those who work with children that childhood is a precious time and that education should be sensitive and should nurture the child's creativity. Bruno Bettelheim has written eloquently about the importance of giving rein to a child's imaginative capacities during the early years. Fairy tales especially allow a child to begin to make sense of the world and the child's place in that world. Children use stories of enchantment to figure out what the consequences of certain actions might be and incorporate aspects of these stories in their own fantasies. This is the kind of play that allows a child to get to know himself better. As Bettelheim says: "To offer a child rational thought as his major instrument for sorting out his feelings and understanding in the world will only confuse him."[24]

Sloan suggests that children are being pushed into adult kinds of thinking at an earlier and earlier age: "We live at a time when the feeling, image-making capacities of the child have been already pushed aside and ignored in modern education by a misplaced emphasis on ever-earlier development of analytical, narrowly conceived functional skills. Are we in danger of now further subjecting the child to a technology that would seem to eliminate entire sources of sensory and living imagery—while accentuating out of all proportion images of a very limited type, all the while inserting the latter directly into the child's mind during its most plastic and formative years?"[25]

Television has had a baneful effect on the ability of children to create their own images. A study comparing the effects of radio and television found that radio was more likely to stimulate children's imagination. Children in two different age groups (grades one to two and three to four) were exposed to one story in a television format and another in a radio format. Two stories were used, with a video and audio version of each. Each presentation was stopped shortly before the ending of the story. The children were assessed on their ability to complete the stories by introducing original elements that had not been part of the story presentation. Radio presentations led to more imaginative story completions than did television presentations.[26]

Although the research is still sketchy and the samplings are small, it would appear that the effect of educational software—so often indistinguishable from computer games—is also destined to decrease the imaginative capacities of children. The *Atlantic Monthly* has reported that using the program *Reader Rabbit* (one of the ten most widely used computer programs in elementary schools) caused a 50 percent drop in the creativity of elementary school students. Forty-nine students used this software reading program for seven months and at the end of this time had difficulty answering open-ended questions, suffered diminished verbal fluency, and could not brainstorm with their original degree of creativity.[27]

Dr. Paul Steinhauer, a staff psychiatrist at the Hospital for Sick Children in Toronto, has observed that many parents are pushing their children into too many structured activities, without enough time for imaginative play and for the development of interpersonal skills. Steinhauer, the chairman of Voices for Children, an organization devoted to improving the quality of life for children, says that the relationship between the parent and child and between the teacher and child is the real foundation for learning, and that the greatest investment in our children's education is to give them a secure relationship with another living, breathing person. "Cognitive and emotional development in children cannot be separated." This is something that arts educators have long recognized.

Nurturing a love of the arts is best done when children are young, since those lucky enough to take school or community arts courses in their youth are more likely to participate in the arts as adults. A 1995 survey in Ontario found that nearly a fifth of Ontarians had never participated in the arts as children.[28] Researchers Louis Bergonzi and Julia Smith of the University of Rochester in New York analyzed data from a 1992 survey conducted by the U.S. Bureau of the Census.[29] While they discovered a correlation between arts education and social class (the higher people were on the socioeconomic ladder, the more arts training they had received), schools tended to mitigate this effect, making arts education more accessible to all.

When one considers the lifelong pleasure, and often profit, to be gained from artistic pursuits, it's worth asking whether the emphasis in primary education should not be on the arts rather than on computer use. Using a computer is, after all, something that most reasonably intelligent adults can learn in a fairly short time. Not to learn this skill in childhood would hardly be a serious disadvantage. There are, however, particular advantages in participating in the arts at a young age. Learning to read music and play a musical instrument, for example, is much easier to do when young—if music is not included in the school curriculum, these abilities might never be acquired. Even more important, the self-discipline and emotional control that children need to perform or create works of art, if instilled at an early age, can be an inestimable advantage to them as they grow up and, indeed, for the rest of their lives. Considering the many benefits of arts education, we must ask ourselves whether we do our children a great disservice by cutting arts programs in order to provide them with computer technology.

11

The Real World of Learning

A computer puts a literal and psychological screen–a barrier–between the child and the real world.

Mary Swift[1]

... without intimacy with nature, we can confuse crimes against the Earth with technological progress.

David Suzuki[2]

On a warm summer's day in August 1995, a group of twelve- and thirteen-year-old students was taking a field trip to visit a farm near Henderson, Minnesota, a town in the south-central part of the state. Several of the kids were chasing frogs when a thirteen-year-old boy by the name of Jeff Fish caught a peculiar-looking specimen. Describing the incident to a reporter sometime later, the teenager said, "When I picked him up I saw that he was missing his right hind leg. My first instinct was that a predator had bitten it off. But I looked him over for sores or scars and I didn't see any, so I showed him to the teacher."[3]

While the teacher examined the frog, her students caught more of the animals. Of the twenty-two frogs collected, eleven had deformities of one kind or another. The students' shaken teacher, Cindy Reinitz, reported their findings to the local wildlife biologist and eventually to Minnesota Pollution Control.

The students' discovery of deformed frogs turned out to be the first of more than a hundred such incidents in Minnesota (and subsequently, frogs with a range of deformities turned up across Wisconsin, Iowa, South Dakota, Missouri, California, Texas, Vermont, and along the St. Lawrence River in Quebec). Numerous amphibians were found with extra legs, webbed legs, paralyzed legs, and missing eyes. In one horribly memorable case, a frog had an eye growing inside its throat. These deformities have been the subject of a number of conferences, and the water quality of the region has been under constant investigation. Chemical pollutants are seen as the likely culprits, but so far no single source has been cited as the cause of the deformities. Meanwhile, people in many areas of the state have taken to drinking bottled water.

Disturbing as their discovery was, it nevertheless taught the students a valuable lesson, and one that they were unlikely to forget. Their first-hand experience of nature in jeopardy brought home to them both the fragility and complexity of the natural world. Something had gone wrong for which there was no obvious or visible cause. There were no neat explanations or easily identifiable solutions. In other words, there were forces at work that were beyond immediate human control.

There is still in some quarters a strong belief that the natural world can be controlled and managed to accommodate our increasingly voracious demands on its resources, a mind-set that persists in spite of much evidence to the contrary. Among scientists, however, there is now a greater recognition of the extraordinary complexity of the Earth's environmental systems, a complexity that we ignore at our peril. To continue our exploitation of this planet regardless of the consequences would no doubt bring devastation to much of the world's population, but to apply simplistic solutions could bring results that would be worse than the problems they seek to resolve.

The environmental challenges facing our own and future generations surely require that our children grow up sensitive to the forces shaping life on this planet and learn to appreciate the threat posed to many types of environments by natural processes and by human intervention. Teachers have long recognized that classroom projects involving living things and field trips to various natural environments have an important part to play in developing such attitudes. The former give children a sense of personal responsibility for other forms of life, while the latter are especially valuable experiences for those who live in urban centers and have little direct contact with nature.

All this is beginning to change with the use of classroom computers. More and more children's experience of the natural world is being confined to images on a computer screen. Multimedia encyclopedias, Internet websites, computer simulation programs—all enable children to visit and experience various types of environments, many of which are far beyond the scope of a one-day excursion from school. Rather than being formed by direct experience, children's perceptions of the natural world are being shaped by the technology through which their experiences are mediated. What this technology presents is a world that is instantly accessible, controllable at will, and subject to arbitrary changes whose consequences can easily be reversed.

The following advertisement for a new electronic atlas sets the scene. It begins: "Mother Nature needed 4.5 billion years to create the original. You'll need ten minutes for your version. Rand McNally now brings you the power to shape the world with New Millennium World Atlas Deluxe software. It's the only atlas that lets you create a personalized view of the world." The advertising copy slickly conveys the power-trip mentality that lies behind this computer-generated vision of the Earth. "If you're in the mood to explore, New Millennium will let you jump instantly to anywhere in the world. Peer into the eye of a dinosaur. Witness the awesome forces that trigger a volcanic eruption. Navigate the most beautifully detailed 3-D maps available." And the tone is reinforced by the closing words of encouragement: "So go ahead. Take your world for a spin."[4] It's as if the planet were a high-powered, luxury automobile.

One of the biggest problems with such computer software is that it gives children a false idea of their relationship to the natural world. Because it is so easy to call up a picture or film clip of a particular animal or habitat, children are given the impression that nature is conveniently at their fingertips, and that its processes can be manipulated or speeded up and served to them in an easy-to-read format. This is poor preparation for appreciating and understanding nature first-hand, since the study of nature requires a good deal of patient observation and sometimes considerable hardship. The natural world does not "perform" on demand, and much of it is in remote areas that are reached with difficulty and have inhospitable climates. Ironically, programs designed to encourage an interest in nature can end up having the opposite effect. When confronted with the real thing, children might either be bored or feel threatened, and might well prefer to settle for the screen version.

Computer programs, of course, are not the first medium to manufacture images of the natural world for human consumption. A large proportion of North American adults, for example, formed their impressions of nature by watching Disney cartoons or nature programs on television which portrayed wild animals as generally cute, if not cuddly, and much like people in the way they respond to the situations in which they find themselves. These impressions have become so deeply embedded that many people behave with a breathtaking disregard for their safety when they come across animals in the wild.

Computer simulations designed to help children understand the workings of natural (and man-made) systems can be even more misleading, because they appear to present a realistic model of how such systems actually work. This is, in fact, far from being the case. Simulations present only a partial, artfully contrived reality, one for which the programmer determines the variables to be included and the effects that changing these variables will have. The impression given is that there are definite answers, when in reality there are often merely tentative hypotheses and further aspects of the situation to explore. Since children, and no doubt many adults as well, do not appreciate these limitations, they will be led to believe that computer-generated solutions can be applied to issues that in reality are far too complex to be resolved in this way.

Learning involves the construction of models from which we form ideas about ourselves and the world around us. These models evolve through a process of experience and reflection—mistaken observations are corrected and false assumptions discarded as we add to our knowledge and refine our ideas. The problem with computer simulations is that the software designer has already made assumptions about how the model works, so in using such software we are relying on someone else's perceptions and judgment. These assumptions are a permanent feature; they cannot be changed. Moreover, they are hidden from the user, and so we do not even know if they are reasonable or accurate.

Computer simulations present children with situations in which they no longer have to consider their real-world experiences or the real-world complexities and constraints with which they have to live. Children are thus limiting their responses to experience when using simulations, since many of the considerations that govern their decisions in the real world can simply be ignored. As Theodore Roszak points out, "the 'universe' which we can create on a computer screen is a small, highly edited simulation of reality. Moreover, it is a universe created by a small, highly edited simulation of *ourselves*. Only one narrow band of our experience is represented in the computer: logical reason. Sensual contact, intuition, inarticulated commonsense judgments, aesthetic taste have been largely, if not wholly, left out. We do not bring the full resources of the self to the computer."[5]

At the same time, simulation programs, especially those for children, contain an element of play. Human interaction with the environment is viewed as a grand experiment, one whose consequences need not be taken too seriously, because a false move can always be corrected—if the worst comes to the worst, one can always start the program again. While there is undoubtedly something to be said for allowing children to exercise their curiosity in a "safe" environment, this will do little to develop in them a sense of responsibility for their actions. When something goes wrong in the real world, you can't just close it down and start again.

Even where there is a serious intent, there is a problem of oversimplification, which leads to an incomplete understanding of the environment studied. To take an interesting example, *The Water Game* is a simulation whose purpose is to teach children about the importance of water and irrigation on a Third World farm. Working in groups of between two and four, children undertake the role of water-carrier, whose task is to supply the farm with water. Water is collected from a variety of sources and stored in tanks, each tank representing a particular use—that is, for washing, for cooking and drinking, for farm animals, and for irrigation of crops. Using keyboard controls, children decide what size of containers to use to collect the water, what sources of water are available, the best route to and from these sources, and how the water should be distributed among the various uses (tanks). The object of the game is to carry and distribute enough (drinkable and other) water so that people, animals, and crops survive. After several simulated days, the results of the children's decisions are revealed in a report that tells how much water has been carried and the state of health of the people, animals, and crops on the farm. It is expected that, at least on the first attempt, the children will fail to keep the farm adequately supplied; thus they will acquire a sense of the "real" difficulties faced by farmers in the Third World.[6]

This simulation clearly has good intentions, and children will no doubt find it an interesting game to play. But it has serious limitations when set against the reality it purports to convey. Each team's score is based on the number of liters successfully carried, the implication being the more water carried the better. But in a "real" situation there are other tasks that are also extremely important, such as gathering fuel, spreading fertilizer, and weeding crops. The collection and storage of water must take these other activities into account. Thus, what really matters is the *optimal* amount of water—enough to nurture the farm while allowing time to meet other essential needs. These other concerns might not be appreciated by the children playing the game. They might well come away with the belief that availability of water is the biggest problem facing Third World farmers and have little idea of the other factors affecting the farm's productivity: the effects of the weather (there are times when too much rain can be devastating), fuel requirements, pesticide use, and the application of chemical fertilizers.

One must also question whether this kind of simulation on its own offers an effective means of fostering an understanding of a way of life that differs so markedly from the children's own. They would surely learn far more about the complex process of planting, nurturing, harvesting, and caring for animals if they were to visit a small local farm and see first-hand the nature of the work involved. Better still, they could grow their own garden, either in the schoolyard or else in a classroom window box, and thus do the work themselves. By observing their efforts over time, children would see the effects of changing weather patterns throughout the year and would come to appreciate the different needs of various plants for water, sunlight, and fertilizer. They would also gain an understanding of the interactions between plant and animal life—for example, the role of bees in pollination. These experiences are far more likely than any computer simulation to lead to an empathetic view of the lives of Third World farmers whose livelihoods depend on the yearly rhythms of the Earth.

Hands-on practical work can also benefit students academically. Evidence of this comes from *NAEP 1996 Trends in Academic Progress*, published by the U.S. Department of Education. Every two years, the National Assessment of Education Progress reports on test scores in math, science, reading, and writing in the fourth, eighth, and eleventh grades (that is, for students aged nine, thirteen, and sixteen). The latest report also provides insights into the home and school experiences that contribute to students' knowledge of subject matter and notes that in 1996 students who worked with living plants obtained higher science scores than those whose assignments excluded hands-on activities.[7]

Although the central role of computer technology in helping us understand natural phenomena is firmly fixed in the public's mind, many scientists now realize that direct observation and practical experience can be of more value in understanding natural processes than computer-generated models. Brian Carson is a geoscientist who heads up a team of volunteers working to restore the Chapman Creek watershed on the Sunshine Coast north of Vancouver, British Columbia. The river was virtually destroyed by logging and the construction of roads, which caused erosion and landslides, removing precious soil from the forest and depositing it in the river. Instead of relying on scientific studies and computerized monitoring of the water quality and flow, Carson spends hours walking around the river, learning its secrets by observing its changes. In fact, he and his team have learned that visual observations of the river are crucial to understanding how it once flowed, before the area was logged. By figuring out how it used to flow, he is in effect letting the river tell him what to do, how best to return it to its original course.

Carson has also drawn on the personal experience of people whose knowledge of rivers is based on years of observation. As he told a reporter, "When I started this project, loggers and old-timers who worked near rivers would tell me things I found unbelievable. Then when I stayed and observed the river continuously, I saw with my own eyes what the locals had reported, and realized they'd been dead right all along. That increased my respect both for nature and for non-scientists."[8]

While it is not always possible to give children wilderness experiences, a hands-on approach to scientific study is one in which children can easily become involved. In Bloomfield, Ontario, a picturesque town on the shores of Lake Ontario, community volunteers and local students have been working for several years to rehabilitate a trout stream, which runs through several farmers' fields before emptying into a lake. Adults and school children have planted more than fifteen thousand spruce and pine trees in an effort to prevent erosion and create a habitat for wildlife. Opting for home-grown, low-tech solutions, they have placed bundles of brush (much of it derived from old Christmas trees collected locally) on the edges of the stream to act as filters. These both prevent sedimentation and, by narrowing the water course, create greater depth. The Warring Creek Improvement Association, as it is called, takes a community-based approach to improving the local environment. Everyone, including children, has an opportunity not only to learn about the environment but also to take an active role in improving its quality.

Students who participated in this project were able to study the water course throughout the process of its rehabilitation. They observed the areas of the stream where soil had washed in from the surrounding cultivated fields and monitored the progress at each stage of rejuvenation. They set up outdoor experiments, measuring air and water temperature with hand-held thermometers and employing string and stakes to measure the depth and speed of the creek. Water color and clarity were also examined as this once muddy stream slowly came back to life.

Based on their own field work, students were able to create their own maps and charts of the stream and the surrounding area. Working in groups, at various times during the course of the project they collected a variety of plant and animal species, including frogs, mosquitoes, spiders, hard-shelled black water striders, cattails, snails, and clam shells, and counted them to see how the population of the animal world changed in response to their efforts. As the process of restoring this once pristine gravel-bed trout stream continues, students will be able to keep track of how well Warring Creek harbors new stocks of trout. Wide stretches have been left on either side of the stream to create habitats for wildflowers, trees, and other plant life, as well as for animals. According to a government hydrologist, "The kids are getting a first-hand lesson here that they'll never forget."[9]

The children became so involved in the project that when a contractor proposed to dig a nearby gravel pit, many of the children and their parents, who had also worked to rehabilitate the stream, rose up to oppose it. The Warring Creek group is convinced that the gravel pit would interfere with the water tables and wells, harming the stream which they now realize flows into West Lake, one of the most heavily touristed areas in the county. Because of the knowledge and understanding gained through hands-on experience, the parents of these children are now taking legal action against local businessmen who wish to mine gravel and clear-cut the nearby woods. The students' scientific studies thus acquired new meaning by being linked to a broader issue affecting their community.

These kinds of intimate experiences of nature are unfortunately all too rare for many school children. Those who are in favor of re-placing real-world outings with digital "field trips" do not take into account the emotional as well as intellectual links that must be forged in order for children to care enough about the environment to want to preserve it.

Being emotionally engaged includes facing up to what some may consider the unpalatable realities of the natural world, not the least of which is the fact that one must be prepared to get one's hands dirty if one is to discover the secrets of ecosystems and of the living organisms that inhabit them. Yet the effect of computer programs is to distance children from the true nature of the material they are learning about.

A notable example is the frog dissection kit that can now be purchased on CD-ROM or else downloaded over the Web. Instead of cutting up a real frog, which can be a messy operation, children can engage in a scalpel-free dissection. By using the mouse, they can simply point and click, removing organ after organ and, if they wish, putting them back in again the same way. These electronic frogs are shown in 3-D and can be viewed from a variety of angles. The organs are color-coded, and should a student fail to identify a part correctly, he need only point and click and the correct anatomical description will appear on screen in the appropriate place.

For those who are squeamish, on-screen dissection offers obvious advantages. They need never experience the smell or feel of an actual frog or the sight of its internal organs. Yet for all that these electronic facsimiles of the natural world save the lives of innocent frogs and sanitize what can be an unpleasant task for sensitive students, both the American Human Anatomy and Physiology Society and the National Association of Biology Teachers in the United States have adopted policies strongly in support of real dissection.

They have good reason to take this position. Those who examine biological organisms know that no two specimens of the same species are ever exactly alike. Neither plants nor animals come with color-coded anatomy, and anyone who has ever dissected a frog or examined a seed under a microscope knows only too well how difficult it is to identify the various parts correctly. It takes a lot of visual acumen, an ability that must be developed through practical experience.

Kids can learn the names of a few organs and their approximate locations from a computer program, but this teaches them nothing about the far more complex anatomical systems and the intricacy of the links among them.

The use of computer technology, so often seen as a one-stop solution, can, then, come between us and a proper understanding of the natural world. The acquisition of scientific knowledge does not necessarily depend on high-tech intervention; human observation and experience are far more essential. We seem to have forgotten this simple truth, dazzled as we are by the wonders of the electronic age. And yet there are peoples for whom this remains a living reality.

The indigenous inhabitants of the Amazon rain forest, for instance, are amazingly knowledgeable about their natural world. They have to be, because they depend on it for survival in a way that many of us, in our thoroughly urbanized existence, would find hard to understand. There, even quite young children are well acquainted with a multitude of edible or healing plants.[10] The uses to which various plants are put shows just how sophisticated this knowledge is. For example, one of the staples of the Amazonian Indians' diet is the poisonous root of the yucca plant, which they have learned to prepare in ways that remove the cyanic material it contains. They make a drink from the pomegranate-like fruit of a palm, rich in vitamin B1, which is otherwise in scarce supply in their diet. They use drops of a tea made from vine leaves to cure eye infections, and a parasitic plant to stop blood flowing from a wound. And they wash themselves and their clothing with plants containing saponins, substances that produce foam when put in water. Indians of the northwestern Amazon also use the poison found in a number of plant species to help them catch fish. One such plant is a forest liana whose bark is scraped off, softened by soaking, and then either thrown into, or placed in a bag and dragged through, the water. The poison affects the functioning of the gills. The fish are stunned and, seeking oxygen, come to the surface, where they are caught. None of the poison is absorbed by the fish, so they are entirely edible.[11]

The Amazonian Indians in fact possess an encyclopedic botanical knowledge that few, if any, Western scientists can match. The Indians' uncanny ability to identify a particular kind of plant indicates that their senses are acutely attuned to the botanical riches of their environment. "The forest peoples' acquaintance with plants is subtle as well as extensive," writes Harvard biologist Richard Evans Schultes. "The Indians often distinguish 'kinds' of a plant that appear indistinguishable, even to the experienced taxonomic botanist."[12]

There has recently been an attempt in some quarters to correct the earlier tendency to underestimate, or overlook altogether, the knowledge of the world's indigenous peoples. The United Nations officially recognizes the vast body of knowledge that is not contained in books, but is passed on down the generations and gleaned from an intimate contact with the natural environment, and a number of projects have been undertaken to document indigenous knowledge and integrate it with Western science in order to reach a better understanding of Earth's natural systems.

Aboriginal peoples gain their knowledge of the natural world through observation and direct experience, and this knowledge is passed on from one generation to the next, so that the longer a people live in an area, the greater their knowledge of it becomes. To take an example from Canada, the National Aboriginal Forestry Association has documented the forest-related traditional knowledge and practices of a number of First Nations peoples across the country. The Crees of Eeyou Astchee in northern Quebec have developed a sophisticated system of resource management in which the land is divided into "wildlife harvesting territories," each under the stewardship of a single "tallyman" and his family. The tallyman is responsible for managing the resources of the territory, but in addition to his own knowledge, he depends upon the knowledge of other families using the land, who pass on information about specific sites so that a detailed picture of local conditions can be developed and shared with all the families concerned. The tallyman's accumulated knowledge includes "local seasonal climatic patterns, movement of animals, location of plants, ages of trees, drainage patterns and wildlife habitat preferences" and is vital to maintaining an optimal yield of resources.[13]

This kind of holistic understanding of the environment is in danger of being lost as young aboriginals absorb the values of the dominant culture through the electronic media. As for children living in urban environments in industrialized countries, they are already losing their connections with the natural world in many ways. Many city children cannot accurately name the flowers or shrubs in their local parks or home gardens and are unaware that many of these plants are not native species. Many cannot tell the difference between an orange and a tangerine, and even fewer realize that there are dozens of species of, for example, apples, potatoes, and tomatoes, rather than the few, common varieties that they normally see. As well, the way in which fruits and vegetables appear year-round in their local grocery stores gives them a sense of a seasonless harvest. When everything is available all the time, the natural constraints of climate and geography no longer seem to matter.

Yet even in the midst of a large city, a sense of being a part of nature can act as a powerful spur to children's imagination and creativity, and making this sense come alive is one of the greatest gifts a teacher can give to her students. Geneticist and environmental activist David Suzuki has praised a Tokyo teacher, Toshiko Toriyama, for her ability to do just this.[14] Aware of the fact that so many children, especially those growing up in noisy, polluted urban areas, lack any real understanding of nature and their place in it, Toriyama gets her students to imagine what it would be like to be an insect such as a praying mantis, moving through its life cycle, or else a tree growing in the forest which is cut down and taken to market. She derives her inspiration from the writing of Buddhist poet Kenji Miyazawa, whose poetry describes the mystery and wonder of the natural world. With Toriyama's guidance, children learn, by invoking their imaginative capabilities, to understand the complex life cycles that bind all living organisms together. In addition, realizing that many children do not understand where their food actually comes from, Toriyama takes her students to visits farms, so that they can observe the life cycle of pigs, for instance, beginning with their birth and ending when the animals are taken to a slaughterhouse. Only through concrete experiences like these, she believes, can children come to understand the human dependency on other living organisms.

An interesting example of how this can be done is provided by the Boyne River Natural Science School in Shelburne, one of a number of field schools for elementary school children in Ontario, which allow kids growing up in cities to experience what it is like to live surrounded by nature.

During their stay, students learn about the natural world by being immersed in it. They spend their days hiking through forests and wetlands, watching birds, identifying insects, and observing the changing weather patterns. On one occasion, a group came across the fresh carcass of a deer and severed the head in order to take it back for further study. For many of the children, this was first time they had ever seen a dead animal.

Students who visit the school during the winter go cross-country skiing and snowshoeing, learning to identify animal tracks and droppings. Orienteering—navigating using a compass and a map—is also taught. Because so many city children have little acquaintance with nature, their time at the Boyne school is precious and life-changing. Many city kids have never walked in a forest, fed chickadees, or seen rabbit tracks on fresh snow. Dave Parsons, a teacher at the school, remembers a child from Toronto who was a recent immigrant to Canada. Having never seen snow before, this child spent the whole time crawling on the ground to get a close as possible to the crystallized water in order to fully appreciate this novel sensation. Other children are captivated by their first bonfire under the stars and moon; for most, the night sky is almost always obscured by the lights of the city. Nothing children can do on a computer can even begin to come close to reproducing the experience of a visit to the Boyne River school.

The highlight for many students is the time spent at the ecology center, a unique structure that stands as an example of alternative technology, of technology in harmony with nature. This "living building" is octagonal in shape, and its north wall has been built into the side of a hill. The roof is made of pine covered by a layer of insulation, a vapor barrier, a layer of gravel, and, finally, a layer of soil in which grass and wildflowers grow. Designed to be self-sufficient in renewable energy sources, this structure uses both passive and active solar energy. Another feature of the building is a "living machine," a system that mimics nature's way of purifying water. Water from the building's sinks and toilets is recycled through a series of tanks containing snails and fish and plant life and moves finally to an indoor marsh and an indoor pond. This system renders human waste and water potable without the use of chlorine. By observing how the building "works," children become aware that there are alternatives to many of the technologies we unthinkingly consider so essential.

This living experiment is precisely the kind of experience children need if they are to grow up to create solutions that are technologically viable and do not add to the environmental problems that already exist on a global scale. The aim of the Boyne River Natural Science School is to educate children so that they "will learn to walk more softly on this earth."

The simple experience of just being in nature exerts more of an influence on the creative, intellectual, and emotional life of children than can ever be accurately measured. Anthropologist-educator-author Loren Eiseley recalled that he had been "created" more by yellow buttercups he saw on a kindergarten picnic than by any laboratory test tubes he encountered. "It is more important to bathe the spirit in natural influences," said the natural history writer John Burroughs, "than to store the mind with facts."

Edith Cobb, a sociologist who analyzed the lives of more than three hundred outstanding individuals from the sixteenth through the twentieth century, concluded that there was a strong link between genius and the experience of being close to the natural world in childhood. Cobb believed that creativity and constructive thinking were not the result of the accumulation of information but rather arose out of what she called "a continued plasticity of response of the whole organism to new information and in general to the outer world."[15] This kind of thinking, which is highly developed in geniuses, has its genesis in the early years of childhood. Einstein acknowledged that his long walks in nature played a formative role in his thinking; and geneticist Barbara McClintock credits her observations of the unique pattern of corn kernels with her breakthroughs in the structure of DNA. The work of writers like Emily Dickinson, Julian Huxley, Lawrence Durrell, and Margaret Atwood attests to the importance of close contact with the natural world as a seminal influence. During adulthood, creative geniuses return again and again to that period of childhood between the ages of five and twelve when their experiences of the natural world and their place in it gave them an intuitive understanding of what so many have called wholeness, oneness, or a sense of harmony with nature. Cobb suggests that this pre-verbal experience of what she terms "aesthetic logic" is the foundation of creative insight. Exposure to nature also sharpens perceptual acuity, which is the foundation of any creative act.

Those who are lucky enough to experience the natural world in childhood have advantages over their peers whose only sense of nature is mediated through images produced by someone else. By learning from direct experience to observe and understand the world around them, children will not only develop greater sensory awareness of their surroundings but will also acquire a fund of knowledge that they can draw upon and return to in their imaginations all their lives.

12

Imagining Alternatives

In school, there is no argument or negotiation with the computer.
Ursula Franklin[1]

We should learn to act even more prudently with computer technology, because bad material delivered electronically can be even more hurtful than badly written material.
Judah Schwartz

When we began work on this book, we knew that there was a tremendous amount of media coverage extolling the benefits of computer use in schools. We expected that the research studies we consulted would support this view. This proved not to be the case. The more we examined research on various aspects of educational computer use, the clearer it became that there is a huge gap between the public's perception and the reality of what is happening in our schools. Even in schools that were considered to be exemplary users of computer technology, there were problems, often serious ones, which have been all but ignored by the media.

Again and again the teachers and parents we met told us that "we have to prepare our children for the future." Often we detected, underlying this insistence, the insecurity felt by many adults who have found it hard to cope with the rapid changes in computer technology in the workplace. What they were really talking about was not their children's education, but rather their children's future employment. Teachers and parents seem to us to have been intimidated into believing that they are

neglectful if they do not provide children with access to computer tech‐
nology, regardless of the way it is used.

What is missing here is any sense of the way computer use can
contribute to *educational* goals.

The fact that computer technology plays an ever larger role in
many aspects of our daily lives does not mean that having children
use computers at the earliest possible age is in their best interests.
Other forms of learning should take precedence during the early
years. As for the technical skills without which, we are constantly
told, our children's future will be at risk, most people can acquire an
adequate level of computer competence in a matter of months.
Access to computers in high school will give students more than
enough experience of the most up-to-date computer applications.
We believe that the overwhelming majority of elementary schools
have not benefited from using computer technology. Technology has
simply added to the workload of overburdened teachers and created
funding problems.

Elementary schools have more important things to do than act as
a training ground for employment. Young children need to develop in‐
tellectual curiosity, learn social skills, and explore the sensuous richness
of daily life. At this stage, children begin a process whereby they learn
to discern, to critically appraise, to make connections, and to approach
life energetically, spurred by curiosity and armed with skepticism.

In pursuit of these goals, nothing is more important than the rela‐
tionship between the teacher and the student. Who among us has not
at least one teacher to thank for igniting an enthusiasm for science,
music, or literature? Curiosity is contagious. And teachers are much
better at arousing the curiosity of children than computers. Good
teachers convey their own interests and excitement in learning. They
are not just concerned with *what* their students learn but with *why* they
should know about certain things and *how* this knowledge can make a
difference to them.

By encouraging questions and debate, teachers create a lively in‐
terplay of ideas and opinions. A computer program doesn't care
what students think (having no thoughts of its own) and offers only

a standardized, predetermined response. Children cannot challenge what it tells them. They cannot appeal to a computer's experience or understanding to discover *why* something is right or wrong or simply ambiguous. Only the presence of a sympathetic adult will stimulate them to ask the kinds of questions that play a crucial role in their learning. Sheer quantity of information, which is what computers can provide, is irrelevant. Grasping a few fundamental ideas is more important for a young child than having access to a vast mountain of raw data. Without a teacher to guide them, children will find it hard to impose any kind of order or coherence on what they learn.

An emphasis on learning with computer software threatens to undermine the student-teacher relationship. Teachers, we found, are often viewed as mere adjuncts to computer technology, responsible for training children in its use. As the principal of one high-tech school told us, there is "a swing away from the learning specialist towards the technology specialist." In many school districts, teachers with technology experience tend to get the preferred teaching jobs, thus implicitly devaluing the creative teacher and narrowing the curriculum. And those teachers who feel obliged to catch up by learning to use the latest software or taking Internet courses will have little time left to learn more about music, math, or visual art, or to plan hands-on science experiments or interesting field trips.

Computer use, we discovered, displaces parts of the curriculum that are most enriching for young children. Arts programs, for example, have often been curtailed and sometimes eliminated in order to free up funds and curriculum time for computers. There is, however, no reason to suppose that replacing the arts with computer technology will improve our schools; in fact, there is a good deal of evidence to the contrary. And though it is often claimed that children enjoy working with computers, it is also evident that they miss the programs they have been deprived of. At a school in Massachusetts, noted for its reliance on computer technology, children spent upwards of four hours per week on a computer, yet music was almost entirely lacking in their lives. One child said regretfully that the only time she sang at school was "at Christmas," while another wished passionately to learn to play a musical instrument.

In contrast, we found that schools with an arts-based curriculum were remarkable for the high quality of student work. When arts are integrated into the curriculum, children are given ample opportunity to develop not only their imaginative and creative capacities but also their social skills. The arts feed the senses, heightening awareness of one another and the world we live in. Mastering any art form requires patience and perseverance and encourages children to become confident and self-disciplined. Surely these must be among the most important educational goals we have for our children.

The fact that the arts are in danger of not being given their rightful place in our children's education is a reflection of a particular view of what education is for. In his seminal book *Technology and Empire*, George Grant said, "The curriculum is itself chiefly determined by what the dominant classes of the society consider important to be known."[2] The most influential of the dominant classes these days is the business elite, and so the corporate agenda looms large. Corporate leaders are adept at paying lip service to the need for creativity and higher thinking skills, but they often have strictly functional requirements in mind when considering educational objectives at the school level.

Many parents today have bought into this way of thinking. In Calgary, Alberta, for instance, there is a proposal to create The Charter School of Commerce, where children would carry briefcases, wear shirts and ties, learn about mortgage tables and stock market movements, and acquire much of their learning through headsets and computers. The single-minded objective of this school is to create high-tech entrepreneurs capable of entering the global economy while by-passing college or university.[3] Yet these students, whose creative lives will have been neglected, may not become the successful entrepreneurs their parents and teachers are hoping to create. What makes a successful entrepreneur are qualities like leadership, self-discipline, perseverance, an ability to deal with other people, drive and energy, and belief in a vision—none of which can be learned by using a computer. Technical expertise is much less important. Even in the business world, creativity and intuition play a crucial role

When visiting schools with a heavy reliance on computer technology, we could not help noticing that computers tended to dominate the classroom, taking precedence over other kinds of tools and techniques for learning. Because the computer has come to be seen as the *primary* scientific and technological tool, children have access to computers, but no acquaintance with microscopes or magnifying glasses, chemistry sets, measuring scales, dissection kits, "bug jars," and other kinds of scientific instruments. All of these earlier and simpler technologies have an advantage over the computer in that they involve direct, hands-on contact with the physical world. The same could be said of technologies associated with the arts such as musical instruments, crayons, paints, pastels, paper, costumes, clay, textiles. All of these technologies are far more "interactive" than any single software program. Given that we are shaped by the tools we use, children who are encouraged to rely on a single, extremely powerful technology during their formative years may become set in too narrow a mold. Children can be discouraged from inventive and imaginative thinking in many ways. Neglecting to give them a *range* of tools to work with is certainly one way of doing so.

It is essential that children become emotionally engaged with, as opposed to emotionally detached from, the material they study. Our faith in one kind of technology has led us to believe, for example, that technical solutions can be imposed on natural ecosystems to suit our needs, whether to increase crop yields, replace old-growth forest with cash-crop plantations, or produce hydroelectric power by building dams. This faith has been bolstered by the fact that the benefits of our technological interventions often arise fairly quickly; the drawbacks emerge over a much longer time, nature working more slowly than humanity in this respect. We have many examples of how scientific detachment and the application of technology without ecological awareness can go wrong: the Aral Sea and its surrounding region, which have been devastated as a result of the large-scale irrigation of cotton plantations and the application of huge amounts of chemical fertilizer and pesticides; the Kissimmee River, Florida, whose straightening in the name of flood control and improved navigation led to the contamination of the state's major source of drinking water.

It is not just the complexity of the wilderness or the rural environment, however, that children need to understand and experience first-hand. The same is true of the cities in which the majority of children now live. Computer simulations like *Sim City* or *My World* purport to allow children to manage a city, but in reality such programs give children a simplistic understanding of urban planning. Far too many decisions have been made about our cities based upon theories that have not taken into account their complexity. Many of our cities have been blighted by urban developments intended to benefit those who live or work in them but which ended up having the opposite effect, diminishing people's sense of personal connection to the place in which they lived. Jane Jacobs, one the most influential critics of misguided urban development, has long insisted that her ideas have come from actually walking around the neighborhoods in which she lives. Her personal observations, coupled with discussions with others in her community, have given rise to ideas that give a more complex and accurate understanding of the dynamics of city life.

The dynamics of human societies mirror those of natural environments in that they consist largely of many local events involving many different and often competing elements. For young children, how these elements interact is best learned through their experiences of living in their local community. It is through such experiences that children develop an understanding of what it means to be part of a community and a sense of the responsibilities they must fulfill if they are to contribute to the community's well-being. As with the natural world, a true understanding of our human environment begins with direct personal experience of local conditions. Such conditions are highly complex and often require us to make difficult compromises. But to ignore them is not only to alienate ourselves from our immediate surroundings but also to deny much of our own identity. As British political philosopher John Gray has said, "We are who we are because of the places in which we grow up, the accents and friends we acquire by chance, the burdens we have not chosen but somehow learn to cope with. Real communities are always local—places in which people have put down roots and are willing to put up with the burdens of living together."[4]

Nicholas Negroponte proclaims that in future "we will socialize in digital neighbourhoods in which physical space will be irrelevant and time will play a different role,"[5] but children who are already getting too little attention from parents and are being overlooked in large classes will find life in a "digital neighborhood" a poor substitute. Children need to live in real time in real space with real people. Just as an infant requires a parent in order to feel safe and secure, children require a real social context in which to learn. Children can have electronic relationships with peers across several time zones, yet still be unable to create friendships with their classmates, and so will have a limited and rather sterile understanding of human relationships. Today's children need more interaction with parents and teachers. There is no substitute for direct experience.

It is entirely possible that the most detrimental effects of computer technology will result from the way in which it pushes aside the experience of children and their teachers, encouraging exploration of an electronic world in which there is a vast proliferation of material but none of it is generated by them, their teachers, or their parents.

The lack of critical appraisal of technology in general has become a serious problem. While it has brought many benefits, technological innovations have often made worse the problems they were designed to solve. Many of these have caused great harm to children. To cite just two examples: the development of antibiotics was a great boon to modern medicine, but the overuse or misapplication of antibiotics has led to a situation in which many different strains of bacteria have become so resistant to these drugs that they now require new kinds of antibiotics to combat them. Bottle-feeding and the development of infant formula is another case in point. The promotion of synthetic formulas by the infant formula manufacturers has created the illusion that breast-feeding is less desirable than bottle-feeding, when in fact there is a wealth of evidence demonstrating that the former is much better for both baby and mother. Imposing computers on young children is yet another of these technological innovations that we might live to regret. The fact is, we don't really know what the long-term effects of regular computer use on children's development will be. The widespread use of computers in our schools is a grand experiment whose outcome is uncertain.

So far, the experiment has not been successful. If there are benefits to be gained from the use of computers in our schools, they have not been realized. And it is not likely that they will be while the integration of computer technology into schools proceeds at its current frantic pace.

What has been lacking up to now is a serious public debate about the nature of this technology and what it should, or could, be used for in our children's education. Such a debate is all the more necessary because so many parents and teachers have been seduced by the blandishments of computer companies and software developers into believing that mastery of computer technology is the key to their children's success.

Used inappropriately, computer technology, far from creating more imaginative and creative opportunities for learning, does more harm than good. Judah Schwartz, the co-director of Harvard's Educational Technology Center, believes in the judicious use of computers, but he warns that, because computer technology is more powerful than the technology of books, "it will be much worse, if used badly, than books, and will be much more effective in doing damage."

Sadly, it seems that the worst use of computers often occurs among those students for whom school computers were to be the great equalizer, providing opportunities that would not be available to them in their computer-less homes. "There is," says Schwartz, "an implicit racism in the rise of mind-numbing software in inner city schools. Lock up such software in the closet." Rather than putting its faith in computer technology, an egalitarian school system would ensure that all children were in small classes, had access to well-stocked libraries, had a curriculum rich in music, visual art, and drama, and were offered good quality physical education as well as hands-on science activities—all of which have been shown to aid children's development.

There are encouraging signs that teachers and parents are beginning to question the use of computers in schools. Parents of children at a Vancouver school recently voted against spending on computer technology, arguing that it was too costly to maintain and that its benefits for their children were far from clear. In New York, technology coordinator Giulia Cox told *The New York Times*: "If someone said to me, you have a choice: you can cut your class size of 37:1 in half or have laptops, I'd choose smaller classes over laptops in a second."[6] And then there's Lakeside School, the elite Seattle private school that has Bill Gates among its alumni. Judy Lightfoot, Lakeside's English department chair, has posted a 3,500-word essay against the purchase of laptop computers on her website. Lakeside was expected to take part in a $1.7-million state program called "The Copernicus Project," in which every student would be given a laptop computer. It ties in with the "Learning with Laptops" campaign currently being mounted by Toshiba and Microsoft. Ironically, reported Mike Romano of *The Seattle Weekly*, the school has just finished one of its most successful fundraising campaigns in secondary school history, thanks to a donation of $10 million from Bill Gates, and other alumni.[7]

Lightfoot points out that the machines are a distraction from learning, as students relate more to them than to each other. Buying them would cost the school annually between $800,000 and $1.6 million—funds better spent on financial aid to students who cannot otherwise afford the school. Laptops are also expensive, fragile, and soon obsolete. Lightfoot estimates that the Lakeside School would throw out between $1 and $1.5 million in laptops every three to five years. She concludes: "It seems unethical to teach students that it is acceptable to waste resources just so they can use similar [up-to-date] machines to do their schoolwork."

It is unethical to push students into a high-tech future and fail to give them the critical skills to understand the limitations that *every* technology possesses. That failure could create a generation unable to envision any other future. And envisioning the best future that can be made from present realities is the critical act for any generation.

The struggle to use technology wisely and well is one of the most important challenges we and our children face, and schools are a crucial arena in which this challenge must be confronted. Children's educational needs are best met by giving them a range of appropriate tools. We cannot rely on a single technology to do the job of educating our children.

If we want a future in which technology is used in a humane and thoughtful way, we must proceed with prudence where our children are concerned. If we want our children to cope with the complexity of the future, we must give them the broadest sense of the alternatives.

Endnotes

Chapter One

1. Jane M. Healy, *Endangered Minds: Why Our Children Don't Think* (New York: Simon & Schuster/Touchstone, 1991), p. 345.

2. Paul Koring, "Computers Mislead Leaders' Wives," *The Globe and Mail*, April 9, 1997, p. A1.

3. Cited in Theodore Roszak, *The Cult of Information,* 2nd ed. (Berkeley, CA: University of California Press, 1994), p. 51.

4. "Timeline of Changes in the Prevailing Wisdom of 'Experts' About How Teachers Should Use Computers in Schools," U.S. Congress, Office of Technology Assessment, *Teachers and Technology: Making the Connection,* OTA-EHR-616 (Washington, D.C.: U.S. Government Printing Office, April 1995), p. 104; Original source: H. J. Becker, "Analysis and Trends of School Use of New Information Technologies," Office of Technology Assessment contractor report, March 1994.

5. Seymour Papert, *The Children's Machine: Rethinking School in the Age of the Computer* (New York: Basic Books, 1993), p. 168.

6. Office of Technology Assessment, *Teachers and Technology,* p. 90.

7. This quote appears in Douglas D. Noble's unpublished paper "Bill of Goods" and is taken from William Aspray's "Interview with Andrew Molnar," *Oral History* 234, September 25, 1991 (Charles Babbage Institute, University of Minnesota), p. 17.

8. Cleborne D. Maddux, "The Internet: Educational Prospects—and Problems," *Educational Technology,* vol. 34, no. 7, Sept. 1994, pp. 37-38 (italics in the original). Maddux points out that what is happening with the Internet is largely a repeat

performance of what occurred with personal computers in the early eighties—the emphasis was on *access*, with "far too much attention given to *technical* considerations and far too little to *educational* questions and concerns."

9. Cleborne D. Maddux, "Preface" to *Computers in the Schools*, Special Issue: Assessing the Impact of Computer-Based Instruction, vol. 5, nos 3/4, 1988, p. 5 (italics in the original).

10. Seymour Papert, *Mindstorms: Children, Computers, and Powerful Ideas* (New York, Basic Books, 1980), p. 155.

11. "Too Good to Last," *The Economist*, March 23, 1996, p. 61.

12. John Davy, "Mindstorms in the Lamplight," in Douglas Sloan (Ed.), *The Computer in Education: A Critical Perspective* (New York: Teachers College Press, 1985), p. 12.

13. Jerry Mander, *Four Arguments for the Elimination of Television* (New York: Quill, 1978), pp. 24, 25.

14. Bill McKibben, *The Age of Missing Information* (New York: Random House, 1992), p. 16.

15. Office of Technology Assessment, *Teachers and Technology*, pp. 1, 92.

16. According to its Home Page on the Web, "'NetDay96' is a statewide cooperative effort by California's technology industries, public schools, and communities to install the wires needed to provide at least 20 percent of the state's 13,000 schools with access to the Internet."

17. British Columbia Ministry of Education, *Technology in British Columbia Public Schools: Report and Action Plan, 1995 to 2000* (1995), p. 1.

18. Oliver Boyd-Barrett, "Schools' Computing Policy as State-directed Innovation," *Educational Studies* (U.K.), vol. 16, no. 2, 1990, pp. 172-73.

19. Centre for Applied Research in Education, *DTI Micros in Schools Support 1981-1984: An Independent Evaluation* (Norwich: University of East Anglia, 1988), cited in Boyd-Barrett, "Schools' Computing Policy as State-directed Innovation," p. 176.

20. Department for Education, *Survey of Information Technology in Schools*, Statistical Bulletin No. 3/95, (February 1995). The actual number of computers available increased from 48,300 to 185,000 in primary schools and from 96,300 to 308,800 in secondary schools.

21. Paul Lima, "Technophobia," *The Toronto Star*, Section G: Fast Forward, June 30, 1994, p. G5.

22. Military research on educational technology has been driven to a large extent by the need to ensure that military personnel can effectively operate the increasingly sophisticated weapon and defense systems on which the military relies. These systems are in fact seen as man-machine systems, combining human decision-making ability with machine computing-power. As Noble writes, "A central element in military systems thinking is the idea of the 'man-machine.'" Computer-based education "was first developed as part of pioneering efforts to understand, and design, new roles for the 'human factor' in advanced military systems." It was also concerned with how best these roles could be learned, for in order for such systems to meet their performance specifications, their human "components" must receive rigorous training in specific tasks and procedures. Douglas D. Noble, *The Classroom Arsenal: Military Research, Information Technology and Public Education* (London: Falmer Press, 1991), p. 36.

23. Ibid., p. 2.

24. David A. Dockterman, "Interactive Learning: It's Pushing the *Right* Buttons," *Educational Leadership*, vol. 53, no. 2, Oct. 1995, p. 59. Dockterman believes that some computer programs do succeed in being truly interactive.

25. Healy, *Endangered Minds*, pp. 183, 185.

26. Larry Cuban, *Teachers and Machines: The Classroom Use of Technology Since 1920* (New York: Teachers College Press, 1986). The Introduction to this book gives a good overview of the history of technology in the classroom and the futile attempts made to incorporate it into teaching strategies.

27. Cuban, *Teachers and Machines*, pp. 19-23.

28. Norman Woelfel and Keith Tyler, *Radio and the School* (Yonkers-on-the-Hudson, NY: World Book Co., 1945), p. 89; cited in Cuban, *Teachers and Machines*.

29. Quoted in McKibben, *The Age of Missing Information*, p. 204.

30. Cuban, *Teachers and Machines*, p. 38.

31. Office of Technology Assessment, *Teachers and Technology*, pp. 107-8.

32. The amount of time students actually use computers, for example, is not much different from the time they spend watching videos in class. U.S. Office of Technology Assessment estimates, based on reports of computer coordinators in schools, indicate that students in all grades spend on average two hours per week at a computer, while students in elementary schools spend one and three-quarters hours. The students themselves reported much less frequent use: 24 minutes per week in grade five; 38 minutes per week in grade eight. *Teachers and Technology*, pp. 101-2. The discrepancies in the figures reported by coordinators and by students may be explained by the fact that some students use computers much more often than others.

33. Michael G. Fullan, Matthew B. Miles, and Stephen E. Anderson, *Strategies for Implementing Microcomputers in Schools: The Ontario Case* (Toronto: Ontario Ministry of Education, 1988), p. 1.4.

34. The higher figure comes from Barbara Wickens, "A 'Nerd' Image Problem," *Maclean's*, May 11, 1992, p. 41.

Chapter Two

1. Ursula Franklin, *The Real World of Technology* (Toronto: CBC Enterprises, 1990), p. 76.

2. Aaron Falbel, "The Computer as a Convivial Tool," *Mothering*, Fall 1990, p. 96.

3. U.S. Congress, Office of Technology Assessment, *Teachers and Technology: Making the Connection*, OTA-EHR-616 (Washington, DC: U.S. Government Printing Office, April 1995), p. 9.

4. Henry Jay Becker, "A Truly Empowering Technology-Rich Education—How Much Will It Cost?" *Educational IRM Quarterly*, vol. 3, no. 1, Fall 1993, p. 31. Becker puts the cost of each computer at $1,250 (Table 2, p. 34). Hardware costs have come down, relatively speaking, since 1993, but the increased capabilities of the machines in use these days tend to offset price reductions.

5. Office of Technology Assessment, *Teachers and Technology*, p. 41. The estimate was made by the Software Publishers Association.

6. Kerry A. White, "School Technology Spending on the Rise, Survey Predicts," *Education Week*, September 3, 1997, p. 19.

7. Office of Technology Assessment, *Teachers and Technology*, pp. 21, 23. Even the cost of installing one PC plus modem per school would run to between $80 million and $390 million, with operating costs ranging between $160 million and $560 million. The OTA acknowledges, however, that these estimates "could easily be far from the mark." Furthermore, they do not take into account the costs of using "additional technological configurations that offer potential, such as cellular telephones and wireless modems."

   For schools interested in laptop technology, a California company called NETSchools Corp was offering, as of 1997, "a comprehensive, tailored package of laptops for every student and teacher at a school, plus management software and an infrared network that transfers data throughout a classroom, reducing the need for wiring." The cost of this package was about $1,600 per student or $1 million per school. With 80,000 public schools in the U.S., this would cost $80 billion if applied across the U.S. public school system. "Schools Plug In to Technology Trend: Student Laptops" (Technology Update), *Education Week*, June 18, 1997, p. 6.

8. Robert C. Johnston, "Wilson Seeks Smaller Classes, More Money for Technology," *Education Week*, January 15, 1997, p. 22; Todd Oppenheimer, "The Computer Delusion," *The Atlantic Monthly*, July 1997, p. 53.

9. Department for Education, *Survey of Information Technology in Schools*, Statistical Bulletin No. 3/95, (February 1995).

10. Peter West, "Computer Theft Is 'Hidden Cost' of Boom in School Technology," *Education Week*, June 5, 1996, pp. 1, 8-9.

11. Quoted in Lynne Schrum, "Educators and the Internet: A Case Study of Professional Development," *Computers and Education*, vol. 24, no. 3, April 1995, pp. 221-28.

12. Paul J. McCarty, "Four Days That Changed the World (and other amazing Internet stories)," *Educational Leadership*, vol. 53, no. 2, Oct. 1995, p. 50.

13. Peter West, "Low-cost Service Should Satisfy Phone-access Mandate, Group Says," *Education Week*, May 15, 1996, p. 16.

14. Cleborne D. Maddux, "The Internet: Educational Prospects—and Problems," *Educational Technology*, vol. 34, no. 7, Sept. 1994, p. 40.

15. Becker, "A Truly Empowering Technology-Rich Education—How Much Will It Cost?" pp. 31-35.

16. Office of Technology Assessment, *Teachers and Technology*, p. 44. The GAO report referred to is *School Facilities: America's Schools Report Differing Conditions*.

17. Kerry A. White, "New Teaching Methods, Technology Add to Space Crunch," *Education Week*, October 2, 1996, p. 12. The GAO report referred to is *School Facilities: America's Schools Not Designed or Equipped for 21st Century*.

18. White, "New Teaching Methods, Technology Add to Space Crunch," p. 12.

19. In its 1994 report, the Ontario government's Royal Commission on Learning singled out the case of Lambton County, "whose information technology project impressed us so greatly," which had "sacrificed its music program in order to move toward the information highway …" *For the Love of Learning, Report of the Royal Commission on Learning* (Queen's Printer for Ontario, 1994), vol. IV, Making It

Happen, p. 18. It's a pity the commission wasn't more impressed by the value of the music program.

20. Oppenheimer, "The Computer Delusion," p. 46.

21. Pamela Mendels, "Teaching Conference Questions Fundamental Role of Computers," *New York Times* Website, December 5, 1997.

22. Douglas D. Noble, "Bill of Goods," *The International Handbook on Teachers and Teaching* (Belgium: Kluwer Press), in press.

23. Jerry Borrell, "America's Shame: How We've Abandoned Our Children's Future," *Macworld*, Sept. 1992, p. 25.

Chapter Three

1. Alfred North Whitehead, "Technical Education and Its Relation to Science and Literature" (1929) in Alfred North Whitehead, *The Aims of Education* (New York: Free Press, 1967), p. 50.

2. This view is held by those who advocate an extreme version of computer functionalism, according to John Searle, Professor of Philosophy at the University of California at Berkeley. John R. Searle, "Consciousness and the Philosophers," *New York Review of Books*, March 6, 1997, p. 44.

3. Seymour Papert, *Mindstorms: Children, Computers, and Powerful Ideas* (New York: Basic Books, 1980), p. vi.

4. Ibid., p. viii.

5. Seymour Papert, *The Children's Machine: Rethinking School in the Age of the Computer* (New York: Basic Books, 1993), p. 33.

6. Papert, *Mindstorms*, p. 9.

7. *The Ontario Curriculum, Grades 1-8, Mathematics* (Toronto: Ministry of Education, 1997), p. 47.

8. Rina Cohen, "Implementing Logo in the Grade Two Classroom: Acquisition of Basic Programming Concepts," *Journal of Computer Based Instruction*, vol. 14, no. 2, 1987, pp. 124-32. Another study involving grade two students abandoned "free-discovery" learning in favor of a "guided discovery" approach because it became apparent that the three-month period of the study would not be long enough for students to attain any significant programming ability. Lloyd P. Rieber, "LOGO and Its Promise: A Research Report," *Educational Technology*, vol. 27, no. 2, Feb. 1987, pp. 12-16.

9. Peter Cope and Malcolm Simmons, "Children's Exploration of Rotation and Angle in Limited Logo Microworlds," *Computers and Education*, vol. 16, no. 2, 1991, p. 140.

10. Janet K. Keller, "Characteristics of Logo Instruction Promoting Transfer of Learning: A Research Review," *Journal of Research on Computing in Education*, vol. 23, no. 1, Fall 1990, pp. 58-59.

11. A similar transition occurred in a two-year study of the use of Logo at the Center for Children and Technology at Bank Street College in New York. The teachers involved "began by seeing Logo as an environment for learning general problem-solving skills but by the second year saw Logo mainly as a way for students to learn about computers and computer programming." Curt Dudley-Marling and

Ronald D. Owston, "Using Microcomputers to Teach Problem Solving: A Critical Review," *Educational Technology*, vol. 28, no. 7, July 1988, p. 30.

12. Theodore Roszak, *The Cult of Information*, 2nd ed. (Berkeley, CA: University of California Press, 1994), p. 85.

13. Gavriel Salomon and D. N. Perkins, "Transfer of Cognitive Skills from Programming: When and How?" *Journal of Educational Computing Research*, vol. 3, no. 2, 1987, pp. 149-69; and D. N. Perkins and Gavriel Salomon, "Are Cognitive Skills Context-Bound?" *Educational Researcher*, vol. 18, no. 1, Jan.-Feb. 1989, pp. 16-25.

14. See, for example, Douglas H. Clements and Bonnie K. Nastasi, "Effects of Computer Environments on Social-Emotional Development: Logo and Computer-Assisted Instruction," *Computers in the Schools*, vol. 2, nos 2/3, 1985, pp. 11-31.

15. David Elkind, "The Impact of Computer Use on Cognitive Development in Young Children: A Theoretical Analysis," *Computers in Human Behavior*, vol. 1, no. 2, 1985, p. 139.

16. Linda R. Krasnor and John O. Mitterer, "Logo and the Development of General Problem-Solving Skills," *The Alberta Journal of Educational Research*, vol. 30, no. 2, 1984, p. 138.

17. Papert, *Mindstorms*, p. 21.

18. Ronald Kotulak, *Inside the Brain: Revolutionary Discoveries of How the Mind Works* (Kansas City, MO: Andrews and McMeel, 1996), p. 5.

19. Maria Montessori, *The Absorbent Mind* (New York: Dell Publishing, 1984), p. 146.

20. George Butterworth, "Starting Point," *Natural History*, May 1997, pp. 14-16.

21. Kotulak, *Inside the Brain*, p. 7.

22. Andrew Trotter, "Software for Preschoolers Makes Market Inroads," *Education Week*, December 11, 1996, p. 5.

23. Vickie M. Brinkley and J. Allen Watson, "Effects of Microworld Training Experience on Sorting Tasks by Young Children," *Journal of Educational Technology Systems*, vol. 16, no. 4, 1987-88, pp. 349-64. The study involved day-care children aged two and three years old. The sorting task involved deciding whether objects should be placed either inside or outside the house.

24. Lilian G. Katz and Sylvia C. Chard, *Engaging Children's Minds: The Project Approach* (Norwood, NJ: Ablex, 1989), pp. 18-19.

25. Anne E. Cunningham and Keith E. Stanovich, "Early Spelling Acquisition: Writing Beats the Computer," *Journal of Educational Psychology*, vol. 82, no. 1, 1990, p. 159.

26. John A. Livingston, *The Rogue Primate* (Toronto: Key Porter Books, 1994), p. 122.

27. John Davy, "Mindstorms in the Lamplight," in Douglas Sloan (Ed.), *The Computer in Education: A Critical Perspective* (New York: Teachers College Press, 1985), p. 12.

28. Papert, *Mindstorms*, p. 118.

29. Theresa H. Escobedo and Ambika Bhargava, "A Study of Children's Computer-Generated Graphics," *Journal of Computing in Childhood Education*, vol. 2, no. 4, Summer 1991, pp. 21-22.

30. N. Miller and L. Malamed, "Neuropsychological Correlates of Academic Achievement." Poster presentation, International Neuropsychological Society, Vancouver, B.C., February 1989.

31. Diane Ackerman, *A Natural History of the Senses* (New York: Random House, 1990), p. xv.

32. Jane M. Healy, *Endangered Minds: Why Our Children Don't Think* (New York: Simon & Schuster/Touchstone, 1991), p. 144.

33. Ibid., pp. 138, 144. (Emphasis in original.)

34. G. N. Getman, "Computers in the Classroom: Bane or Boon?" *Academic Therapy*, vol. 18, no. 5, May 1983, p. 519.

35. Papert, *Mindstorms*, p. 11.

36. Bill Gates, *The Road Ahead* (New York: Penguin Books, 1995), p. 217.

Chapter Four

1. D. LaMont Johnson and Cleborne D. Maddux, "The Birth and Nurturing of a New Discipline," *Computers in the Schools*, vol. 8, nos 1/2/3, 1991, p. 9.

2. *The Economist*, April 20, 1996, Review, p. 11.

3. *Home PC*, June 1994, pp. 40-41.

4. See, for example, James A. Kulik, Chen-Lin C. Kulik, and Robert L. Bangert-Drowns, "Effectiveness of Computer-Based Education in Elementary Schools," *Computers in Human Behavior*, vol. 1, no. 1, 1985, pp. 59-74; Richard P. Niemiec and Herbert J. Walberg, "Computers and Achievement in the Elementary Schools," *Journal of Educational Computing Research*, vol. 1, no. 4, 1985, pp. 435-40; Richard Niemiec *et al.*, "The Effects of Computer Based Instruction in Elementary Schools: A Quantitative Analysis," *Journal of Research on Computing in Education*, vol. 20, no. 2, 1987, pp. 85-103; M. D. Roblyer, W. H. Castine, and F. J. King, "A Review of Recent Research," *Computers in the Schools*, Special Issue: Assessing the Impact of Computer-Based Instruction, vol. 5, nos 3/4, 1988, pp. 11-149. (This research team examined several previous reviews as well as conducting one of their own.); Chen-Lin C. Kulik and James A. Kulik, "Effectiveness of Computer-Based Instruction: An Updated Analysis," *Computers in Human Behavior*, vol. 7, nos. 1-2, 1991, pp. 75-94; Yuen-Kuang Cliff Liao and George W. Bright, "Effects of Computer Programming on Cognitive Outcomes: A Meta-Analysis," *Journal of Educational Computing Research*, vol. 7, no. 3, 1991, pp. 251-68; Alice W. Ryan, "Meta-analysis of Achievement Effects of Microcomputer Applications in Elementary Schools," *Educational Administration Quarterly*, vol. 27, no. 2, May 1991, pp. 161-84; Ahmad Khalili and Lily Shashaani, "The Effectiveness of Computer Applications: A Meta-Analysis," *Journal of Research on Computing in Education*, vol. 27, no. 1, Fall 1994, pp. 48-61; Claire M. Fletcher-Flinn and Breon Gravatt, "The Efficacy of Computer Assisted Instruction (CAI): A Meta-Analysis," *Journal of Educational Computing Research*, vol. 12, no. 3, 1995, pp. 219-42.

5. Kulik and Kulik, "Effectiveness of Computer-Based Instruction: An Updated Analysis," pp. 75, 80. The 254 studies cover learners of all ages, from kindergarten to adult students. Of these, 48 studies involved elementary school students.

6. Roblyer, Castine, and King, "A Review of Recent Research."

7. Ibid., pp. 113-14.

8. Richard D. Klimpston *et al.*, "The Effects of Integrating Computers Across a Primary Grade Curriculum," *Journal of Computing in Childhood Education*, vol. 2, no. 2, Winter 1990/91, pp. 31-45.

9. Henry Jay Becker, "Computer-based Integrated Learning Systems in the Elementary and Middle Grades: A Critical Review and Synthesis of Evaluation Reports," *Journal of Educational Computing Research*, vol. 8, no. 1, 1992, pp. 1-41.

10. Harold L. Miller, Jr., "Quantitative Analyses of Student Outcome Measures," *International Journal of Educational Research*, vol. 27, no. 2, 1997, p. 135.

11. Henry Jay Becker, "A Model for Improving the Performance of Integrated Learning Systems: Mixed Individualized/Group/Whole Class Lessons, Cooperative Learning, and Organizing Time for Teacher-Led Remediation of Small Groups," *Educational Technology*, vol. 32, no. 9, Sept. 1992, p. 7.

12. Lani M. Van Dusen and Blaine R. Worthen, "Can Integrated Instructional Technology Transform the Classroom?" *Educational Leadership*, vol. 53, no. 2, Oct. 1995, p. 30.

13. Ibid., p. 32 (emphasis added).

14. Mary-Alice White, "Are ILSs Good Education?" *Educational Technology*, vol. 32, no. 9, Sept. 1992, p. 49.

15. Henry Jay Becker and Nira Hativa, "History, Theory and Research Concerning Integrated Learning Systems," *International Journal of Educational Research*, vol. 21, no. 1, 1994, pp. 6, 8. The authors state that ILSs are used in Austria, Canada, Germany, Guatemala, Hungary, Israel, Kenya, Namibia, South Africa, Spain, the U.K., and the U.S.

16. Douglas D. Noble, "The Educational Engineer Meets Wayne's World," *Rethinking Schools*, vol. 8, no. 2, 1993, p. 15.

17. For example, an analysis of sixty-five studies of the effects of computer programming found that while the effects on students' performance were "slightly positive," the studies of less than three months showed more positive results than those of longer duration (Liao and Bright, "Effects of Computer Programming on Cognitive Outcomes: A Meta-Analysis," pp. 251-68.) A possible explanation for this difference is that the students did better in the shorter studies because the novelty of programming would have worn off before the end of the longer studies. The University of Michigan research review mentioned earlier recorded similar results, though in this case computer-based instruction was found to be "especially effective when the duration of treatment was limited to four weeks or less" (Kulik and Kulik, "Effectiveness of Computer-Based Instruction: An Updated Analysis," p. 88).

18. Kathy A. Krendl and Mary Broihier, "Student Responses to Computers: A Longitudinal Study," *Journal of Educational Computing Research*, vol. 8, no. 2, 1992, pp. 215-27.

19. Keiko T. Miyashita, "Effect of Computer Use on Attitudes Among Japanese First- and Second-Grade Children," *Journal of Computing in Childhood Education*, vol. 5, no. 1, 1994, pp. 72-83.

20. A meta-analysis of computer-based instruction in U.S. colleges found that there was a significant effect in favor of computer-based instruction when different teachers taught the computer-based and conventional classes, but that there was far less difference in results when the same teacher taught both types of classes. It is reasonable to suppose that the same would hold true for younger students in school. Gavriel Salomon and Howard Gardner, "The Computer as Educator: Lessons From Television Research," *Educational Researcher*, vol. 15, no. 1, Jan. 1986, p. 14.

21. Don Tapscott, "A Data Tonic for Schooling and Medicine, *The Globe and Mail*, May 25, 1994, p. A11; Gene Wilburn, "Kids Programs Put the Accent on Fun," *The Toronto Star*, May 12, 1994, p. G6; Paul Lima, "Technophobia," *The Toronto Star*, Section G: Fast Forward, June 30, 1994, p. G1.

22. *San Jose Mercury News*, "Exploring the Link between Academic Achievement and Investment in Classroom Technology," November 21, 1995.

23. Christopher H. Schmitt, "Computer in Schools: Do Students Improve?" *San Jose Mercury News*, January 14, 1996, p. 8A. The strong link between poorer school districts and improved achievement with computer use suggests that students from disadvantaged backgrounds may get a moral boost from having access to new equipment. Gleaming new computers and fancy software may give students, especially those who feel neglected, a feeling of greater control over their own lives and a sense, however brief, of being valued.

24. Herbert Kohl, *Basic Skills: A Plan for Your Child, A Program for All Children* (Boston: Little, Brown, 1982), p. 16. For an excellent discussion on testing and the bell curve, see pp. 12-17, 217-31.

25. William Hines, "Kudos to Our Classrooms," *The Globe and Mail*, August 11, 1996, p. D1.

26. Ibid., p. D1. (See also Herbert Kohl's *Basic Skills* or David Owen's *None of the Above*.)

27. James H. Wiebe and Nancy J. Martin, "The Impact of a Computer-Based Adventure Game on Achievement and Attitudes in Geography," *Journal of Computing in Childhood Education*, vol. 5, no. 1, 1994, p. 61.

28. Sharon McCoy Bell, "World Processing: The Magic of Carmen Sandiego," *Home PC*, June 1994, pp. 68, 70.

29. Roblyer, Castine, and King, "A Review of Recent Research," p. 12.

Chapter Five

1. Bruno Bettelheim and Karen Zelan, *On Learning to Read: The Child's Fascination with Meaning* (New York: Knopf, 1982), p. 5.

2. Foreword by Chester E. Finn, Jr., Assistant Secretary, Office of Educational Research and Improvement, U.S. Department of Education, to *Becoming a Nation of Readers: What Parents Can Do* (D. C. Heath, March 1988), p. iii.

3. Ontario Ministry of Education, *Literacy for Life: Report on Partnerships for Children's Literacy* (Toronto: Queen's Printer for Ontario, 1991), p. 7.

4. Child psychologist Margaret Donaldson points out that young children do not necessarily realize "that the flow of speech, which they have been producing and interpreting unreflectingly for years, is composed of *words*." (Emphasis in original.) Margaret Donaldson, *Children's Minds* (London: Fontana Press, 1986), p. 97.

5. Marilyn Jager Adams, *Beginning to Read: Thinking and Learning About Print* (Cambridge, MA: MIT Press, 1990), p. 321.

6. Reported in Ronald Kotulak, *Inside the Brain: Revolutionary Discoveries of How the Mind Works* (Kansas City. MO: Andrews and McMeel, 1996), p. 32. The comment was made by Janellen Huttenlocher of the University of Chicago with reference to early TV watching, but with television and multimedia computers rapidly converging, it could just as well apply to early computer use.

The shortcomings of voices from the screen have also been demonstrated by studies conducted in Manchester and London, England, by Dr. Sally Ward, a leading authority on children's speech development. Her studies showed that television can be a major factor in delaying speech development in children under three years of age. Children who spent too much time in front of the television were prevented from learning to talk by the constant noise from the TV set. The children, however, soon recovered if parents turned the TV off and spent more time talking to them.

7. Margaret Donaldson, "Speech and Writing and Modes of Learning" in *Awakening to Literacy*, edited by Hillel Goelman, Antoinette Oberg, and Frank Smith (Portsmouth, NH: Heinemann, 1984), p. 174.

8. Frank Smith, "The Creative Achievement of Literacy," in *Awakening to Literacy*, p. 144.

9. Yetta Goodman, "The Development of Initial Literacy," in *Awakening to Literacy*, p. 102.

10. This is one of the findings of the Bristol Study of Language Development.

11. James Fallows, "Navigating the Galaxies," *The Atlantic Monthly*, April 1996, p. 105.

12. Jane M. Healy, *Endangered Minds: Why Our Children Don't Think* (New York: Simon & Schuster/Touchstone, 1991), p. 231.

13. R. C. Anderson *et al.*, *Becoming a Nation of Readers: The Report of the Commission on Reading*, 1985, p. 23; Adams, *Beginning to Read*, p. 86. The Bristol Study of Language Development found that the frequency with which parents read stories to their children had a positive effect on children's knowledge of what books are for and how they are used, which in turn affected their success in their early years at school.

14. Bruno Bettelheim and Karen Zelan, "Why Children Don't Like to Read," *The Atlantic Monthly*, November 1981, pp. 25-31.

15. Hilary McLellan, "Hyper Stories: Some Guidelines for Instructional Designers," *Journal of Research on Computing in Education*, vol. 25, no. 1, Fall 1992, p. 31.

16. Personal communication from Celia Lottridge.

17. Smith, "The Creative Achievement of Literacy," p. 152.

18. Adams, *Beginning to Read*, p. 54.

19. Jeanne S. Chall, *Learning to Read: The Great Debate* (New York: McGraw-Hill, 1967), p. 270. Bettelheim and Zelan agree with Chall that "children may enjoy the exercise of reading drills when they first learn reading, just as they enjoy practicing other new skills. ... It matters little what is decoded; it is the fact that he can decode that delights the child." Bettelheim and Zelan, *On Learning to Read*, p. 7.

20. Adams, *Beginning to Read*, pp. 286-87. Chall says she often observed that children were "listless and bored" when doing workbook exercises on their own. Chall, *Learning to Read: The Great Debate*, p. 272.

21. Laura D. Goodwin *et al.*, "Cognitive and Affective Effects of Various Types of Microcomputer Use by Preschoolers," *American Educational Research Journal*, vol. 23, no. 3, Fall 1986, pp. 348-56; Dolores A. Gore *et al.*, "A Study of Teaching Reading Skills to the Young Child Using Microcomputer Assisted Instruction," *Journal of Educational Computing Research*, vol. 5, no. 2, 1989, pp. 179-85; Anne E. Cunningham and Keith E. Stanovich, "Early Spelling Acquisition: Writing Beats the Computer," *Journal of Educational Psychology*, vol. 82, no. 1, March 1990, pp. 159-62. The first of these studies involved children aged between three and five years, the second children aged five years, and the third children in grade one.

In Goodwin *et al.*, three software programs were used: *The Stickybear ABC*, *Alphabet Zoo-ABC Time*, and *Early Games—Match Letters and Alphabet*. All these programs are intended for children aged three to six years old and all claim to teach letter matching and recognition. In Gore *et al.*, the software used was: *Charlie Brown ABC's* (Random House); *Memory: A First Step* (Sunburst Communications); *Sesame Street Letter Go Round* (CBS Software); *Kinder Koncepts Reading* (Queque Inc); *Easy as ABC* (Springboard Software); *First Letter Fun* (MECC); *Preschool I.Q. Builder* (Program Design Inc); *Stickybear ABC's* (Weekly Reader Software); *Early Games for Young Children* (Learning Tools); *Early Elementary 1* (Compu-Tations Inc).

22. Goodwin *et al.*, "Cognitive and Affective Effects of Various Types of Microcomputer Use by Preschoolers," p. 355. All it took, in fact, was a twenty-minute orientation session. The authors comment, "One would expect the novelty effect, if there were one, to be made of sterner stuff."

23. The five stations are:

   1. Computer station. Children learn phonemes (the sounds of spoken language) by listening to and repeating key words. One activity has them fill in blanks in words with the correct phonemes.

   2. Work Journal station. This provides further practice with phonemes. Children listen to pre-recorded lessons using headphones and fill in blanks in a workbook.

   3. Writing-Typing station. Children write words they have learned by typing on the computer or using pencil and paper. They can continue a story, start a new one, print a story, or read a story previously written.

   4. Listening-Library station. Stories are read to children at reduced speeds while they follow along in a written version.

   5. Make Words station. Children use various materials—sticks, clay, wire, paper cutouts—to form words, letters, and sentences.

24. Douglas D. Noble, "A Bill of Goods: The Early Marketing of Computer-Based Education and Its Implications for the Present Moment" (draft ms, April 1995), p. 102.

25. Nancy R. Preston, "ERIC Research Abstracts," *Journal of Computer-Based Instruction*, vol. 19, no. 4, 1992, p. 138: "IBM's Writing to Read Program: The Right Stuff or Just High Tech Fluff?" by Balwant Singh. Paper presented at the Annual Meeting of the Florida Educational Research Association, November 1991; Betty Collis, Lloyd Ollila, and Kathleen Ollila, "*Writing to Read*: An Evaluation of a Canadian Installation of a Computer-Supported Initial Language Environment," *Journal of Educational Computing Research*, vol. 6, no. 4, 1990, p. 416.

26. Kathy A. Krendl and Russell B. Williams, "The Importance of Being Rigorous: Research on Writing to Read," *Journal of Computer-Based Instruction*, vol. 17, no. 3, 1990, pp. 81, 84.

27. "Often as many as three or four adults are present with only 15 students in the lab during Writing to Read instruction." Krendl and Williams, "The Importance of Being Rigorous," p. 81. With another class of "almost 30 students" three adults staffed the lab, "the paraprofessional who ran the lab, the classroom teacher, and the paraprofessional from the class." Dorothy Huenecke, "An Artistic Criticism of a Computer-Based Reading Program," *Educational Technology*, vol. 32, no. 7, July 1992, p. 55.

28. Collis *et al.*, "*Writing to Read*: An Evaluation of a Canadian Installation," pp. 414-16. In addition, parent-volunteers often forgot that *WTR* starts children off on phonemes (language sounds) and requires children "to write as they hear." They often corrected children's spelling, and in doing so got them confused.

29. As recommended in Richard C. Overbaugh, "Word Processors and Writing-Process Software: Introduction and Evaluation," *Computers in Human Behavior*, vol. 8, no. 1, 1992, p. 142.

30. Collis *et al.*, "*Writing to Read*: An Evaluation of a Canadian Installation," p. 416.

31. Huenecke, "An Artistic Criticism of a Computer-Based Reading Program," pp. 55, 56. Huenecke observed children using the *WTR* program from the spring of their kindergarten year until the end of their first-grade year.

32. Quoted in Noble, "A Bill of Goods," p. 16.

33. Chall, *Learning to Read: The Great Debate*, p. 270. (Emphasis in original.)

34. Bettelheim and Zelan, *On Learning to Read*, p. 236.

35. Healy, *Endangered Minds*, p. 210.

Chapter Six

1. Marilyn Cochran-Smith, "Word Processing and Writing in Elementary Classrooms: A Critical Review of Related Literature," *Review of Educational Research*, vol. 61, no. 1, Spring 1991, p. 114.

2. David N. Dobrin, "A Limitation on the Use of Computers" in Deborah H. Holdstein and Cynthia L. Selfe (Eds.), *Computers and Writing: Theory, Research, Practice* (New York: Modern Language Association of America, 1990), p. 56.

3. One researcher has suggested that "The most significant effect of computers on children's writing may be that they increase the amount of peer collaboration in classrooms. ... Cooperation among children is important because of its positive effects on children's affective, social and intellectual development." David K. Dickinson, "Cooperation, Collaboration, and a Computer: Integrating a Computer into a First-Second Grade Writing Program," *Research in the Teaching of English*, vol. 20, no. 4, Dec. 1986, p. 358.

4. Thomas T. Barker, "Computers and the Instructional Context" in Holdstein and Selfe (Eds), *Computers and Writing: Theory, Research, Practice*, p. 16.

5. Colette Daiute of Harvard University, writing in the mid-1980s, noted that research to date had not provided any overwhelming evidence that children aged nine to thirteen produced more text, or better text, using computers than they did with pen and paper. Colette Daiute, *Writing and Computers* (Reading, MA: Addison-Wesley, 1985), pp. 170-71.

 Nearly ten years later, an analysis of the results of twenty-eight studies of students' writing indicated slightly more positive effects. It found that two-thirds of these studies "concluded that access to word processing during writing instruction improved the quality of students' writing," though the author notes that overall the improvement was "fairly small." (Robert L. Bangert-Drowns, "The Word Processor as an Instructional Tool: A Meta-Analysis of Word Processing in Writing Instruction," *Review of Educational Research*, vol. 63, no. 1, Spring 1993, pp. 77, 87.) There were nine studies in which word processors were used to provide remedial writing instruction, and these yielded the most positive results.

Positive results are also reported in Margarie Montague, "Computers and Writing Process Instruction," *Computers in the Schools*, vol. 7, no. 3, 1990, pp. 5-20; Ronald D. Owston, Sharon Murphy, and Herbert H. Wideman, "On and Off Computer Writing of Eighth Grade Students Experienced in Word Processing," *Computers in the Schools*, vol. 8, no. 4, 1991, pp. 67-87; and Ronald D. Owston, Sharon Murphy, and Herbert H. Wideman, "The Effects of Word Processing on Students' Writing Quality and Revision Strategies," *Research in the Teaching of English*, vol. 26, no. 3, Oct. 1992, pp. 249-76. In the second of these studies the authors speculate that, having become used to writing with computers, students may have had negative attitudes towards writing by hand, and this may have had an effect on students' performance: "... it could be that the students' extensive and relatively positive experience with word processing reduced their willingness to write and revise by hand since it made handwritten effort seem more onerous by comparison" (p. 84).

A review of research on computer use in writing since 1987 found that students wrote more but not necessarily better and that, in the case of one study, students using computers were too quick to start drafting and ignored the prewriting stages more often than students who wrote by hand. W. Michael Reed, "Assessing the Impact of Computer-Based Writing Instruction," *Journal of Research on Computing in Education*, vol. 28, no. 4, Summer 1996, pp. 418-37.

Negative or insignificant effects are reported in Ruth J. Kurth, "Using Word Processing to Enhance Revision Strategies During Student Writing Activities," *Educational Technology*, vol. 27, no. 1, Jan. 1987, pp. 13-19; Aviva Freedman and Linda Clarke, *The Effect of Computer Technology on Composing Processes and Written Products of Grade 8 and Grade 12 Students* (Toronto: Ontario Ministry of Education, 1988); Edward L. Shaw, Jr., Ann K. Nauman, and Debbie Burson, "Comparisons of Spontaneous and Word Processed Compositions in Elementary Classrooms: A Three-Year Study," *Journal of Computing in Childhood Education*, vol. 5, no. 3/4, 1994, pp. 319-27; Lois Mayer Nichols, "Pencil and Paper Versus Word Processing: A Comparative Study of Creative Writing in the Elementary School," *Journal of Research on Computing in Education*, vol. 29, no. 2, Winter 1996, pp. 159-66; Edward W. Wolfe et al., "A Study of Word Processing Experience and Its Effects on Student Essay Writing," *Journal of Educational Computing Research*, vol. 14, no. 3, 1996, pp. 269-83. In this last study, involving grade ten students, the negative effects were confined to students with little computer experience. However, in Nichols, "Pencil and Paper Versus Word Processing," the sixth-grade students had all received a year and a half of word processing instruction.

6. Shaw, Nauman, and Burson, "Comparisons of Spontaneous and Word Processed Compositions in Elementary Classrooms: A Three-Year Study," p. 325.

7. Evidence of positive effects on students' attitudes to writing is reported in Kurth, "Using Word Processing to Enhance Revision Strategies During Student Writing Activities"; Owston, Murphy, and Wideman, "On and Off Computer Writing of Eighth Grade Students Experienced in Word Processing"; Lori Seawel et al., "A Descriptive Study Comparing Computer-Based Word Processing and Handwriting on Attitudes and Performance of Third and Fourth Grade Students Involved in a Program Based on a Process Writing Approach," *Journal of Computing in Childhood Education*, vol. 5, no. 1, 1994, pp. 43-59; Reed, "Assessing the Impact of Computer-Based Writing Instruction." Little change in attitudes is reported in Margaret A. Moore and Stuart A. Karabenick, "The Effects of Computer

Communications on the Reading and Writing Performance of Fifth-Grade Students," *Computers in Human Behavior*, vol. 8, no. 1, 1992, Special Issue: Computer Use in the Improvement of Writing, pp. 27-38.

8. One researcher has suggested that "attitude toward writing itself may not be the chief determinant of engagement in word processing. Students may become more enthusiastic about word processing, not because of more positive attitudes toward writing, but because they enjoy working on the computer." Bangert-Drowns, "The Word Processor as an Instructional Tool: A Meta-Analysis of Word Processing in Writing Instruction," p. 88.

9. Reported in Daiute, *Writing and Computers*, p. 43.

10. Cochran-Smith, "Word Processing and Writing in Elementary Classrooms," p. 145.

11. Colette Daiute, "Physical and Cognitive Factors in Revising: Insights from Studies with Computers," *Research in the Teaching of English*, vol. 20, no. 2, May 1986, pp. 141-59; Elana Joram *et al.*, "The Effects of Revising With a Word Processor on Written Composition," *Research in the Teaching of English*, vol. 26, no. 2, May 1992, pp. 167-93; Wolfe *et al.*, "A Study of Word Processing Experience and Its Effects on Student Essay Writing." In this last study, the students who had a medium or high level of comfort and experience with word processing wrote essays of about the same length on the computer as they did by hand.

12. Herbert H. Wideman *et al.*, "The Development of Children's Writing in a High Computer Access Environment: A Three Year Study," Centre for the Study of Computers in Education, York University, Technical Report 94-3, Nov. 1994. The study compared students' writing abilities in each grade with those of a comparable group of students at the other school. Students' writing folders were evaluated in the spring of each year, separate scores being given for the meaning and content of a text and surface features of the writing, such as grammar, spelling, use of words, typographical errors, and length. The specific meaning and content features considered were: "general writing development (writing in the first, second or third person), sense of audience, purpose for writing, story quality (overall meaning, unity, detail), story structure (setting, character, plot, outcome), lexical choice, cohesion (logical flow), ability to share feelings" (p. 13). This study is also discussed in Ronald D. Owston and Herbert H. Wideman, "Word Processors and Children's Writing in a High-Computer-Access Setting," *Journal of Research on Computing in Education*, vol. 30, no. 2, Winter 1997, pp. 202-20.

13. One of the lead researchers confirmed that this indeed seemed to be the case, but stressed that this was a qualitative judgment and was not based on quantitative analysis. Personal communication from Herbert Wideman.

14. In one of the computer-using classes, the students, as part of a special project, each had the use of "their own" PowerBook laptop computer. It's quite possible that the provision of a laptop computer for each student created a new relationship between the students and their work. The report states that their teacher "became more intensely involved with what students were doing with their PowerBooks. She showed more excitement in class, and was more prepared to advise, monitor, question and make changes to student work." And the students responded. They were "thrilled that 'the teacher' had enough confidence in them as mature people and competent users by eventually allowing them to take the PowerBooks home. Although the exercise was planned as part of the pilot project, the students

interpreted it as but another reflection of their status as special students" (p. 142). The fact that the students could take their laptops home added to the time they could spend on their projects. It is surely not a coincidence that the students in this class wrote far more than any other class in either school, on average producing texts that were twice as long.

15. The following excerpts are fairly typical of the writing done by the three students.

Low rated

> Then behind Jim there was Grendel, Grendel "said, lets see you take on my baby Lobo" Jim "said OK unless you want to see your baby get his but kicked" Go fight him Lobo" OK daddy" Lobo took out a knife come on Lobo lets fight fare and square, ok in two seconds Jim wiped Lobo out the window and he landed in the mail box ... (p. 170)

Average rated

> Time was running out because there was an old saying that if you were on Mercury for about 2-3 days you could get this disease or you could get a very very very bad cold and you would have to [The text is broken this way in the original.]

> go to this special shooting star "which is really a special hospital" and get stunned by a needle as long as a keyboard and where ever you got stunned by the needle it would bleed and bleed and bleed. I was just hoping so bad that someone would just come and pick me up and I would never have to go back to this eerie,frightening, [sic] weird place ever again. Anyway I tried to get up but it was just impossible to get up after I had tried about fifty times to see if I could get up for the 56th time and I finally got up thank goodness for getting up. (p. 172)

High rated

> I slowly edge closer to the window. I can see the moon, it looks alone, like me. I crawl away from the window again, my leg still hurting from being thrown into my new prison. The ground is cold and slippery, with a layer of dust. I felt something crawling up my arm. I scream and brush it away. I slowly stand up, and limp over to the window. There was something comforting about it. I stared out into the darkness, feeling to confused and scared to think. Tall shadows of trees stretched out across the bare land, that seemed to carry on forever. They seemed so free. A cool breeze scurried the dirt, and lifted the hair on my shoulders. I closed my eyes. The comfort was gone. The muffled sound of restless leaves, sounded like slow, dragging footsteps. I shivered. (p. 177)

It's a pity that none of the work done by students not using computers was included for comparison.

16. River East School Division Literacy Initiative 1988-1996, Executive Summary, p. 1. The Literacy Initiative comprised three separate projects: Writing for Meaning, which was piloted twice, in 1990 and 1991; Networking for Learning (1993-94), which extended Writing for Meaning to include networking students to other schools and to business partners through wide area networks; and the School-wide Literacy Project (1994-95), in which the writing of all students from grades two to five was assessed in one of the River East elementary schools.

17. As described by Dr. Richard Freeze, Professor of Educational Psychology at the University of Manitoba, who conducted four studies during the course of the project, "*KnowledgeBuilder* contains fours windows which can be opened individually or in combination on the same screen. The 'Knowledge Base' window acts like an electronic interactive resource book which students, teachers, and writing partners can use to access, input, withdraw and reference information. [For example, students can post materials they have found or reports they have written to the Knowledge Base; in this way they can share their research and writing with others.] The 'Organizer' window is designed to prompt students' organizational skills to map concepts, write outlines, or conduct research. The 'Draftwriter' window guides students through the composition process and may be used in combination with the Knowledge Base or Organizer window on the same screen. The 'Publisher' window offers a wide selection of editing and formatting features and enables students to print their final product, save it to the Knowledge Base or send it to a partner on the LAN or WAN [local or wide area network]." D. Richard Freeze, "Networking for Thinking and Writing: An Evaluation of Students' Reflective Writing in the Networking for Learning Project," p. 4.

18. Bill Wresch, "What I Learned in Wabeno," *Computers in Human Behavior*, vol. 8, no. 1, 1992, Special Issue: Computer Use in the Improvement of Writing, p. 11. Wresch is author of the *Writer's Helper* software program. (Emphasis added.)

19. Gene Wilburn, "Kids Programs Put the Accent on Fun," *The Toronto Star*, May 12, 1994, p. G6. It would be nice to think that the last sentence contained a touch of humor, but this does not seem to be the case.

20. Blaine H. Moore and Helen Caldwell, "Drama and Drawing for Narrative Writing in Primary Grades," *Journal of Educational Research*, vol. 8, no. 2, Nov/Dec 1993, pp. 100-10.

21. Theodore Roszak, *The Cult of Information*, 2nd ed. (Berkeley, CA: University of California Press, 1994), p. 80.

22. Wideman *et al.*, "The Development of Children's Writing in a High Computer Access Environment: A Three Year Study," p. 122.

23. Owston, Murphy, and Wideman, "The Effects of Word Processing on Students' Writing Quality and Revision Strategies," p. 264.

24. Michael Peacock and Chris Breese, "Pupils with Portable Writing Machines," *Educational Review* (U.K.), vol. 42, no. 1, 1990, p. 48.

25. Several researchers have pointed out that there is little research to support the claim that word processors improve the quality of writing because they make it easier to revise. Joram *et al.*, "The Effects of Revising with a Word Processor on Written Composition" cites a number of studies which indicate that word processing revision tends to consist mainly of surface changes "and other revising activities that are typical of immature writers" (pp. 168-69). The author of another paper points out that few studies of revision with word processing "report increased quality." Gail E. Hawisher, "The Effects of Word Processing on the Revision Strategies of College Freshmen," *Research in the Teaching of English*, vol. 21, no. 2, May 1987, p. 146.

26. Owston, Murphy, and Wideman, "The Effects of Word Processing on Students' Writing Quality and Revision Strategies." The drafts and final versions of the first two students were both about 200 words in length. One of these students

did divide her draft into three paragraphs in the final version, which indicates some concern about the structure of her piece, but otherwise she merely corrected eight typographical errors (two of these being identical), combined two sentences which had previously been correctly separated, and failed to address five grammatical mistakes. The other student corrected five typographical errors (two of them identical) and missed two others. With so few changes being made, one wonders just how these two students spent their time at the revision stage.

27. When a group of third and fourth grade students were asked how they felt about using the computer, they said that recopying was boring. Other comments were that: handwriting made their hands tired, whereas word processing did not; it was easier to revise and edit when using the computer; and their work looked neater. Seawel *et al.*, "A Descriptive Study Comparing Computer-Based Word Processing and Handwriting on Attitudes and Performance of Third and Fourth Grade Students," p. 51.

28. Daiute, "Physical and Cognitive Factors in Revising," pp. 153, 156.

29. Freedman and Clarke, *The Effect of Computer Technology on Composing Processes and Written Products*, p. 100.

Chapter Seven

1. Michael Heim, *The Metaphysics of Virtual Reality* (New York: Oxford University Press, 1993), p. 145.

2. Steve James, "Throwing the Book at the Internet," *The Guardian Weekly*, July 7, 1996, p. 24. Researching another topic, the costs of producing "a supposedly BSE-free, organically-reared cow," proved just as troublesome. One search engine listed 6,000 entries on organic farming, an impossible number to scroll through, while another engine sidetracked him into a completely different field by interpreting the BSE acronym as Breast Self-Examination.

3. John W. Merck Jr., "Mesozoic Errors," *The Sciences*, September/October 1995, pp. 40-43.

4. Paul Roberts, "Virtual Grub Street, Sorrows of a Multimedia Hack," *Harper's*, June 1996, pp. 73-74.

5. "Booting Electronic Books," *The Economist*, September 3, 1994, pp. 83-84.

6. Personal communication from Anne Letain; Lesley Kreuger, "Teacher-librarians More Necessary than Ever," *The Globe and Mail*, January 19, 1996, p. A22.

7. This is a particularly severe problem for most Canadian publishers of children's books, which tend to have very small print runs. Indeed, small presses often print few copies of their high-quality books and consequently rely on reviews to bring their material to the attention of teachers and parents. If librarians don't hear about a book fairly quickly, it may be out of print before they have the chance to purchase it.

8. In Canada, library use virtually doubled between 1972 and 1992. In the same period it tripled in Quebec.

9. Thomas A. Childers, "California's Reference Crisis," *The Library Journal*, April 15, 1994, p. 33.

10. In one classroom in northern California, I observed a computer technician giving a lesson on African wildlife. With the use of a software program, a series of

images of various animals were projected on the screen. The class of grade-one children, about twenty-five of them, were clustered around one monitor, making it difficult to see. The technician clicked on each image and said the words "giraffe," "hyena," or "hippopotamus," as each new image appeared on the screen. Meanwhile the children were given about forty-five seconds to study the images and make quick sketches of them. Like trying to sketch the animals on a revolving carousel, not only is this kind of rushed instruction indicative of a complete lack of understanding of how children learn, it is also a poor use of the technology.

11. Gary Marchionini, "Hypermedia and Learning: Freedom and Chaos," *Educational Technology*, vol. 28, no. 11, Nov. 1988, p. 9.

Chapter Eight

1. "Opportunity Knocks," *The Economist*, September 13, 1997, p. 63.

2. Message from M & M's website library.

3. "Boys/Girls: Online Paths Diverge," *Digital Kids*, March 1997.

4. David Leonhardt and Kathleen Kerwin, "Hey Kid, Buy This," *Business Week*, June 30, 1997, p. 62. Another source indicates that in the U.S. children between the age of three and twelve control about $47 billion of spending a year. ("Shop for Little Horrors," *The Economist*, June 5, 1997, p. 66.)

5. Erica Gruen's remarks were also reported in "Children Get Growing Online Attention: Marketers Discuss How to Make Connections with the New Wave of Interactive Kids," *Interactive Marketing News*, November 10, 1995, p. 2.

6. Michael Brody, "Children in Cyberspace: Targets for Corporate Marketers," *Psychiatric News*, February 7, 1997, p. 13.

7. Jeremy Hoey, "Web Free?" *Adbusters*, Autumn 1997, p. 61.

8. Kathryn Montgomery and Shelley Pasnik, *The Web of Deception: Threats to Children from Online Marketing* (Washington, DC: Center for Media Education, 1996).

9. Center for Media Education, *Alcohol and Tobacco on the Web: New Threats to Youth* (Washington, D.C., 1997), p. 29.

10. Center for Media Education, *An Update of Children's Web Sites' Information Collection Practices* (Washington, D.C., 1997), p. 2.

11. Anne Reilly Dowd, "Protect Your Privacy," *Money*, August 1997, p. 112.

12. Jared Sandberg, "Ply and Pry: How Business Pumps Kids on Web," *The Wall Street Journal*, June 9, 1997, p. B11.

13. *FTC News* (Federal Trade Commission, Washington, D.C.), July 16, 1996, pp. 2, 3.

14. When a group of marketers held a conference in Toronto in 1995 called "Kid Power Marketing," concerned to a large extent with Internet and computer-related advertising, they issued a pamphlet which suggested that the conference would tell advertisers "how to get your product past the gatekeepers"—that is, how to pitch directly to children without adult interference.

15. One example is the Book It program sponsored by Pizza Hut. Under this program, students who read a prescribed number of books are rewarded with free pizza coupons. Book It is used in more than 60,000 American and Canadian classrooms. Many teachers and parents, however, are uncomfortable with this

program, believing that children should not have to be rewarded with fast food in return for the pleasure of reading.

16. It is interesting to note, however, that one of the advantages of the ScreenAd contract put to the board was that the revenue would have offset the costs of providing Internet access to students.

17. Some preschoolers may spend up to one-third of their waking hours in front of the TV. Stephen Kline, *Out of the Garden: Toys and Children's Culture in the Age of TV Marketing* (Toronto: Garamond Press, 1993), p. 17. According to the American Medical Association, "The amount of time spent in front of a television or video screen is the single biggest chunk of time in the waking life of an American child." American Medical Association, "Physician Guide to Media Violence," July 1996, p. 9.

In the U.S., the FTC guidelines restricting children's TV advertising time to nine minutes per hour on Saturday and Sunday morning have been relaxed. The Children's Television Act of 1990 increased commercial time to ten minutes per hour on weekends and twelve minutes per hour on weekdays. In Canada, on the other hand, the Quebec provincial government, under the Parti Québécois, has legislated a provincial ban on children's television advertising. Kline, *Out of the Garden*, pp. 214-18.

18. Kline, *Out of the Garden*, p. 141.

19. By creating their fantasies for them, advertising limits children's imaginative responses to problems they experience in their lives. Their imagination is so crowded with characters and plots from commercials that these become a touchstone for children in talking about and determining their behavior. In other words, children are being culturally conditioned to the point that they cannot express their feelings without the mediation of their favorite on-screen characters.

Michael Brody has an extensive collection of character dolls which he uses in his medical practice. His stock includes everything from Barney and Baby Bop, the Little Mermaid, Teenage Mutant Ninja Turtles, and the Power Rangers to oldies like Cinderella, Mickey Mouse, Donald Duck, Batman, and Spiderman. When children come to him for treatment, he finds that he must use these dolls in order to put the children at ease. Such characters, he has found, figure prominently in the imaginative life of his young patients. In many respects, one can say that a child is inhabited by the characters he or she chooses as role models, and in Brody's experience many children choose fantasy characters as role models. Unfortunately, the coping strategies these role models have in dealing with difficulties in their lives are not necessarily ones that are available to children, and they certainly don't constitute viable options or strategies for dealing with daily life.

Chapter Nine

1. Emil Pascarelli and Deborah Quilter, *Repetitive Strain Injury: A Computer User's Guide* (New York: John Wiley, 1994), p. 3.

2. Jane Greening and Bruce Lynn, "Vibration Sense in the Upper Limb in Patients with Repetitive Strain Injury and a Group of At-risk Office Workers," *International Archives of Occupational and Environmental Health*, vol. 71, issue 1, 1998, pp. 29-34.

3. Deborah Quilter, "Computer Injuries: The Next Generation," *VDT News*, Nov./Dec. 1995, p. 8.

4. Alison Dickie, "Computer Caution: This Machine Could Be Hazardous to Your Child's Health," *Home and School Magazine*, May 1995, pp. 37-38.

5. Factors specific to the video screen that can cause eyestrain include:

   • *Glare:* Glare associated with VDTs can come from the reflection of artificial or natural light, from white paper placed near the screen, and even from white clothing worn by the person at the keyboard. Glare can reduce the contrast between characters/images and their background, making them harder to distinguish. Anti-glare screens can address this problem, but they reduce character/image sharpness and make the screen darker. Compensating for this by increasing the brightness tends to reduce sharpness even more.

   • *Resolution and Color Problems:* Lack of sharpness can lead to excessive and futile efforts by the eye to bring characters into focus. Unusual fonts, with small or tightly spaced characters, impair legibility and create problems in distinguishing among characters. Too many colors on the screen simultaneously can be visually confusing, and colors widely separated on the spectrum can blur together, owing to their differing focal points.

   • *Flicker:* Commonly known as "flicker," the scan-line refresh rate is the number of times per second an image is redrawn on the screen. Many see a potential source of eyestrain in the instability of flicker at lower refresh rates, suggesting higher refresh rates produce a more stable image and thus reduce eyestrain. However, Alan Kennedy and Wayne Murray of the University of Dundee in Scotland write that they "have evidence that disturbances to eye movement control occur at, or above, refresh rates of 100Hz, well beyond the point at which users report a display as appearing stable." Kennedy and Murray found the eye makes an increasing number of small corrective movements as the refresh rate increases, and this may impair reading performance and contribute to visual fatigue.

   • *Jitter:* Individual characters on VDT screens can also oscillate. This "jitter" can lead to poor legibility and may be one of the main causes of the vision problems VDT workers experience, according to Dr. Kjell Hansson Mild of Sweden's National Institute of Occupational Health (NIOH). Dr. Mild notes that electromagnetic fields below a certain frequency cause movement in characters on the screen that cannot be seen with the naked eye. Other researchers at NIOH have shown that "jitter" on the screen may be caused by electromagnetic fields from other nearby electrical sources, not the VDT itself. They argue that building wiring, or electrical devices such as low voltage lamps and microfiche readers, can distort characters displayed on VDTs.

6. W. Jaschinski-Kruza, "Transient Myopia after Visual Work," *Ergonomics*, vol. 27, no. 11, 1984, pp. 1181-89; H. Yoshikawa and I. Hara, "A Case of Rapidly Developed Myopia among VDT Workers," *Japanese Journal of Industrial Health*, vol. 31, no. 1, 1989, pp. 24-25.

7. Shirley Palmer, "Does Computer Use Put Children's Vision at Risk?" *Journal of Research and Development in Education*, vol. 26, no. 2, Winter 1993, pp. 59-65.

8. Marian C. Fish and Shirley C. Feldman, "Learning and Teaching in Microcomputer Classrooms: Reconsidering Assumptions," *Computers in the Schools*, vol. 7, no. 3, 1990, p. 91.

9. Warren E. Hathaway, "The Effects of Type of School Lighting on Physical Development and School Performance of Children" (Edmonton: Alberta

Department of Education, March 1994), pp. 1-19. The two-year project, which involved 327 children in grades five and six at five Edmonton-area schools, tested the scholastic development and physical development of children who were exposed to full-spectrum lighting versus those whose classrooms were lit by high-energy sodium-vapor lights.

10. The study was cited in William D. Graf, *Pediatrics* magazine, April 1994. In December 1997, a TV cartoon based on Nintendo's popular Pocket Monster caused about five hundred Japanese children to suffer epileptic seizures after an explosion followed by a five-second flash from the eyes of the most popular character.

11. Researchers have identified emissions of the following chemicals from computers and VDTs: n-Butanol, 2-Butanone, 2-Butoxyethanol, Caprolactam, Cresol, Dimethylbenzene, Ethylbenzene, Heptadecane, Hexanedioic acid, Ozone, Phenol, Phosphoric acid, Toluene, Xylene, Butyl 2-methylpropyl phthalate, Decamethyl cyclopentasiloxane, Dodecamethyl cyclohexasiloxane, 2-Ethoxyethylacetate, 4-Hydroxy benzaldehyde, 2-Methyl-2-propanoic acid, and 2-tetra-butylazo-2-methyozy-4-methyl-pentane. Cited in EPA, *Office Equipment: Design, Indoor Air Emissions, and Pollution Prevention Opportunities.*

12. Ibid.

13. An interdisciplinary study carried out by the Office Illness Project in northern Sweden found 450 cases of mucosal and dermatological symptoms among the 5,986 office workers surveyed.

14. For years, electric utility companies and computer manufacturers denied that there was any effect, deleterious or otherwise, from low-level exposure to EMFs. But epidemiological studies have led many scientists, both inside and outside the industry, to accept that these fields do affect living organisms. Denver researchers Nancy Wertheimer and Ed Leeper were the first to discover a link between childhood leukemia and EMFs, among children living in homes located near electrical transformers. The mortality rate from leukemia for children living near these transformers was two to three times higher than the normal rate among the general population. Other findings, including three pooled studies from Denmark, Finland, and Sweden, by Drs. Anders Ahlbom, Mari Feychting, Jorgen Olson, and Pia Verkasalo, concluded there was evidence to "support the hypothesis that exposure to magnetic fields of the type generated by transmission lines has some etiological role in the development of leukemia in children." They reported a doubling of the risk of childhood leukemia for long-term residential exposures greater than 2 mG (milliGauss). *The Lancet*, November 20, 1993. Cited in *VDT News*, Nov./Dec. 1993.

15. Indira Nair and Jun Zhang, "Distinguishability of the Video Display Terminal (VDT) as a Source of Magnetic Field Exposure," *American Journal of Industrial Medicine*, vol. 28, no. 1, July 1995, pp. 23-29.

16. Russel J. Reiter and Jo Robinson, *Melatonin: Your Body's Natural Wonder Drug* (New York: Bantam Books, 1995), p. 170.

17. "The exposure of humans or animals to light (visible electromagnetic radiation) at night rapidly depresses pineal melatonin production and blood melatonin levels. Likewise, the exposure of animals to various pulsed static and extremely low frequency magnetic fields also reduces melatonin levels. Because it is a potent oncostatic agent and prevents both the initiation and promotion of cancer, reduction

of melatonin, at night, by any means, increases cells' vulnerability to alteration by carcinogenic agents. Thus, if in fact artificial electromagnetic field exposure increases the incidence of cancer in humans, a plausible mechanism could involve a reduction in melatonin which is the consequence of such exposures." Russel J. Reiter, "Melatonin Suppression by Static and Extremely Low Frequency Electromagnetic Fields; Relationship to the Reported Increased Incidence of Cancer," *Reviews on Environmental Health*, vol. 10, no. 3-4, 1994, p. 171.

18. C. Chociolko and W. Leiss, *Risk and Responsibility* (Montreal/Kingston: McGill-Queen's University Press, 1994).

19. Fitness levels in Canada begin declining as early as age twelve. Seventy-six per cent of elementary school girls and 26 percent of the boys cannot do one chin-up, indicating a lack of upper-body strength, which is precisely what they need in order to operate a computer keyboard without undue strain.

20. Millicent Lawton, "More Children Becoming Overweight, Study Finds," *Education Week*, October 11, 1995, p. 6.

21. Robert C. Klesges, Mary L. Shelton, and Lisa M. Klesges, "Effects of Television on Metabolic Rate: Potential Implications For Childhood Obesity," *Pediatrics*, vol. 91, no. 2, Feb. 1993, p. 281.

22. Joe Levy, "Couch-Potato Kids Spawn Fitness Crisis," *Toronto Star*, April 25, 1993, p. G2.

23. Janetta A. Wilson, "Computer Laboratory Workstation Dimensions: Scaling Down for Elementary School Children," *Computers in the Schools*, vol. 8, no. 4, 1992, pp. 41-48.

24. Virtual reality (VR) is seen by its proponents as having great potential to improve education: taking field trips without leaving the classroom is an often cited example.

Early forms of VR have been in use since the 1950s as flight simulators, and there is a broad range of associated health problems on record. These include excessive salivation, fatigue, headaches, nausea, vomiting, coordination problems, and finally dramatic disorientation. Flashbacks are also commonly reported. Young people seem more susceptible to these wide-ranging symptoms, as reported in the July 1995 issue of *Technology Review*.

The most common explanation for such simulator sickness is that the senses are confused, not knowing how to choose between the subject's actual situation and what they think they are seeing. Robert Kennedy, a psychologist with the Orlando branch of Essex Corporation, suggests that 30 percent of all people who use simulators of some kind display symptoms of motion sickness, such as cold sweats, nausea, and vomiting. One of Kennedy's studies showed that 14 percent of helicopter pilots trained in a simulator reported symptoms of motion sickness lasting longer than six hours. Sega canned its $200 home Genesis 16 VR game when it was found 40 percent of its users were experiencing simulator sickness.

Those for whom VR was first developed take simulator sickness seriously. NASA and the U.S. Air Force, Army, Navy, and Marines—none will let those suffering from simulator sickness fly or drive until twenty-four hours after the symptoms subside.

While the effects of simulator sickness are thoroughly documented, they are rarely mentioned in discussions of the technology. According to Kennedy, "it is not until after the design is frozen that the effect of a game on humans is considered."

But this technology is expected to occupy one-third of the home video game market by the turn of the century.

Chapter Ten

1. Michael W. Apple, "The New Technology: Is It Part of the Solution or Part of the Problem in Education?" *Computers in the Schools*, vol. 8, nos 1/2/3, 1991, p. 75.

2. Nan Elsasser, executive director of Working Classroom, Inc., Albuquerque, New Mexico. Quoted in Judith Humphreys Weitz, *Coming Up Taller: Arts and Humanities Programs for Children and Youth At Risk* (Washington, DC: President's Committee on the Arts and the Humanities, 1996), p. 29. Working Classroom, Inc. is a multidisciplinary arts program offering visual arts, theater, and creative-writing workshops.

3. *For the Love of Learning, Report of the Royal Commission on Learning* (Toronto: Queen's Printer for Ontario, 1994), *Volume II: Learning: Our Vision for Schools*, p. 41.

4. Douglas Sloan, "Introduction: On Raising Critical Questions about the Computer in Education," in Douglas Sloan (Ed.), *The Computer in Education: A Critical Perspective* (New York: Teachers College Press, 1985), p. 3.

5. Robert J. Sternberg, *Successful Intelligence* (New York: Simon & Schuster, 1996); Daniel Goleman, *Emotional Intelligence* (New York: Bantam Books, 1995).

6. Robert J. Sternberg, "Successful Intelligence: An Expanded Approach to Understanding Intelligence," February 1997, pp. 3, 4.

7. Ibid., p. 16.

8. Nancy Welch *et al.*, *Schools, Communities, and the Arts,: A Research Compendium* (Washington, D.C.: National Endowment for the Arts, June 1995), pp. 13-15; Richard L. Luftig, *The Schooled Mind: Do the Arts Make a Difference? Year 2, An Empirical Evaluation of the Hamilton Fairfield SPECTRA+ Program, 1992-1994* (Oxford, OH: Center for Human Development, Learning, and Teaching, Miami University).

9. Sternberg, "Successful Intelligence," p. 21.

10. Goleman, *Emotional Intelligence*, p. xii.

11. Ibid., p. 80.

12. Ibid., pp. 81-82. "The third of children who at four grabbed for the marshmallow most eagerly had an average verbal score of 524 and quantitative (or 'math') score of 528; the third who waited longest had average scores of 610 and 652, respectively—a 210-point difference in total score."

13. Ibid., p. 160.

14. Patricia Crawford and Priscilla Galloway, "The Effect of Creative Drama on Student Discipline, Social Maturity, and Creative Writing" (Toronto: Ontario Ministry of Education). For some strange reason, this report was made available on microfiche only.

15. Ontario Ministry of Education, *The Arts in Ontario Schools* (Toronto: Queen's Printer for Ontario, 1991), p. 8.

16. Crawford and Galloway, "The Effect of Creative Drama," quoted in Ontario Ministry of Education, *The Arts in Ontario Schools*, pp. 8-9.

17. Goleman, *Emotional Intelligence*, p. 237.

18. On the surface, certain kinds of work may look rational and analytic, when in fact a much greater range of thinking is involved. For example, Stephen Fast, a

software support engineer who has worked for large multinational computing companies, says that much of his work is people-oriented and involves trying to empathize with the client. "Often when I am working with a client, whether they are in Switzerland or in Texas, I am trying to figure out what they are seeing on the computer screen at the other end. I have to try to understand what the problem is from only very sketchy information they provide me." Although he has a highly technical understanding of software, his work depends as much on his "people skills" as on his technical expertise.

In fact, in many technologically based occupations, there appears to be a stage at which technical expertise gives way to other, more intuitive forms of knowing. Hubert and Stuart Dreyfus of the University of California at Berkeley instance the example of experienced Air Force pilots.

> In the Air Force, instructor pilots teach beginning pilots, among other things, how to scan their instruments. The instructor pilots teach the beginning pilots the rule for instrument scanning that they, the instructor pilots, were taught, and, as far as they know, still use. At one point, however, Air Force psychologists studied the eye movement of the instructors as they actually flew and found, to everyone's surprise, that the instructor pilots were not following the rule they were teaching. In fact, as far as the psychologists could determine, they were not following any rule at all. ... The instructors, after years of experience, had learned to scan the instruments in flexible and situationally appropriate ways. [Hubert L. Dreyfus and Stuart E. Dreyfus, "Putting Computers in Their Proper Place: Analysis versus Intuition in the Classroom" in Sloan (Ed.), *The Computer in Education*, p. 58.]

The seasoned pilots who were teaching had years of experience and were using this experience intuitively in ways that had been refined over a long period of time. They had developed a "feel" for their handling of the aircraft that defied rational analysis. Thus the rules that had been devised for pilot training and were taught during computer-simulated flight became at some point irrelevant.

19. Howard Gardner, *Frames of Mind: The Theory of Multiple Intelligences* (New York: Basic Books, 1993), p. 23.

20. Ronald Kotulak, *Inside the Brain: Revolutionary Discoveries of How the Mind Works* (Kansas City, MO: Andrews and McMeel, 1996), p. 141.

21. A. J. S. Rayl, "Striking a Neural Chord: Musical Links for Scientists and Mathematicians of Tomorrow," *Omni*, Winter 1995, p. 14.

22. Blaine H. Moore and Helen Caldwell, "Drama and Drawing for Narrative Writing in Primary Grades," *Journal of Educational Research*, vol. 8, no. 2, Nov./Dec. 1993, pp. 100-10. Quoted in Welch *et al.*, *Schools, Communities, and the Arts*, pp. 46, 47.

23. Reported in Welch *et al.*, *Schools, Communities, and the Arts*, pp. 16-18.

24. Bruno Bettelheim, *The Uses of Enchantment* (New York: Vintage Books, 1977), p. 119.

25. Sloan, "Introduction: On Raising Critical Questions about the Computer in Education," pp. 7-8.

26. Patricia Greenfield, Dorathea Farrar, and Jessica Beagles-Roos, "Is the Medium the Message?: Effects of Radio and Television on Imagination," *Journal of Applied Developmental Psychology*, vol. 7, no. 3, 1986, pp. 201-18.

27. Todd Oppenheimer, "The Computer Delusion," *The Atlantic Monthly*, July 1997, p. 52.

28. Ontario Arts Council, *The Arts and the Quality of Life: The Attitudes of Ontarians* (Toronto: Ontario Arts Council, 1995), p. 28.

29. The survey was carried out for the National Endowment for the Arts and was known as the Survey of Public Participation in the Arts (SPPA92). Bergonzi and Smith's analysis is reviewed in Welch *et al.*, *Schools, Communities, and the Arts*, pp. 111-12.

Chapter Eleven

1. Mary Swift, "Computers in Pre-School Centres?" *Australian Journal of Early Childhood*, vol. 10, no. 3, Sept. 1985, p. 22.

2. David Suzuki, "A Buddhist Way to Teach Kids Ecology," *The Toronto Star*, June 18, 1994, C2.

3. William Souder, "Deformed Frogs Rattle Experts," *The Toronto Star*, October 5, 1996, p. C6.

4. *Natural History*, November 1997, p. 3.

5. Theodore Roszak, *The Cult of Information*, 2nd ed. (Berkeley, CA: University of California Press, 1994), pp. 70-71.

6. *The Water Game* (CWDE Software, 1989) is featured in a study by Peter Kutnick and David Marshall, "Development of Social Skills and the Use of the Microcomputer in the Primary School Classroom," *British Educational Research Journal*, vol. 19, no. 5, 1993, pp. 517-33. The British students taking part in the study were in year five, aged nine to ten.

7. Linda Jacobson, "Long-Term Achievement Study Shows Gains, Losses," *Education Week*, September 3, 1997, p 12.

8. Bill Atkinson, "The Prince of Muddy Waters," *The Globe and Mail*, May 3, 1997, p. D5.

9. Kevin Wood, "Students Work to Improve Environment," *The Picton Gazette*, Spring 1994, p. 5.

10. By contrast, few of our children would recognize, say, camomile by its shape, color, or smell, or know that it can settle an upset stomach and is useful for soothing rashes. Yet this medicinal plant can be found growing in many North American cities. On the other hand, many of our children would know the whereabouts of the nearest pharmacy, although they would not necessarily be able to pick out the appropriate cure (assuming it was available over the counter) when they got there.

11. Richard Evans Schultes, "Burning the Library of Amazonia," *The Sciences*, March/April 1994, pp. 24, 30.

12. Ibid., p. 24

13. National Aboriginal Forestry Association, "Aboriginal Forest-Based Ecological Knowledge in Canada," Canadian Forest Service, Natural Resources Canada, August 30, 1996, pp. 42-43. The paper presents case studies on the Algonquins of Barriere Lake, Quebec; the Gitxsan, of northwestern British Columbia; the Nuu-Chah-Nulth of Clayoquot Sound, Vancouver Island; the Cree, Dene, and Métis of northeastern Alberta; and the Crees of Eeyou Astchee in northern Quebec.

14. Suzuki, "A Buddhist Way to Teach Kids Ecology," p. C2.

15. Edith Cobb, "The Ecology of Imagination in Childhood," *Daedalus*, vol. 88, 1959, p. 538.

Chapter Twelve

1. Ursula Franklin, *The Real World of Technology* (Toronto: CBC Enterprises, 1991), p. 51.

2. George Grant, *Technology and Empire* (Toronto: House of Anansi Press, 1969), p. 113.

3. Alanna Mitchell, "Calgary School for Business Kids Stirs Up a Fuss," *The Globe and Mail*, May 4, 1998, pp. A1, A6.

4. John Gray, "Cyberspace Offers a Hollow Freedom," *The Guardian Weekly*, April 16, 1995, p. 12.

5. Nicholas Negroponte, *Being Digital* (New York: Vintage Books, 1996), p. 7.

6. Mike Romano, "... With Liberty and Laptops for All?" *The New York Times*, February 26, 1998.

7. Mike Romano, "Lapping it Up," *The Seattle Weekly*, February 5, 1998, p. 7.

Bibliography

Books

Ackerman, Diane. *A Natural History of the Senses*. New York: Random House, 1990.

Adams, Marilyn Jager. *Beginning to Read: Thinking and Learning About Print*. Cambridge, MA: MIT Press, 1990.

Barlow, Maude, and Robertson, Heather-jane. *Class Warfare: The Assault on Canada's Schools*. Toronto: Key Porter Books, 1994.

Bettelheim, Bruno. *The Uses of Enchantment*. New York: Vintage Books, 1977.

Bettelheim, Bruno, and Zelan, Karen. *On Learning to Read: The Child's Fascination with Meaning*. New York: Knopf, 1982.

Bowers, C. A. *The Cultural Dimensions of Educational Computing: Understanding the Non-Neutrality of Technology*. New York: Teachers College Press, 1988.

Bormann, F. Herbert, and Kellert, Stephen R., eds. *Ecology, Economics, Ethics: The Broken Circle*. New Haven/London: Yale University Press, 1991.

Brod, Craig. *Technostress: The Human Cost of the Computer Revolution*. Reading, MA: Addison-Wesley, 1984.

Capra, Fritjof. *The Web of Life*. New York: Anchor Books, 1996.

Chall, Jeanne S. *Learning to Read: The Great Debate*. New York: McGraw-Hill, 1967.

Cooley, Mike. *Architect or Bee?: The Human Price of Technology*, new ed. London: Hogarth Press, 1987.

Cuban, Larry. *Teachers and Machines: The Classroom Use of Technology Since 1920*. New York: Teachers College Press, 1986.

Daiute, Colette. *Writing and Computers*. Reading, MA: Addison-Wesley, 1985.

Donaldson, Margaret. *Children's Minds*. London: Fontana Press, 1986.

Franklin, Ursula. *The Real World of Technology*. Toronto: CBC Enterprises, 1991.

Gardner, Howard. *Frames of Mind: The Theory of Multiple Intelligences*. New York: Basic Books, 1993.

Gates, Bill. *The Road Ahead*. New York: Penguin Books, 1995.

Goelman, Hillel; Oberg, Antoinette; and Smith, Frank, eds. *Awakening to Literacy*. Portsmouth, NH: Heinemann, 1984.

Goleman, Daniel. *Emotional Intelligence*. New York: Bantam Books, 1995.

Healy, Jane M. *Endangered Minds: Why Our Children Don't Think*. New York: Simon & Schuster/Touchstone, 1991.

Heim, Michael. *The Metaphysics of Virtual Reality*. New York: Oxford University Press, 1993.

Hunt, Morton. *The Universe Within: A New Science Explores the Human Mind*. New York: Simon & Schuster, 1982.

Jacoby, Russell, and Glauberman, Naomi, eds. *The Bell Curve Debate: History, Documents, Opinions*. New York: Times Books, 1995.

Kagan, Jerome. *The Nature of the Child*. New York: Basic Books, 1984.

Katz, Lilian G., and Chard, Sylvia C. *Engaging Children's Minds: The Project Approach*. Norwood, NJ: Ablex Publishing, 1989.

Kline, Stephen. *Out of the Garden: Toys and Children's Culture in the Age of TV Marketing*. Toronto: Garamond Press, 1993.

Kotulak, Ronald. *Inside the Brain: Revolutionary Discoveries of How the Mind Works*. Kansas City, MO: Andrews and McMeel, 1996.

Livingston, John A. *The Rogue Primate*. Toronto: Key Porter Books, 1994.

Livingstone, David. *The Education-Jobs Gap*. Boulder, CO: Westview Press, 1998.

Mander, Jerry. *Four Arguments for the Elimination of Television*. New York: Quill, 1978.

Mander, Jerry. *In the Absence of the Sacred*. San Francisco: Sierra Club Books, 1992.

McKibben, Bill. *The Age of Missing Information*. New York: Random House, 1992.

Montessori, Maria. *The Absorbent Mind*. New York: Dell Publishing, 1984.

Nabham, Gary Paul, and Trimble, Stephen. *The Geography of Childhood*. Boston, MA: Beacon Press, 1994.

Negroponte, Nicholas. *Being Digital*. New York: Vintage Books, 1996.

Noble, David. *Progress without People*. Toronto: Between the Lines Press, 1995.

Noble, Douglas D. *The Classroom Arsenal: Military Research, Information Technology and Public Education*. London: Falmer Press, 1991.

Norman, Donald A. *Things That Make Us Smart: Defending Human Attributes in the Age of the Machine*. Reading, MA: Addison-Wesley, 1993.

Quilter, Deborah. *The Repetitive Strain Injury Recovery Book*. New York: Walker & Co., 1998.

Papert, Seymour. *Mindstorms: Children, Computers, and Powerful Ideas*. New York: Basic Books, 1980.

Papert, Seymour. *The Children's Machine: Rethinking School in the Age of the Computer*. New York: Basic Books, 1993.

Pascarelli, Emil, and Quilter, Deborah. *Repetitive Strain Injury: A Computer User's Guide*. New York: John Wiley, 1994.

Penrose, Roger. *The Emperor's New Mind*. London: Vintage Books, 1989.

Perkins, David. *Smart Schools: From Training Memories to Educating Minds*. New York: Free Press, 1992.

Perkins, Michael C., and Nuñez, Celia H. *Kidware: The Parents' Guide to Software for Children*. Rocklin, CA: Prima Publishing, 1995.

Postman, Neil. *Technopoly: The Surrender of Culture to Technology*. New York: Knopf, 1992.

Postman, Neil. *The Disappearance of Childhood* (with a new preface by the author). New York: Vintage Books, 1994.

Postman, Neil. *The End of Education: Redefining the Value of School*. New York: Knopf, 1995.

Reiter, Russel J., and Robinson, Jo. *Melatonin: Your Body's Natural Wonder Drug*. New York: Bantam Books, 1995.

Restack, Richard. *The Brain Has a Mind of Its Own*. New York: Harmony Books, 1991.

Roszak, Theodore. *The Cult of Information*, 2nd ed. Berkeley, CA: University of California Press, 1994.

Setzer, Valdemar. *Computers in Education*. Edinburgh: Floris Books, 1989.

Sloan, Douglas, ed. *The Computer in Education: A Critical Perspective*. New York: Teachers College Press, 1985.

Smith, Frank. *Reading*, 2nd ed. Cambridge: Cambridge University Press, 1985.

Smith, Frank. *Understanding Reading: A Psycholinguistic Analysis of Reading and Learning to Read*, 2nd. ed. New York: Rinehart and Winston, 1978.

Smith, Frank. *Writing and the Writer*. Hillsdale, NJ: Lawrence Erlbaum, 1982.

Stoll, Clifford. *Silicon Snake Oil*. New York: Doubleday, 1995.

Turkle, Sherry. *The Second Self: Computers and the Human Spirit*. New York: Simon & Schuster/Touchstone, 1985.

Weikart, Phyllis, and Carlton, Elizabeth B. *Foundations in Elementary Education Movement*. Ypsilanti, MI: High/Scope Press, 1995.

Weizenbaum, Joseph. *Computer Power and Human Reason: From Judgment to Calculation*, (reprinted with new preface). Harmondsworth: Penguin Books, 1993.

Reports and Resource Documents

Artsvision/The Royal Conservatory of Music. *Community Arts & Education Partnership, Towards a Comprehensive Arts and Education Program for Metropolitan Toronto through*

Community Partnerships: Assessment and Recommendations. Toronto: The RCM Pedagogy Institute, June 20, 1994.

British Columbia Ministry of Education. *Technology in British Columbia Public Schools: Report and Action Plan, 1995 to 2000,* 1995.

Center for Media Education. *Alcohol and Tobacco on the Web: New Threats to Youth.* Washington, DC: Center for Media Education, 1997.

Center for Media Education. *An Update of Children's Web Sites' Information Collection Practices.* Washington, DC: Center for Media Education, 1997.

Childers, Thomas A. *Reference Performance in California Public Libraries, 1994-95.* Philadelphia, PA: College of Information, Science, and Technology, Drexel University, 1995.

Computers in Education: A Critical Look. Invitational Symposium, University of California, Berkeley, June 3-5, 1995. Summary of discussions and conclusions synthesized by Fritjof Capra. Berkeley, CA: Center for Ecoliteracy.

Emmett, Terry S., and Roberts, Lily. *California's Investment in Site-Based Educational Technology: Volume I, Evaluation of the Model Technology Schools Levels I and II; Volume II, Evaluation of the School-Based Educational Technology Grant Projects.* Research, Evaluation, and Technology Division, California Department of Education, Feb. 1995.

Freedman, Aviva, and Clarke, Linda. *The Effect of Computer Technology on Composing Processes and Written Products of Grade 8 and Grade 12 Students.* Toronto: Ontario Ministry of Education, 1988.

Freeze, D. Richard. "An Evaluation of the Writing for Meaning Project." Winnipeg: River East School Division/The Apple Canada Education Foundation, 1990.

Freeze, D. Richard. "Networking for Thinking and Writing: An Evaluation of Students' Reflective Writing in the Networking for Learning Project." Winnipeg: River East School Division/The Apple Canada Education Foundation, 1994.

Freeze, D. Richard. "Report #2, Writing for Meaning in an Integrated Learning Environment: Control Group Comparison." Winnipeg: River East School Division/The Apple Canada Education Foundation, 1991.

Fullan, Michael G.; Miles, Matthew B.; and Anderson, Stephen E. *Strategies for Implementing Microcomputers in Schools: The Ontario Case.* Toronto: Ontario Ministry of Education, 1988.

Hathaway, Warren E. "The Effects of Type of School Lighting on Physical Development and School Performance of Children." Edmonton: Alberta Department of Education, March 1994.

Luftig, Richard L. *The Schooled Mind: Do the Arts Make a Difference? Year 2, An Empirical Evaluation of the Hamilton Fairfield SPECTRA+ Program, 1992-1994.* Oxford, OH: Center for Human Development, Learning, and Teaching, Miami University.

Montgomery, Kathryn, and Pasnik, Shelley. *The Web of Deception: Threats to Children from Online Marketing.* Washington, DC: Center for Media Education, 1996.

National Aboriginal Forestry Association. "Aboriginal Forest-Based Ecological Knowledge in Canada." Canadian Forest Service, Natural Resources Canada, Aug. 1996.

Nye, Barbara. *Project Challenge Fifth-Year Summary Report: An Initial Evaluation of The Tennessee Department of Education "At-Risk" Student/Teacher Ratio Reduction Project in Sixteen Counties, 1989-90 through 1993-94.* Nashville, TN: Center of Excellence for Research and Policy on Basic Skills, Tennessee State University, 1995.

Nye, Barbara. *The Lasting Benefits Study: A Continuing Analysis of the Effect of Small Class Size in Kindergarten Through Third Grade on Student Achievement Test Scores in Subsequent Grade Levels.* Nashville, TN: Center of Excellence for Research and Policy on Basic Skills, Tennessee State University, 1995.

Ontario Government. *For the Love of Learning: Report of the Royal Commission on Learning.* 5 volumes. Toronto: Queen's Printer for Ontario, 1994.

"River East School Division Literacy Initiative, 1988-1995: A Summary Report." Winnipeg, September 1995.

San Jose Mercury News. "Exploring the Link Between Academic Achievement and Investment in Classroom Technology," Nov. 21, 1995.

Toews, Otto B. "Networking for Thinking and Writing." Winnipeg: River East School Division, Sept. 1993.

Toronto Board of Education. *Learning with Computer Technologies: Future Directions, 1991-1995, A Report on the Curricular Use of Computers and Related Technologies in Toronto Schools,* Nov. 1991.

U.K. Department for Education. *Survey of Information Technology in Schools,* Statistical Bulletin No. 3/95, Feb. 1995.

U.S. Congress, Office of Technology Assessment. *Teachers and Technology: Making the Connection,* OTA-EHR-616. Washington, DC: U.S. Government Printing Office, April 1995.

U.S. Environmental Protection Agency. *Office Equipment: Design, Indoor Air Emissions, and Pollution Prevention Opportunities.* Washington, DC, March 1995.

Welch, Nancy, *et al. Schools, Communities, and the Arts: A Research Compendium.* Washington, DC: National Endowment for the Arts, June 1995.

Wellburn, Elizabeth. "Information, Telecommunications and Learning: A Review of the Research Literature," British Columbia Education Technology Centre, 1991.

Wideman, Herbert H., *et al. The Development of Children's Writing in a High Computer Access Environment: A Three Year Study.* North York, ON: Centre for the Study of Computers in Education, York University, Technical Report 94-3, Nov. 1994.

Unpublished Papers

Noble, David. "Digital Diploma Mills: Part I, The Automation of Higher Education," Oct. 1997.

Noble, Douglas D. "A Bill of Goods: The Early Marketing of Computer-Based Education and Its Implications for the Present Moment," April 1995.

Sternberg, Robert J. "Successful Intelligence: An Expanded Approach to Understanding Intelligence," Feb. 1997.

Articles

Achilles, Charles M. "Students Achieve More in Smaller Classes," *Educational Leadership*, Feb. 1996, pp. 76-77.

Apple, Michael W. "The New Technology: Is It Part of the Solution or Part of the Problem in Education?" *Computers in the Schools*, vol. 8, nos 1/2/3, 1991, pp. 59-81.

Bangert-Drowns, Robert L. "The Word Processor as an Instructional Tool: A Meta-Analysis of Word Processing in Writing Instruction," *Review of Educational Research*, vol. 63, no. 1, Spring 1993, pp. 69-93.

Becker, Henry Jay. "A Model for Improving the Performance of Integrated Learning Systems: Mixed Individualized/Group/Whole Class Lessons, Cooperative Learning, and Organizing Time for Teacher-Led Remediation of Small Groups," *Educational Technology*, vol. 32, no. 9, Sept. 1992, pp. 6-15.

Becker, Henry Jay. "A Truly Empowering Technology-Rich Education—How Much Will It Cost?" *Educational IRM Quarterly*, vol. 3, no. 1, Fall 1993, pp. 31-35.

Becker, Henry Jay. "Computer-based Integrated Learning Systems in the Elementary and Middle Grades: A Critical Review and Synthesis of Evaluation Reports," *Journal of Educational Computing Research*, vol. 8, no. 1, 1992, pp. 1-41.

Becker, Henry Jay. "How Exemplary Computer-Using Teachers Differ from Other Teachers: Implications for Realizing the Potential of Computers in Schools," *Journal of Research on Computing in Education*, vol. 26, no. 3, Spring 1994, pp. 291-321.

Becker, Henry Jay. "Mindless or Mindful Use of Integrated Learning Systems," *International Journal of Educational Research*, vol. 21, no. 1, 1994, pp. 65-79.

Becker, Henry Jay. "The Importance of a Methodology That Maximizes Falsifiability: Its Applicability to Research About Logo," *Educational Researcher*, vol. 16, no. 5, June-July 1987, pp. 11-16.

Becker, Henry Jay, and Hativa, Nira. "History, Theory and Research Concerning Integrated Learning Systems," *International Journal of Educational Research*, vol. 21, no. 1, 1994, pp. 5-12.

Bennett, Neville. "Class Size in Primary Schools: Perceptions of Headteachers, Chairs of Governors, Teachers and Parents," *British Educational Research Journal*, vol. 22, no. 1, 1996, pp. 33-56.

Bettelheim, Bruno, and Zelan, Karen. "Why Children Don't Like to Read," *The Atlantic Monthly*, November 1981, pp. 25-31.

Bigelow, Bill. "On the Road to Cultural Bias: A Critique of *The Oregon Trail* CD-ROM," *Language Arts*, vol. 74, Feb. 1997, pp. 84-93.

Borrell, Jerry. "America's Shame: How We've Abandoned Our Children's Future," *Macworld*, Sept. 1992, pp. 25-30.

Boyd-Barrett, Oliver. "Schools' Computing Policy as State-directed Innovation," *Educational Studies* (U.K.), vol. 16, no. 2, 1990, pp. 169-85.

Brinkley, Vickie M., and Watson, J. Allen. "Effects of Microworld Training Experience on Sorting Tasks by Young Children," *Journal of Educational Technology Systems*, vol. 16, no. 4, 1987-88, pp. 349-64.

Brown, John Seeley. "Process versus Product," *Journal of Educational Computing Research*, vol. 1, no. 2, 1985, pp. 179-201.

Budin, Howard R. "Technology and the Teacher's Role," *Computers in the Schools*, vol. 8, nos 1/2/3, 1991, pp. 15-26.

"Canadian Perspectives on *The Bell Curve*." Special issue of *The Alberta Journal of Educational Research*, vol. 41, no. 3, Sept. 1995.

Childers, Thomas A. "California's Reference Crisis," *The Library Journal*, April 15, 1994, pp. 32-35.

Clements, Douglas H., and Nastasi, Bonnie K. "Effects of Computer Environments on Social-Emotional Development: Logo and Computer-Assisted Instruction," *Computers in the Schools*, Special Double Issue: Logo in the Schools, vol. 2, nos 2/3, 1985, pp. 11-31.

Clements, Douglas H.; Nastasi, Bonnie K.; and Swaminathan, Sudha. "Young Children and Computers: Crossroads and Directions From Research," *Young Children*, vol. 48, no. 2, Jan. 1993, pp. 56-64.

Cobb, Edith. "The Ecology of Imagination in Childhood," *Daedalus*, vol. 88, 1959, pp. 537-48.

Cochran-Smith, Marilyn. "Word Processing and Writing in Elementary Classrooms: A Critical Review of Related Literature," *Review of Educational Research*, vol. 61, no. 1, Spring 1991, pp. 107-55.

Cohen, Rina. "Implementing Logo in the Grade Two Classroom: Acquisition of Basic Programming Concepts," *Journal of Computer-Based Instruction*, vol. 14, no. 2, 1987, pp. 124-32.

Collis, Betty; Ollila, Lloyd; and Ollila, Kathleen. "*Writing to Read*: An Evaluation of a Canadian Installation of a Computer-Supported Initial Language Environment," *Journal of Educational Computing Research*, vol. 6, no. 4, 1990, pp. 411-27.

Cope, Peter, and Simmons, Malcolm. "Children's Exploration of Rotation and Angle in Limited Logo Microworlds," *Computers and Education*, vol. 16, no. 2, 1991, pp. 133-41.

Cunningham, Anne E., and Stanovich, Keith E. "Early Spelling Acquisition: Writing Beats the Computer," *Journal of Educational Psychology*, vol. 82, no. 1, March 1990, pp. 159-62.

Daiute, Colette. "Physical and Cognitive Factors in Revising: Insights from Studies with Computers," *Research in the Teaching of English*, vol. 20, no. 2, May 1986, pp. 141-59.

Dickinson, David K. "Cooperation, Collaboration, and a Computer: Integrating a Computer into a First-Second Grade Writing Program," *Research in the Teaching of English*, vol. 20, no. 4, Dec. 1986, pp. 357-78.

Dockterman, David A. "Interactive Learning: It's Pushing the *Right* Buttons," *Educational Leadership*, vol. 53, no. 2, Oct. 1995, pp. 58-59.

Dudley-Marling, Curt, and Owston, Ronald D. "Using Microcomputers to Teach Problem Solving: A Critical Review," *Educational Technology*, vol. 28, no. 7, July 1988, pp. 27-33.

Elkind, David. "The Impact of Computer Use on Cognitive Development in Young Children: A Theoretical Analysis," *Computers in Human Behavior*, vol. 1, no. 2, 1985, pp. 131-41.

Ely, Donald P. "Computers in Schools and Universities in the United States of America," *Educational Technology*, vol. 33, no. 9, Sept. 1993, pp. 53-57.

Eraut, Michael. "Groupwork with Computers in British Primary Schools," *Journal of Educational Computing Research*, vol. 13, no. 1, 1995, pp. 61-87.

Escobedo, Theresa H., and Bhargava, Ambika. "A Study of Children's Computer-Generated Graphics," *Journal of Computing in Childhood Education*, vol. 2, no. 4, Summer 1991, pp. 3-25.

Eurich-Fulcer, Rebecca, and Schofield, Janet Ward. "Wide-area Networking in K-12 Education: Issues Shaping Implementation and Use," *Computers and Education*, vol. 24, no. 3, April 1995, pp. 211-20.

Falbel, Aaron. "The Computer As a Convivial Tool," *Mothering*, Fall 1990, pp. 91-96.

Fay, Anne Louise, and Mayer, Richard E. "Children's Naive Conceptions and Confusions About Logo Graphics Commands," *Journal of Educational Psychology*, vol. 79, no. 3, 1987, pp. 254-68.

Fish, Marian C., and Feldman, Shirley C. "Learning and Teaching in Microcomputer Classrooms: Reconsidering Assumptions," *Computers in the Schools*, vol. 7, no. 3, 1990, pp. 87-96.

Fletcher-Flinn, Claire M., and Gravatt, Breon. "The Efficacy of Computer Assisted Instruction (CAI): A Meta-Analysis," *Journal of Educational Computing Research*, vol. 12, no. 3, 1995, pp. 219-42.

Fletcher-Flinn, Claire M., and Suddendorf, Thomas. "Do Computers Affect 'The Mind'?" *Journal of Educational Computing Research*, vol. 15, no. 2, 1996, pp. 97-112.

Getman, G. N. "Computers in the Classroom: Bane or Boon?" *Academic Therapy*, vol. 18, no. 5, May 1983, pp. 517-24.

Ginther, Dean W., and Williamson, James D. "Learning Logo: What Is Really Learned?" *Computers in the Schools*, Special Double Issue: Logo in the Schools, vol. 2, nos 2/3, 1985, pp. 73-78.

Goodwin, Laura D., *et al.* "Cognitive and Affective Effects of Various Types of Microcomputer Use by Preschoolers," *American Educational Research Journal*, vol. 23, no. 3, Fall 1986, pp. 348-56.

Gore, Dolores A., *et al.* "A Study of Teaching Reading Skills to the Young Child Using Microcomputer Assisted Instruction," *Journal of Educational Computing Research*, vol. 5, no. 2, 1989, pp. 179-85.

Greenfield, Patricia; Farrar, Dorathea; and Beagles-Roos, Jessica. "Is the Medium the Message?: Effects of Radio and Television on Imagination," *Journal of Applied Developmental Psychology*, vol. 7, no. 3, 1986, pp. 201-18.

Hadler, Nortin M. "Arm Pain in the Workplace: A Small Area Analysis," *Journal of Occupational Medicine*, Feb. 1992, pp. 113-18.

Hawisher, Gail. "The Effects of Word Processing on the Revision Strategies of College Freshmen," *Research in the Teaching of English*, vol. 21, no. 2, May 1987, pp. 145-59.

Heller, Rachelle S. "The Role of Hypermedia," *Journal of Research on Computing in Education*, vol. 22, no. 4, Summer 1990, pp. 431-44.

Henniger, Michael L. "Computers and Preschool Children's Play: Are They Compatible?" *Journal of Computing in Childhood Education*, vol. 5, nos. 3/4, 1994, pp. 231-39.

Hickey, M. Gail. "Computer Use in Elementary Classrooms: An Ethnographic Study," *Journal of Computing in Childhood Education*, vol. 4, nos. 3/4, 1993, pp. 219-28.

Hoko, J. Aaron. "SIS: A Futuristic Look at How Computerized Classroom Can Enhance Rather than Diminish Teachers' Pedagogical Power," *Computers in the Schools*, vol. 6, nos 1/2, 1989, pp. 135-43.

Huenecke, Dorothy. "An Artistic Criticism of a Computer-Based Reading Program," *Educational Technology*, vol. 32, no. 7, July 1992, pp. 53-57.

Irwin, Martha E. "Connections: Young Children, Reading, Writing, and Computers," *Computers in the Schools*, vol. 4, no. 1, 1987, pp. 37-51.

Jaschinski-Kruza, W. "Transient Myopia after Visual Work," *Ergonomics*, vol. 27, no. 11, 1984, pp. 1181-89.

Johnson, D. LaMont, and Maddux, Cleborne D. "The Birth and Nurturing of a New Discipline," *Computers in the Schools*, vol. 8, nos 1/2/3, 1991, pp. 5-14.

Jonassen, David H. "Designing Structured Hypertext and Structured Access to Hypertext," *Educational Technology*, vol. 28, no. 11, Nov. 1988, pp. 13-16.

Jones, Ithel. "The Effect of a Word Processor on the Written Composition of Second-Grade Pupils," *Computers in the Schools*, vol. 11, no. 2, 1994, pp. 43-54.

Jones, Ithel, and Pellegrini, A. D. "The Effects of Social Relationships, Writing Media, and Microgenic Development on First-Grade Students' Written Narratives," *American Educational Research Journal*, vol. 33, no. 3, Fall 1996, pp. 691-718.

Joram, Elana, *et al.* "The Effects of Revising With a Word Processor on Written Composition," *Research in the Teaching of English*, vol. 26, no. 2, May 1992, pp. 167-93.

Kahn, Jessica, and Freyd, Pamela. "Touch Typing for Young Children: Help or Hindrance?" *Educational Technology*, vol. 30, no. 2, Feb. 1990, pp. 41-45.

Karger, Howard Jacob. "Children and Microcomputers: A Critical Analysis," *Educational Technology*, vol. 28, no. 12, Dec. 1988, pp. 7-11.

Keller, Janet K. "Characteristics of Logo Instruction Promoting Transfer of Learning: A Research Review," *Journal of Research on Computing in Education*, vol. 23, no. 1, Fall 1990, pp. 55-71.

Kinzer, Charles, *et al.* "Different Logo Learning Environments and Mastery: Relationships Between Engagement and Learning," *Computers in the Schools*, Special Double Issue: Logo in the Schools, vol. 2, nos 2/3, 1985, pp. 33-43.

Klimpston, Richard D., *et al.* "The Effects of Integrating Computers Across a Primary Grade Curriculum," *Journal of Computing in Childhood Education*, vol. 2, no. 2, Winter 1990/91, pp. 31-45.

Krasnor, Linda R., and Mitterer, John O. "Logo and the Development of General Problem-Solving Skills," *The Alberta Journal of Educational Research*, vol. 30, no. 2, 1984, pp. 133-44.

Krendl, Kathy A., and Broihier, Mary. "Student Responses to Computers: A Longitudinal Study," *Journal of Educational Computing Research*, vol. 8, no. 2, 1992, pp. 215-27.

Krendl, Kathy A., and Williams, Russell B. "The Importance of Being Rigorous: Research on Writing to Read," *Journal of Computer-Based Instruction*, vol. 17, no. 3, 1990, pp. 81-86.

Kulik, Chen-Lin C., and Kulik, James A. "Effectiveness of Computer-Based Instruction: An Updated Analysis," *Computers in Human Behavior*, vol. 7, nos. 1-2, 1991, pp. 75-94.

Kulik, James A.; Kulik, Chen-Lin C.; and Bangert-Drowns, Robert L. "Effectiveness of Computer-Based Education in Elementary Schools," *Computers in Human Behavior*, vol. 1, no. 1, 1985, pp. 59-74.

Kurth, Ruth J. "Using Word Processing to Enhance Revision Strategies During Student Writing Activities," *Educational Technology*, vol. 27, no. 1, Jan. 1987, pp. 13-19.

Kutnick, Peter, and Marshall, David. "Development of Social Skills and the Use of the Microcomputer in the Primary School Classroom," *British Educational Research Journal*, vol. 19, no. 5, 1993, pp. 517-33.

Lee, William B., and Kazlauskas, Edward John. "The Ecole Moderne: Another Perspective on Educational Technology," *Educational Technology*, vol. 35, no. 2, Mar.-Apr. 1995, pp. 14-20.

Levin, Diane E., and Carlsson-Page, Nancy. "The Mighty Morphin Power Rangers: Teachers Voice Concern," *Young Children*, Sept. 1995, pp. 67-72.

Liao, Yuen-Kuang Cliff, and Bright, George W. "Effects of Computer Programming on Cognitive Outcomes: A Meta-Analysis," *Journal of Educational Computing Research*, vol. 7, no. 3, 1991, pp. 251-68.

Linn, Marcia C. "The Cognitive Consequences of Programming Instruction in Classrooms," *Educational Researcher*, vol. 14, no. 5, May 1985, pp. 14-16, 25-29.

Maddux, Cleborne D. "Logo: Scientific Dedication or Religious Fanaticism in the 1990s?" *Educational Technology*, vol. 29, no. 2, Feb. 1989, pp. 18-23.

Maddux, Cleborne D. "Preface," to *Computers in the Schools*, Special Issue: Assessing the Impact of Computer-Based Instruction, vol. 5, nos 3/4, 1988, pp. 1-10.

Maddux, Cleborne D. "The Internet: Educational Prospects—and Problems," *Educational Technology*, vol. 34, no. 7, Sept. 1994, pp. 37-42.

Maddux, Cleborne D. "The Merger of Education and the Private Sector: Panacea or Pandora's Box," *Computers in the Schools*, vol. 9, nos 2/3, 1993, pp. 23-34.

Maddux, Cleborne D. "The World Wide Web and the Television Generation," *Computers in the Schools*, vol. 12, nos. 1/2, 1996, pp. 23-30.

Maddux, Cleborne D., and Johnson, D. LaMont. "Logo: A Retrospective," *Computers in the Schools*, vol. 14, nos. 1/2, 1997, pp. 1-8.

Marchionini, Gary. "Hypermedia and Learning: Freedom and Chaos," *Educational Technology*, vol. 28, no. 11, Nov. 1988, pp. 8-12.

Matthew, Kathryn. "A Comparison of the Influence of Interactive CD-ROM Storybooks and Traditional Print Storybooks on Reading Comprehension," *Journal of Research on Computing in Education*, vol. 29, no. 3, Spring 1997, pp. 263-75.

McCarty, Paul J. "Four Days That Changed the World (and other amazing Internet stories)," *Educational Leadership*, vol. 53, no. 2, Oct. 1995, pp. 48-50.

McLellan, Hilary. "Hyper Stories: Some Guidelines for Instructional Designers" *Journal of Research on Computing in Education*, vol. 25, no. 1, Fall 1992, pp. 28-49.

Miller, Harold L., Jr., et al. "The New York City Public Schools Integrated Learning Systems Project: Evaluation and Meta-Evaluation," *International Journal of Educational Research*, vol. 27, no. 2, 1997, pp. 89-184.

Miller, Larry, and Olson, John. "How Computers Live in Schools," *Educational Leadership*, vol. 53, no. 2, Oct. 1995, pp. 74-77.

Miyashita, Keiko T. "Effect of Computer Use on Attitudes Among Japanese First- and Second-Grade Children," *Journal of Computing in Childhood Education*, vol. 5, no. 1, 1994, pp. 73-82.

Montague, Margarie. "Computers and Writing Process Instruction," *Computers in the Schools*, vol. 7, no. 3, 1990, pp. 5-20.

Moore, Blaine H., and Caldwell, Helen. "Drama and Drawing for Narrative Writing in Primary Grades," *Journal of Educational Research*, vol. 8, no. 2, Nov/Dec. 1993, pp. 100-10.

Moore, Margaret A., and Karabenick, Stuart A. "The Effects of Computer Communications on the Reading and Writing Performance of Fifth-Grade Students," *Computers in Human Behavior*, vol. 8, no. 1, 1992, Special Issue: Computer Use in the Improvement of Writing, pp. 27-38.

"NAEYC Position Statement: Technology and Young Children—Ages Three through Eight," *Young Children*, Sept. 1996, pp. 11-16.

Nair, Indira, and Zhang, Jun. "Distinguishability of the Video Display Terminal (VDT) as a Source of Magnetic Field Exposure," *American Journal of Industrial Medicine*, vol. 28, no. 1, July 1995, pp. 23-29.

Nichols, Lois Mayer. "Pencil and Paper Versus Word Processing: A Comparative Study of Creative Writing in the Elementary School," *Journal of Research on Computing in Education*, vol. 29, no. 2, Winter 1996, pp. 159-66.

Niemiec, Richard, *et al.* "The Effects of Computer Based Instruction in Elementary Schools: A Quantitative Synthesis," *Journal of Research on Computing in Education*, vol. 20, no. 2, 1987, pp. 85-103.

Niemiec, Richard P.; Sikorski, Christian; and Walberg, Herbert J. "Learner-Control Effects: A Review of Reviews and a Meta-Analysis," *Journal of Educational Computing Research*, vol. 15, no. 2, 1996, pp. 157-74.

Niemiec, Richard P., and Walberg, Herbert J. "Comparative Effects of Computer-Assisted Instruction: A Synthesis of Reviews," *Journal of Educational Computing Research*, vol. 3, no. 1, 1987, pp. 19-37.

Niemiec, Richard P., and Walberg, Herbert J. "Computers and Achievement in the Elementary Schools," *Journal of Educational Computing Research*, vol. 1, no. 4, 1985, pp. 435-40.

Noble, Douglas D. "The Educational Engineer Meets Wayne's World," *Rethinking Schools*, vol. 8, no. 2, 1993, pp. 14-15.

O'Neil, John. "On Technology and Schools: A Conversation with Chris Dede," *Educational Leadership*, vol. 53, no. 2, Oct. 1995, pp. 6-12.

Oppenheimer, Todd. "The Computer Delusion," *The Atlantic Monthly*, July 1997, pp. 45-62.

Overbaugh, Richard C. "Word Processors and Writing-Process Software: Introduction and Evaluation," *Computers in Human Behavior*, vol. 8, no. 1, 1992, Special Issue: Computer Use in the Improvement of Writing, pp. 121-48.

Owston, Ronald D.; Murphy, Sharon; and Wideman, Herbert H. "On and Off Computer Writing of Eighth Grade Students Experienced in Word Processing," *Computers in the Schools*, vol. 8, no. 4, 1991, pp. 67-87.

Owston, Ronald D.; Murphy, Sharon; and Wideman, Herbert H. "The Effects of Word Processing on Students' Writing Quality and Revision Strategies," *Research in the Teaching of English*, vol. 26, no. 3, Oct. 1992, pp. 249-76.

Owston, Ronald D., and Wideman, Herbert H. "Word Processors and Children's Writing in a High-Computer-Access Setting," *Journal of Research on Computing in Education*, vol. 30, no. 2, Winter 1997, pp. 202-20.

Palmer, Shirley. "Does Computer Use Put Children's Vision at Risk?" *Journal of Research and Development in Education*, vol. 26, no. 2, Winter 1993, pp. 59-65.

Papert, Seymour. "Teaching Children Thinking" in *The Computer in the School: Tutor, Tool, Tutee*, edited by Robert P. Taylor. New York: Teachers College Press, 1980.

Peacock, Michael, and Breese, Chris "Pupils with Portable Writing Machines," *Educational Review* (U.K.), vol. 42, no. 1, 1990, pp. 41-56.

Pearlman, Robert. "Can K-12 Education Drive on the Information Superhighway?" in National Research Council, *The Changing Nature of Telecommunications/Information Infrastructure*. Washington, DC: National Academy Press, 1995.

Perkins, D. N., and Salomon, Gavriel. "Are Cognitive Skills Context-Bound?" *Educational Researcher*, vol. 18, no. 1, Jan-Feb 1989, pp. 16-25.

Reed, W. Michael. "Assessing the Impact of Computer-Based Writing Instruction," *Journal of Research on Computing in Education*, vol. 28, no. 4, Summer 1996, pp. 418-37.

Reiter, Russel J. "Melatonin Suppression by Static and Extremely Low Frequency Electromagnetic Fields: Relationship to the Reported Increased Incidence of Cancer," *Reviews on Environmental Health*, vol. 10, no. 3-4, 1994, pp. 171-86.

Rieber, Lloyd P. "LOGO and Its Promise: A Research Report," *Educational Technology*, vol. 27, no. 2, Feb. 1987, pp. 12-16.

Roberts, Paul. "Virtual Grub Street: Sorrows of a Multimedia Hack," *Harper's*, June 1996, pp. 71-77.

Roblyer, M. D.; Castine, W. H.; and King, F. J. "A Review of Recent Research," *Computers in the Schools*, Special Issue: Assessing the Impact of Computer-Based Instruction, vol. 5, nos 3/4, 1988, pp. 11-115.

Rothstein, Russell I., and McKnight, Lee. "Technology and Cost Models of K-12 Schools on the National Information Infrastructure," *Computers in the Schools*, vol. 12, nos. 1/2, 1996, pp. 31-57.

Ryan, Alice W. "Meta-analysis of Achievement Effects of Microcomputer Applications in Elementary Schools," *Educational Administration Quarterly*, vol. 27, no. 2, May 1991, pp. 161-84.

Salomon, Gavriel, and Gardner, Howard. "The Computer as Educator: Lessons From Television Research," *Educational Researcher*, vol. 15, no. 1, Jan. 1986, pp. 13-19.

Salomon, Gavriel, and Perkins, D. N. "Transfer of Cognitive Skills from Programming: When and How?" *Journal of Educational Computing Research*, vol. 3, no. 2, 1987, pp. 149-69.

Schrum, Lynne. "Educators and the Internet: A Case Study of Professional Development," *Computers and Education*, vol. 24, no. 3, April 1995, pp. 221-28.

Schultes, Richard Evans. "Burning the Library of Amazonia," *The Sciences*, March/April 1994, pp. 24-30.

Schwartz, Judah L. "Intellectual Mirrors: A Step in the Direction of Making Schools Knowledge-Making Places," *Harvard Educational Review*, vol. 59, no. 1, 1989, pp. 51-61.

Seawel, Lori, *et al.* "A Descriptive Study Comparing Computer-Based Word Processing and Handwriting on Attitudes and Performance of Third and Fourth Grade Students Involved in a Program Based on a Process Writing Approach," *Journal of Computing in Childhood Education*, vol. 5, no. 1, 1994, pp. 43-59.

Shavelson, Richard J., and Salomon, Gavriel. "Information Technology: Tool and Teacher of the Mind," *Educational Researcher*, vol. 14, no. 5, May 1985, p. 4.

Shaw, Edward L. Jr.; Nauman, Ann K.; and Burson, Debbie. "Comparisons of Spontaneous and Word Processed Compositions in Elementary Classrooms: A Three-Year Study," *Journal of Computing in Childhood Education*, vol. 5, nos. 3/4, 1994, pp. 319-27.

Shore, Ann, and Johnson, Marilyn F. "Integrated Learning Systems: A Vision for the Future," *Educational Technology*, vol. 32, no. 9, Sept. 1992, pp. 36-39.

Sparkes, R. A. "An Investigation of Year 7 Pupils Learning CONTROL LOGO," *Journal of Computer Assisted Learning*, vol. 11, no. 3, 1995, pp. 182-91.

Swift, Mary. "Computers in Pre-School Centres?" *Australian Journal of Early Childhood*, vol. 10, no. 3, Sept. 1985, pp. 22-23.

Tetenbaum, Toby Jane, and Mulkeen, Thomas A. "Computers as an Agent for Educational Change," *Computers in the Schools*, vol. 2, no. 4, 1985, pp. 91-103.

Underwood, J., *et al.* "Are Integrated Learning Systems Effective Learning Support Tools?" *Computers and Education*, vol. 26, no. 1-3, 1996, pp. 33-40.

Vaidya, Sheila, and McKeeby, John. "Computer Turtle Graphics: Do They Affect Children's Thought Processes?" *Educational Technology*, vol. 24, no. 9, Sept. 1984, pp. 46-47.

Van Dusen, Lani M., and Worthen, Blaine R. "Can Integrated Instructional Technology Transform the Classroom?" *Educational Leadership*, vol. 53, no. 2, Oct. 1995, pp. 28-33.

Van Dusen, Lani M., and Worthen, Blaine R. "The Impact of Integrated Learning System Implementation on Student Outcomes: Implications for Research and Evaluation," *International Journal of Educational Research*, vol. 21, no. 1, 1994, pp. 13-24.

White, Mary-Alice. "Are ILSs Good Education?" *Educational Technology*, vol. 32, no. 9, Sept. 1992, pp. 49-50.

Wiebe, James H. "At-Computer Programming Success of Third-Grade Students," *Journal of Research on Computing in Education*, vol. 24, no. 2, 1991, pp. 214-29.

Wiebe, James H., and Martin, Nancy J. "The Impact of a Computer-Based Adventure Game on Achievement and Attitudes in Geography," *Journal of Computing in Childhood Education*, vol. 5, no. 1, 1994, pp. 61-71.

Witz, Klaus G. "Science with Values and Values for Science Education," *Journal of Curriculum Studies*, vol. 28, no. 5, 1996, pp. 597-612.

Wolfe, Edward W., *et al.* "A Study of Word Processing Experience and Its Effects on Student Essay Writing," *Journal of Educational Computing Research*, vol. 14, no. 3, 1996, pp. 269-83.

Wresch, Bill. "What I Learned in Wabeno," *Computers in Human Behavior*, vol. 8, no. 1, 1992, Special Issue: Computer Use in the Improvement of Writing, pp. 9-16.

Yoshikawa, H., and Hara, I. "A Case of Rapidly Developed Myopia among VDT Workers," *Japanese Journal of Industrial Health*, vol. 31, no. 1, 1989, pp. 24-25.

Zane, Thomas, and Frazer, Connell G. "The Extent to Which Software Developers Validate Their Claims," *Journal of Research on Computing in Education*, vol. 24, no. 3, Spring 1992, pp. 410-19.

Index